The Chartered Institute of Marketing

Introductory Certificate in Marketing

STUDY Workbook

Unit 1 What is Marketing
Unit 2 Understanding Customer Relationships

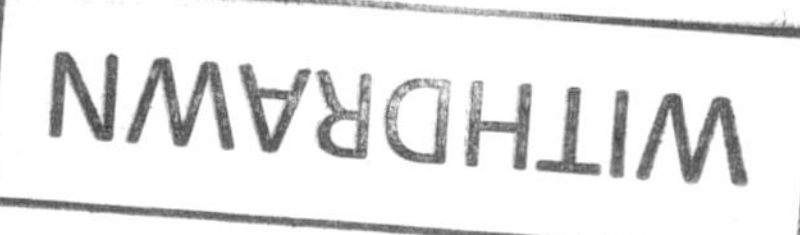

For exams in 2009/2010/2011

First edition March 2009

ISBN 9780 7517 5169 7

British Library Cataloguing-in-Publication Data
A catalogue record for this book
is available from the British Library

Published by

BPP Learning Media Ltd
Aldine House, Aldine Place
London W12 8AA

www.bpp.com/learningmedia

Printed in the United Kingdom

We are grateful to the Chartered Institute of Marketing for permission to reproduce in this text the syllabus, tutor's guidance notes and past examination questions. We are also grateful to Superbrands and The Centre for Brand Analysis for their support of our online feature 'A Word From...'

Author and CIM Publishing Manager: Dr Kellie Vincent
Photography: Terence O'Loughlin

Your learning materials, published by BPP Learning Media Ltd, are printed on paper sourced from sustainable, managed forests.

Contents

1 Aim of the Study Text

This book has been deliberately referred to as a 'Study workbook' rather than *text book ,study text or revision kit* because it is designed to be a mix all three.

So, why is it similar to but not actually a text book? Well, the CIM have identified key texts that you should become familiar with. The purpose of this workbook is not to replace these texts but to pick out the important parts that you will definitely need to know in order to pass and, to suggest a few areas within the texts that will provide good additional reading but that are not absolutely essential. We know that some of you will prefer to read text books from cover to cover whilst others amongst you will prefer to pick out relevant parts or dip in and out of the various topics. This text will help you to ensure that if you are a 'cover to cover' type, then you will not miss the emphasis of the syllabus. If you are a 'dip in and out' type, then we will make sure that you find the parts which are essential for you to know. Unlike a standard text which will have been written to be used across a range of alternative qualifications, this workbook has been specifically for your CIM course, therefore if a topic appears in the book then it is part of the syllabus and therefore will be an area which may be examined.

So now to the issue about why we use the term 'work book' rather than study text or revision kit. To achieve the Introductory Certificate in Marketing, it is essential that you learn to apply the ideas of marketing as you study key marketing theories. One of the reasons that the CIM have chosen to assess the course partly by online exam and partly by work based project is because they require that you can demonstrate both the ability to understand core marketing *theories* (tested via the online exam) but that you are also able to *apply* these theories to a real situation (tested via work based project). The workbook style helps you to learn the theory but also provides tips about planning your project work. Throughout the material you will also find real examples of marketing in practice as well as key concepts highlighted. Specific activities will also be interspersed to help you practice and think about marketing in the workplace. You should complete these activities and also use the checklists , worksheets and planners to help you complete your learning and work based project.

To complete the entire level and obtain your award, you must complete two individual units. The workbook is divided into three core sections. Sections 1 and 2 present the relevant theory and content for the two units. Section 3 guides you through the assessment elements for both units.

2 Studying for CIM qualifications

There are a few key points to remember as you study for your CIM qualification:

(a) You are studying for a **professional** qualification. This means that you are required to use professional language and adopt a business approach in your work.

(b) You are expected to show that you have 'read widely'. Make sure that you read the quality press (and don't skip the business pages), read Marketing, The Marketer, Research and Marketing Week avidly.

(c) Become aware of the marketing initiatives you come across on a daily basis, for example, when you go shopping look around and think about why the store layout is as it is, consider the messages, channel choice and timings of ads when you are watching TV. It is surprising how much you will learn just by taking an interest in the marketing world around you.

(d) Get to know the way CIM write their exam papers and assignments. They use a specific approach which is referred to as The Magic Formula to ensure a consistent approach when designing assessment materials. Make sure you are fully aware of this as it will help you interpret what the examiner is looking for (a full description of the Magic Formula appears later and is heavily featured within the chapters).

(e) Learn how to use Harvard referencing. This is explained in detail later in the Study Workbook

(f) Ensure that you read very carefully all assessment details sent to you from the CIM. They are very strict with regard to deadlines, completing the correct paperwork to accompany any assignment or project and making sure you have your CIM membership card with you at the exam. Failing to meet any assessment entry deadlines or completing written work on time will mean that you will have to wait for the next round of assessment dates and will need to pay the relevant assessment fees again.

3 The Introductory Certificate Syllabus

The Professional Certificate in Marketing is aimed at anyone who is employed in supporting marketing role such as Marketing Co-ordinator or Executive. You may also be a manager with a senior role within in a small or medium sized company where marketing only forms part of a wider work remit. Possibly you may be looking to move into your first marketing role or you wish to become more specialist.

The aim of the qualification is to provide a strong foundation for marketing knowledge. You will develop the breadth of knowledge of marketing theory but also appreciate issues faced within the organisation as CIM qualifications concentrate on applied marketing within real work-places.

The complete qualification is made from two units:

- Unit 1 What is Marketing
- Unit 2 Understanding Customer Relationships

The CIM stipulate that each module should take 30 guided learning hours to complete. Guided learning hours refer to time in class, using distance learning materials and completing any work set by your tutor. Guided learning hours do not include the time it will take you to complete the necessary reading for your studies. You should add an additional 30 hours self study.

The syllabus as provided by the CIM can be found below with reference to our coverage within this workbook.

Unit 1 What is Marketing

Unit characteristics

This unit outlines what marketing is and how it is defined. This unit focuses on the role of marketing, its cross-functional importance and its contribution to business success. It also looks at the role of marketing as a service provider within the organisation.

The unit also provides a basic understanding of the internal and external marketing environment and the marketing mix, with consideration of how these factors differ from one sector to another.

Overarching learning outcomes

By the end of this unit, students should be able to:

- Define marketing in the context of an exchange process
- Determine the importance of marketing as a cross-functional activity contributing towards business success
- Explain the importance of understanding the organisation's marketing environment and the impact it has upon an organisation's ability to satisfy customer needs and wants
- Identify each element of the marketing mix in the context of customer needs and achieving customer satisfaction
- Apply the marketing mix to a range of different organisational sectors and contexts

SECTION 1 – Understanding the role and function of marketing (weighting 15%)

		Covered in chapter(s)
1.1	Define marketing as an exchange process: • Definition: Marketing is the management process responsible for identifying, anticipating and satisfying customer requirements. • The exchange process being the exchange between the organisation, its customers and suppliers	1
1.2	Explain the role of marketing in achieving customer satisfaction: • Marketing and its involvement in analysis and planning • Making customer satisfaction a business objective • Ensuring marketing practices secure customer retention	1
1.3	Determine the importance of the role of marketing as a cross-functional activity within the organisation. The links with marketing and: • Research and Development • Human resources • Production/operations/logistics • Linking the role of marketing with information technology within the organisation (i.e. websites, intranets and extranets.) • Customer service provision	1
1.4	Explain the key differences between internal and external marketing and the role of marketing as an internal service provider within the organisation: • Identification of internal and external customers, including their different needs and wants • Marketing providing services internally including Intranet services for HR, IT Internal Recruitment, briefings and announcements • Extranet services for supporting supply chain activities	1

SECTION 2 – Understanding the Marketing Environment (weighting 30%)

		Covered in chapter(s)
2.1	Explain the importance of understanding the organisation's marketing environment in order to effectively manage the marketing process, and satisfy customer needs: • Defining the internal, micro and external marketing (macro) environment • An appreciation of controllable and uncontrollable factors.	2
2.2	Explain the concept of the PESTEL model and show how each of these factors impact upon the organisation, its ability to undertake marketing activities successfully, cost-effectively and competitively, including identifying: • **Political environment:** Government policy; Changing Governments; International environment and the impact of local government policy. • **Economic factors**: Interest rates; exchange rates; GNP and GDP; Taxation and how it affects viability of the business. • **Social factors**: Increased mobility; societal marketing; representation of family; international and cultural differences and changing social values.	2

	• **Technological factors:** Enhanced production capability and technique; product development; enhanced and effective communications within service provision. • **Environmental factors:** Waste; packaging; sustainability; climate change; corporate social responsibility. • **Legal factors** : Consumer protection legislation (Sales of Goods Act) and Data Protection Act (1998 – upgraded 2000)	
2.3	Identify the key characteristics of the micro-marketing environment, including an understanding of: • Customers • Stakeholders • Competitors • Suppliers • Distributors • Employees.	2
2.4	Explain the processes that can be used for monitoring the marketing environment: • Market scanning • Collection of secondary data through journals, websites, etc	2

SECTION 3 – The marketing mix- 7Ps (weighting 40%)

		Covered in chapter(s)
3.1	Explain the importance of the 7 Ps of the marketing mix as a series of tools co-ordinated to develop and delivered to meet customer needs and wants: • **Product**: Core, augmented and potential product; features and benefits including the tangible nature of the product; NPD; product extension; product modification. • **Price:** Revenue generation; balance of cost versus profitability in meeting financial objectives; monitoring and responding to competitor pricing; customer expectation. • **Place:** Role of distribution; nature of distribution; distribution channels; maximising accessibility; changing role of logistics; differing customer needs; online and offline purchasing • **Promotion:** Communicating the marketing proposition; sales; advertising; sales promotion; public relations; direct marketing; e-communications and personal selling • **People:** Role of people in service delivery; reliance on people to deliver and maintain transactional marketing; role of people in customer relationships. • **Process:** The importance of process in enabling delivery of the customer proposition; end-to-end customer service support to enable transactions. • **Physical evidence:** Point at which service is delivered; physical evidence as part of the marketing proposition; environment; ambiance; corporate image.	3

SECTION 4 – How marketing is applied in different contexts (weighting 15%)

		Covered in chapter(s)
4.1	Explain the different ways in which customers (Business to Business) and consumers (Business to Consumer) make their buying decisions: • The buying-decision making process • The buying decision making unit	4

4.2	4.2 Explain the different ways in which the marketing mix is used in different organisations to influence the buying-decision making units of each the following: • FMCG's (Fast Moving Consumer Goods) • Business-to-Business organisations • Service organisations • Voluntary and not-for-profit organisations • Internet (online) business	4

Unit 1 'What is Marketing' is assessed via an online multiple choice examination. Chapter 9 will provide some tips.

Unit 2 Understanding Customer Relationships

This unit focuses on developing an understanding of internal and external customers and considers how a knowledge and understanding can assist in designing marketing activities to engage and support customers to achieve long-term customer loyalty.

Insight into how to develop internal and external relationships through networking, collaboration and other techniques are covered. In addition, how communications techniques can be used to enhance these relationships to improve the success of marketing activities is also covered.

Information management and collection in order to aid this process and understand customers through the use of marketing research and database development completes the scope of the unit.

Overarching learning outcomes

By the end of this unit, students should be able to:

- Explain the importance of understanding customers and how marketing information aids the better development of marketing activities to achieve customer satisfaction
- Explain the value and importance of internal and external relationships of the organisation and the importance of networking , collaboration and co-operation in order to develop and maintain relationships
- Recognise the importance of internal relationships as an aid to the marketing function establishing its cross functional presence
- Explain the different ways in which to communicate with both internal and external customers in order to develop , maintain and strengthen customer relationships

SECTION 1 – Understanding customers(weighting 20%)

		Covered in chapter(s)
1.1	Discuss the need for organisations to understand: • The difference between the customer and user • Differing needs and wants of the customer base • Benefits of a marketing orientated approach	5
1.2	Recognise the importance of collecting information to gain a better understanding of customer needs from: • Internal and external sources • Secondary data sources • Primary data from research • Understanding some of the limitations of data collected	5

1.3	Explain how information collected from a range of sources can be stored in order to create and maintain a customer database: • Control access to the database to stored information across the organisation • Aid understanding of the organisations database	5
1.4	Explain how customer information can help with: • Identifying differing customer needs and wants • Understanding why customers purchase • Developing appropriate and effective marketing mix activities to meet those needs • Identifying the factors that influence decision making	5

SECTION 2 – Building and maintaining effective internal and external customer relationships (weighting 30%)

		Covered in chapter(s)
2.1	Explain the different types and characteristics of people with which an organisation develops relationships including: • Customers • Users • Connected Stakeholders • Other stakeholders • Differentiating between internal and external customers	6
2.2	Describe the links between the marketing concept , a customer focus and the relationship marketing approach including: • Difference between customer acquisition and retention • An understanding of the benefits of retaining customers • Theoretical aspects such as Pareto and Ladder of loyalty	6
2.3	Explain how marketing activities help to: • Support relationships with external customers • Aid customer retention and loyalty	6
2.4	Explain the importance of developing and sustaining customer, supplier and distributor relationships through: • Developing networking skills • Collaboration and co-operation between intermediaries • Successful negotiation between the various parties within the supply chain	6
2.5	Describe approaches used to build and develop relationships both within the marketing function and across the organisation in order to gain: • Internal co-operation • Commitment to organisational objectives • Internal support for marketing initiatives	6

2.6	Identify Key colleagues within the organisation with whom it is important to develop relationships: • Other marketing team members • Finance • Research & development • Human resources • Purchasing • Manufacturing	6
2.7	Identify potential areas of conflict that can occur between the functions of an organisation including: • The possible causes of conflict – poor, confusing mistimed, unclear communications , different objectives, agendas and focus • The potential effect of conflict on individuals and the organisation	6
2.8	Describe the methods that can be used to overcome conflict between organisational functions • Co-operation • Conciliation • Internal Arbitration	6
2.9	Discuss the need to take into account the views of others within the organisation when undertaking marketing activities including: • Contributing constructive ideas with colleagues to aid plans for improving marketing activities • Co-operating with others to follow plans • Keeping commitments made to others • Identify with others how joint efforts to follow plans can achieve improved performance	6

SECTION 3 – Communicating with internal and external customers (weighting 30%)

		Covered in chapter(s)
3.1	Explain the importance of communication as a tool to aid the development and maintenance of long-term relationships: • Keeping internal and external customers up to date and informed on key issues • A means of exchanging information relevant to the customer/ supplier relationships • A means of gaining Attention, Interest, Desire, Action in the context of marketing	7
3.2	Explain the nature and scope of the communications cycle including: • The Schramm Model • Aspects of encoding the message in relation to customer needs • The effect of 'noise' in the communication process	7
3.3	Explain the various business formats required for communicating both internally and externally with customers, including: • Letters • Memos • Informal Reports • Emails	7

3.4	Explain the importance of good verbal and non-verbal communications: • Kinetics- body language such as facial expressions, eye movements and gestures • Meta – communications – the importance of silences in communications ie, actions speak louder than words • Paralanguage – the use of tone	7
3.5	Identify the strengths and weakness of the following promotional activities in a range of different marketing scenarios designed to aid relationship management including: • Sales Promotions • Public relations • Intranet • Extranet • Internet / Wed based promotion • Digital technologies • Personal Selling from a customer perspective	7
3.6	Describe the processes involved in undertaking a range of tactical direct marketing campaigns including: • e-mail campaigns • e- newsletters • Web pages • Leaflet drops / direct marketing • Sales promotional activities • Tele- messaging • Digital messaging	7
3.7	Discuss how customer databases can be used to support tactical marketing communications activities targeting: • Internal market • External Market • Connected Stakeholders	7
3.8	Explain the process used for effectively managing a communications budget for specific communications tasks, including apportioning costs effectively: • Identification of costs associated with the project • Allocating costs accordingly • Working to a set budget and planning expenditure activities • Using Excel spreadsheet to record and report budget information	7
3.9	Identify and explain the different methods available for monitoring and measuring the success of internal and external tactical communications campaigns: • Inquiry levels • Sales increases • Media evaluation • Satisfaction Surveys	7

SECTION 4 – Providing customer service for internal and external customers (weighting 20%)

		Covered in chapter(s)
4.1	Describe the concept of customer care and customer service and its importance in different sectors including: • Consumer (FMCG markets) • Business-to-business markets • Not-for-profit and public sector organisations	8
4.2	Explain the relationship between customer care, customer focus, relationship marketing: • Customer satisfaction being a marketing objective of a market oriented organisation • Customer service an element of the marketing mix • The link between quality, marketing and customer service being the key to successful relationship marketing	8
4.3	Describe the different stages of a customer care programme and discuss why these programmes are important to delivering a consistent level of customer service and customer support: • Identify customer needs and perceptions • Establish a mission statement • Set service level standards • Establish a management process and communicate it to staff • Establish a complaints system • Develop control systems	8
4.4	Explain the importance of obtaining formal and informal customer feedback and identify a range of methods for collecting information including: • Questionnaires • Feedback cards • Telephone surveys • Suggestion boxes • Online forums • Informal methods i.e. discussions, questions at point of sale	8
4.5	Describe the measures that can be used to monitor the success of customer service support activities: • Number of complaints • Measuring/recording service standards for customer responses • Level of sales growth and decline (new business from existing customers) • Customer retention • Existing customer data	8
4.6	Explain how an understanding of information technology and databases are essential to managing customer care and customer service activities: • The importance of a database and its potential applications • Data components that may be included within a customer/prospect data- base (including geographic, demographic, psychographic and buying pattern data) • Ensuring the database is up to date • Meeting the legal and ethical requirements regarding collection, storage and use of information	8

4.7	Explain the process for managing own self in a disciplined, time orderly and customer conscious way: • Working to achieve your personal objectives • Utilising resources effectively • Completing tasks on time • Seeing through what you have started and closing customer enquiries • Delivering on promises • Monitoring personal achievement and success	8, 10

Unit 2 is assessed via a work based project. Chapter 10 takes you through the process of completing your project.

The CIM Magic Formula

The Magic Formula is a tool used by the CIM to help both examiners write exam and assignment questions and you to more easily interpret what you are being asked to write about. It is useful for helping you to check that you are using an appropriate balance between theory and practice for your particular level of qualification.

Contrary to the title, there is nothing mystical about the Magic Formula and simply by knowing it (or even mentioning it in an assessment) will not automatically secure a pass. What it does do however is to help you to check that you are presenting your answers in an appropriate format, including enough marketing theory and applying it to a real marketing context or issue. After passing the Introductory Certificate in Marketing, if you continue to study for higher level CIM qualifications, you would be expected to evaluate more and apply a more demanding range of marketing decisions. As such the Magic Formula is weighted with an even greater emphasis on evaluation and application as you move to the Professional Diploma and Postgraduate CIM levels.

You can see from the icons used throughout the workbook (also shown below) that for the Introductory Certificate marks are awarded in the following proportions:

- 

Presentation and format – 10%

  Remember, you are expected to present your work professionally which means that it should ALWAYS be typed and attention should be paid to making it look as visually appealing as possible (at higher levels of CIM qualifications this is also the case even in an exam situation). It also means that the CIM will stipulate the format that you should present your work in. The assessment formats you will be given will be varied and can include things like reports to write, slides to prepare, emails, memos, formal letters, press releases, discussion documents, briefing papers, agendas, and newsletters.

- 

Concept – 45%

  Concept refers to your ability to state, recall and describe marketing theory. The definition of marketing is a core CIM syllabus topic. If we take this as an example, you would be expected to recognise, recall, and write this definition to a word perfect standard to gain the full marks for concept. Understanding marketing concepts is clearly the main area where marks will be given within your assessment.

- 

Application – 30%

  Application based marks are given for your ability to apply marketing theories to real life marketing situations. For example, you may be asked to discuss the definition of marketing, and how it is applied within your own organisation. Within this sort of question 30% of the marks would have been awarded within the 'concept' aspect of the Magic Formula. You will gain the rest of the marks through your ability to evaluate to what extent the concept is applied within your own organisation. Here you are not only using the definition but are applying it in order to consider the market orientation of the company.

-  **Evaluation – 15%**

  Evaluation is the ability to asses the value or worth of something sometimes through careful consideration or related advantages and disadvantages or weighing up of alternatives.. Results from your evaluation should enable you to discuss the importance of an issue using evidence to support your opinions.

  Using the example of you being asked whether or not your organisation adopts a marketing approach, if you were asked to 'evaluate' this, it would be expected that you would provide reasons and specific examples why you thought they might take this approach but to also consider issues why they may not be marketing orientated before coming to a final conclusion.

4 A guide to the features of the Study Workbook

Each of the chapter features (see below) will help you to break down the content into manageable chunks and ensure that you are developing the skills required for a professional qualification.

Chapter feature	Relevance and how you should use it	Corresponding icon
Chapter topic list	Study the list. Each numbered topic denotes a numbered section in the chapter. Identified as a key concept within the syllabus	–
Introduction	Shows why topics need to be studied and is a route guide through the chapter.	–
Syllabus linked Learning Objectives	Outlines what you should learn within the chapter based on what is required within the syllabus	–
Format & Presentation	Outlines a key marketing presentation format with reference to the Magic Formula	
Concept	Key concept to learn with reference to the Magic Formula	
Application	An example of applied marketing with reference to the Magic Formula	
Evaluation	An example of evaluation with reference to the Magic Formula	
Worksheet Activity	An application based activity for you to complete, these will feature in chapters 1-4	
Key text links	Emphasises key parts to read in a range of other texts and other learning resources	
Marketing at work	A short case study to illustrate marketing practice	
Work based project tip	Key advice based on the work based project, these will feature within chapters 5-8 in order for you to develop a portfolio to use when you complete your assignment	
Quick quiz	Check your learning in the same format as the exam in chapters 1-4.	
Objective check	Review what you have learnt	

5 A note on Pronouns

On occasions in this Study Workbook, 'he' is used for 'he or she', 'him' for 'him or her' and so forth. Whilst we try to avoid this practice it is sometimes necessary for reasons of style. No prejudice or stereotyping accounting to sex is intended or assumed.

6 Additional resources

6.1 The CIM's reading lists

We have already mentioned that the CIM requires you to demonstrate your ability to 'read widely' . The CIM issue an extensive reading list for each unit. For this unit they recommend supplementary reading. Within the study text we have highlighted within the wider reading links specific topics where these resources would help. The reading lists for this level as provided by CIM are:

Unit 1 What is Marketing

Core Texts

Palmer, A. (2004) Introduction to marketing. Oxford, Oxford University Press.

Baines, P., Fill, C. and Page, K. (2008) Marketing. Oxford, Oxford University Press.

Supplementary Readings

Blois, K. (2000) The Oxford textbook of marketing. Oxford, Oxford University Press.

Blythe, J. (2006) Principles and practice of marketing. London, Thomson.

Brassington, F. and Pettitt, S. (2006) Principles of marketing. 4th edition. Harlow, Prentice Hall.

Cartwright, R. (2001) Mastering the business environment. London, Palgrave.

Palmer, A. (2008) Principles of services marketing. 5th edition. Maidenhead, McGraw-Hill.

Wright, R. (2006) Consumer behaviour. London, Thomson. Blythe, J. (2005) Essentials of marketing communications. 3rd edition. Harlow, Prentice Hall.

Unit 2 Understanding Customer Relationships

Core Texts

Brassington, F. and Pettitt, S. (2007) Essentials of marketing. 2nd edition. Harlow, Prentice Hall.

Egan, J. (2008) Relationship marketing; exploiting relationship strategies in marketing. 3rd edition. Harlow, Prentice Hall.

Supplementary Readings

Arussy, L. (2002) The experience: how to wow your customers and create a passionate workplace. San Francisco, CMP Books.

Boden, A. and Hailstone, P. (2001) Handling complaints. Management Pocketbooks.

Cook, S. (2007) Customer care excellence: how to create an effective customer service focus. 5th edition. London, Kogan Page.

Doole, I., Lancaster, G. and Lowe, R. (2004) Understanding and managing customers. Harlow, Prentice Hall.

Ettinger, B. and Perfetto, E. (2007) Business English: writing in the workplace. Harlow, Prentice Hall. [Available from CIM Direct]

Hill, N., Brierley, J. and MacGougall, R. (2003) How to measure customer satisfaction. 2nd rev edition. Gower.

Hill, E. and O'Sullivan, T. (2004) Foundation marketing. 3rd edition. Harlow, Prentice Hall.

Ober, S. (2006) Contemporary business communication. 6th edition. Boston, Houghton Mifflin.

Palmer, A. (2008) Principles of services marketing. 5th edition. Maidenhead, McGraw-Hill.

Quilliam, S. (2004) Body language: make the most of your professional and personal life by learning to read and use the body's secret signals. London, Carlton Books.

6.2 Assessment preparation materials from BPP Learning Media

To help you pass the Introductory Certificate in Marketing we have created a complete study package. Our A6 set of spiral bound **Passcards** are handy revision cards are ideal to reinforce key topics and practice for the online examination.

6.3 BPP Learning Media's Online Material

To complement this Study Workbook we have also produced some online materials for both students and tutors. These materials have not been designed to remain static but we will be developing more and adding to the content over time. If you have purchased a product within our CIM range then you will be able to access the online materials for free at:

www.bpp.com/lm/cim

Typical content will include:

- Links to the most useful websites for marketers
- Syllabus links to key marketing developments and 'big news' stories
- Pro forma's for key marketing documents such as Marketing Plans, Research Proposals etc

7 Your personal study plan

Preparing a Study Plan (and sticking to it) is one of the key elements to learning success.

The CIM have stipulated that there should be a minimum of 30 guided learning hours spent on each Unit. Guided learning hours will include time spent in lesson, working on fully prepared distance learning materials, formal workshops and work set by your tutor. We also know that to be successful, students should spend *at least* an additional 30 hours conducting self study. This means that for the entire qualification with two units you should spend 60 hours working in a tutor guided manner and at least an additional 60 hours completing recommended reading, working on your project, and revising for the exam. This study workbook will help you to organise this 30 hour portion of self study time.

Now think about the exact amount of time you have (don't forget you will still need some leisure time!) and complete the following tables to help you keep to a schedule.

	Date	Duration in weeks
Course start		
Course finish		Total weeks of course:
Examination date	Revision to commence	Total weeks to complete revision:
Project received:	Submission date:	Total weeks to complete:

Content chapter coverage plan

Chapter	To be completed by	Revised or considered in relation to the work based project ?
1 The role of marketing		
2 The marketing environment		
3 The marketing mix		
4 Marketing in different contexts		
5 Understanding customers		
6 Effective relationships		
7 Marketing communications and promotion		
8 Effective customer service		
9 Preparing for the exam		
10 Completing the work based project		

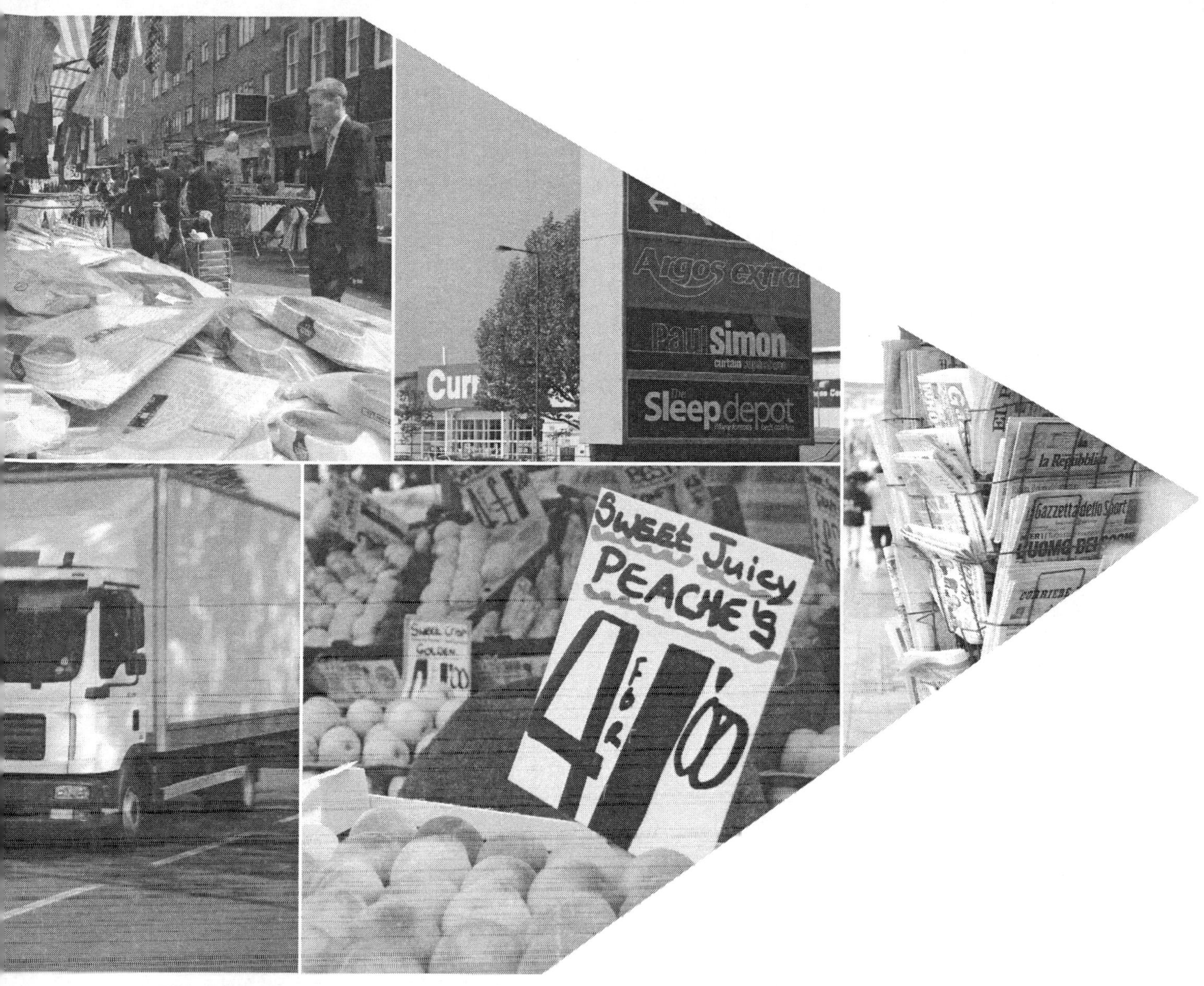

Chapter 1
The role of marketing

Topic list

1 Marketing defined
2 The role of marketing
3 Marketing as a cross functional activity
4 Internal and external marketing

Introduction

This chapter introduces the concept of marketing and defines marketing as an exchange process. Marketing is a term which has many connotations, not all of which are positive and we will address why they have evolved. We will focus on the CIM's definition of marketing and explore the key issue of marketing as an exchange process between the organisations, its customers and suppliers.

In the second section we explain the role of marketing and specifically in relation to helping to achieve customer satisfaction. We look at the range of marketing activities and how it performs the role of putting customer satisfaction at the heart of business objectives. One of the central themes of marketing is to ensure that satisfied customers remain with the organisation, how this is achieved is also briefly explored.

The third section looks at the links between marketing and the wider organisation. When properly applied, marketing should involve cross functional activities to ensure that the organisation is working together to meet overall business aims and customer satisfaction. Key working relationships between the marketing function and other key departments are discussed.

Finally, the fourth section looks at the concept of internal marketing and compares this to external marketing relationships. Internal marketing refers to individuals working within the organisation being considered as customers in their own right. Considerations about how these internal customers' needs and wants may differ to external customers are considered along with some examples of how internal marketing may work in practice.

Syllabus linked learning objectives

By the end of the chapter you will be able to:

Learning objectives		Syllabus link
1	Define marketing as an exchange process	1.1
2	Explain the role of marketing	1.2
3	Describe concepts of analysis and planning and marketing's involvement	1.2
4	Identify the role of marketing in achieving customer satisfaction and retention	1.2
5	Discuss marketing as a cross functional activity	1.3
6	Recognise the key internal functional relationships that are important to the marketing function	1.3
7	Define internal marketing	1.4
8	State the difference in needs between internal and external customers	1.4

1 Marketing defined

When you think of the term marketing, you probably will not come up with exactly the same definition as another person. One of the reasons for this is that we are all customers. As customers, we exist within society filled with marketing initiatives and are increasingly aware of some of the more visible aspects of marketing. Think of a typical morning, you may wake up to the radio. Depending on which station you listen to you may have woken to the advertising jingle of a local pizzeria, showered using the body wash you selected specifically because you liked the packaging (and subconsciously quite fancied entering the on-pack competition to win an exotic holiday). Next, you may have switched on the television to watch the early morning weather forecast, watching it, you are quickly reminded that yesterday you bought the microwave porridge from the manufacturer who are currently sponsoring the weather. On the way to the kitchen to prepare your porridge you may have tripped over a large pile of 'junk mail' in the hallway which also reminded you about the frustrating double glazing sales person who you couldn't get rid of the day before. So, even before leaving the house in the morning you will have been influenced by advertising, packaging design, promotional competitions, and TV sponsorship, annoying elements of direct mail and high pressure sales tactics. It is no wonder that marketing often receives bad press and is viewed as being concerned with persuading people to buy things they do not need or want (Blythe, 2006). These aspects of marketing and are what many customers will understandable yet wrongly regard as a full definition of marketing. In reality, although it is the most visible aspect of marketing, this promotional element represents only part of the concepts full meaning. Clearly, in this example, some of the connotations that can be attached to marketing are not exactly positive. Hill and O'Sullivan (2004) point out that:

"Organisations who see their marketing activity as no more than a ploy to take them (it's products) to their customers are missing the point altogether. The discipline of marketing is both broader and more meaningful that this." pg 2

Marketing should be considered a business philosophy as much as a function within an organisation (Baker, 1992). At its core is the notion of meeting customer needs because it is only this way that the organisation will succeed. On a practical level, think about a product or service you bought and regretted because it was either poor quality, you hadn't really wanted it in the first place or you were unhappy with aftercare service. It is highly unlikely that you would purchase from this company again or recommend it to others. The view that good marketers take is that a satisfied customer is a happy one who will return again. So the best starting place is to identify what customers want and then try to meet these needs.

KEY CONCEPT

concept

The CIM's definition of marketing is;

"Marketing is the management process responsible for identifying, anticipating and satisfying customer requirements profitably"

Marketing has existed as a business function for a relatively short time. Marketing departments began to emerge in the late 1950's with an emphasis on the advertising, selling, distribution, market research and product development (Baker, 1992). In nearly all general marketing text books you are very likely to find a large opening discussion about what marketing actually means. This is largely because is it often misunderstood and there can be vast differences in marketing practice between organisations.

MARKETING AT WORK

application

Marketing is a relatively new business discipline. It was first properly recognised as a distinct discipline in the US after the second world war despite being discussed by British economist Adam Smith in 1776 in his groundbreaking work ' The Wealth of Nations' (Hill & O'Sullivan, 2004). There are also examples of marketing activity becoming popular during the Edwardian period. Scott of the Antarctic was no stranger to the promotional aspects of marketing as he funded his explorations by sponsorship deals from brands of the day including Heinz, Typhoo, and Lyle's among others looking to gain positive connotations from his success. Scott would return from expeditions with photographs of himself and his team perched on

boxes of Fry's chocolate. Sponsoring manufacturers provided funding for the expeditions and product as supplies in return for the opportunity for featuring the explorer in their advertising and benefiting from an early form of celebrity endorsement. (BBC 4, 2007) Although the major growth in marketing departments being introduced into organisations saw it's heyday in 1950's and early 1960's America, the Edwardian period saw the rise of the brand with many of today's recognised food brands such as Cadbury, PG Tips, Perrier, Marmite, and Colmans Mustard first becoming popular because they were regarded as products to be trusted because of their superior quality and high safety standards These brands developed during a time when most loose food products which were packaged at the point of purchase by grocers. Edwardian customers had been warned by many press reports that there was a widespread problem with loose products which were contaminated or diluted with inferior products. Spent tea for example was often mixed with fresh leaves and then sold by unscrupulous importers or grocers. Packaged tea was therefore believed to be protected from such contamination. The rise of mass advertising also emerged at this time, Rachel Jardine, the producer of the BBC4 documentary, The Edwardian Larder commented that during this period;

"This is the moment when food manufacturers began to understand how to manipulate people's perceptions – targeting the working classes or seeking to appeal to the middle class woman with aspirations (as with Perrier, which was promoted by The Daily Mail)." (Jardine, 2007)

1.1 Common features in marketing definitions

If we return for a moment to formal definitions of marketing, we can look at similarities and differences between the three most commonly cited examples, the CIM and American Marketing Association along with those from well known marketing gurus.

The CIM's Definition:

> *'Marketing is the management process responsible for identifying, anticipating and satisfying customer requirements profitably.'* (CIM: www.cim.co.uk)

The American Marketing Association's Definition:

> *'Marketing is the process of planning and executing the conception, pricing, promotion, and distribution of ideas, goods, and services to create exchanges that satisfy individual and organisational objectives.'* (AMA: www.marketingpower.com)

Christian Gronroos' Definition:

> *'Marketing is to establish, maintain and enhance long-term customer relationships at a profit, so that the objectives of the parties involved are met. This is done by mutual exchange and fulfilment of promises.'* (Gronroos, 1990)

These definitions have several key points in common.

- They all stress the importance of customer satisfaction, making marketing a 'mutual exchange' between buyer and seller.
- They all make it clear that there has to be some motivation for the selling organisation such as 'profit' or, more broadly, satisfied 'organisational objectives'.
- They all see marketing as a process that is planned and managed.

There are also some subtle differences, most notably the reference to 'enhancing long-term customer relationships' in the third definition: this is of great importance in the latest ideas about relationship marketing.

1.2 An exchange process

It is important to think about the 'exchange' element of marketing. In other words there is a trade in something that both organisations and customers want. Marketing grew out of exchange.

- In early societies trade is by barter: exchanging goods for other goods.
- When a society becomes capable of producing more than is necessary for individual survival (a surplus), the extra can be traded for other goods and services.
- And as societies develop, trade takes place using an agreed medium of exchange, usually money.

The relevance of this is that for an exchange to take place, a market has developed.

KEY CONCEPT

A market consists of all the potential customers sharing a particular need or wants who might be willing and able to engage in exchange to satisfy that need or want (Kotler, 1994). For example, the immediate market for CIM study work books will include all of you who need or want to pass the CIM's Introductory Certificate in Marketing and are able to purchase a copy. In this example, there will also be a secondary market which will include course tutors and study centre librarians who may purchase the texts. In this market the motivating needs and wants will differ from yours and may stem from their desire to increase pass rates for the study centre or meet objectives to provide a range of relevant texts for the library. . There may even be a third separate market which includes individuals who are interested in learning more about marketing but do not wish to study for a qualification.

The marketing issue to consider here, is to recognise that these alternative markets exist and to consider whether it is possible to meet the needs of all three groups or to focus primarily on the needs of one.

For a profit-making organisation, the exchange of mutual benefits will be an exchange of products/services (supplied to customers) for money (supplied by customers in payment) and other resources (such as customer feedback information). Lancaster & Witney (2005) emphasise, however, that this is not the only type of exchange. Government units, charities, churches and other voluntary/not-for-profit organisations are also now seen as engaging in marketing. In such organisations, the nature of the exchange is different. Services, advocacy, membership, information (and so on) are supplied to a variety of 'customers' (or stakeholders) in exchange for a range of returns: allegiance, volunteer labour, donations, information and so on.

1.3 Organisational motivations to adopt a marketing approach

Earlier, we discussed that it was in the interests of organisations to adopt a marketing approach because only satisfied customers are likely to return. To identify what is likely to satisfy customers, careful analysis of the overall market trends and competitive activity is required. It isn't enough for a company to look at whether their customers are satisfied with their products or services at the present time, an overall awareness of what they may need and want in the future is needed because market places are becoming increasingly dynamic.

MARKETING AT WORK

application

Looking through a just single edition of a weekly marketing journal such as 'Marketing' you are likely to find several examples of products and services which have been hugely popular and well liked by customers in the past but have diminished over time because the needs of the overall market has changed. Companies that fail to adapt to changing needs are pretty much in a no-win situation. For example, attitudes towards diet and healthier lifestyles have meant that the appeal of Diet Coke and its 'cool' status has finally begun to diminish (The Times, 31.01.08) and non-carbonated drinks and fruit based smoothies are increasingly popular. To maintain competitive in this market, Coca-cola launched 'Coke Plus' with the functional benefits of containing added anti-oxidants to appeal to health conscious women. The company also began to focus more on their non-carbonated offerings and invested in new products such as 'Fanta Still' (Marketing, 30.1.08).

Within the women's weekly magazine market, once popular celebrity focussed titles such as Reveal, Now, Heat, Bella and Closer have experienced declining circulation declined as readers turned to the growing range of free daily newspapers (particularly in London) which also feature a celebrity slant. Mid-end of the market magazines such as OK!, Hello Grazia and Glamour however increased their circulation at this time as the desire for higher quality titles grew. Within the market during 2000 and 2007 there had been a flurry of new low priced magazine launches and established titles such as Bella had also been re-positioned to focus more on celebrity gossip to meet the 'current' trends. The impact of these launches, all targeted at similar groups of customers, meant that there was an oversupply in the market, prices were pushed down further and the ability to appeal to advertisers (a key source of additional revenue for the publishers) was increasingly difficult.

The table below shows the market figures published at the end of January

Magazine Title	Growth / Decline	Details
Bella (H Bauer)	↓30%	Relaunched in 2007 (Year on year figure)
Heat (Emap)	↓10%	Significant investment in advertising at this time (Year on year figure)
Closer (Emap)	↓10%	(Year on year figure)
Now (IPC)	↓10%	
Reveal (ACP-Natmag)	↓8%	(Period on period figure)
OK (Northern and Shell)	↑20%	Mid market (Period on period figure)
First (Emap)	↑6%	Mid market (Year on year figure)
Grazia (Emap)	↑5%	Mid market (Year on year figure)

Source: Based on 'Celebrity weeklies lose appeal' Marketing 30.1.08

Dibb et al(1997) outlined why a marketing approach improved business performance by stating that:

"Marketing puts an emphasis on satisfying customers. Marketing analyses should lead a business to develop a marketing strategy that takes into account market trends, aims to satisfy customers and is aware of competitive activity and targets the right customers with a clear positioning strategy. In doing so, a business should benefit from customer loyalty and advantages over its rivals, while making the most efficient use of resources'. Hence, marketing should provide both a financial benefit and a greater sense of wellbeing for the organisation".

For the marketing orientated organisation, perfecting the balance between efficiency (producing products at minimum cost to maximise profits) and effectiveness (producing products to meet the exact needs of customers) is a key consideration. For organisations to be able to achieve this balance, it would not be possible for them to just use it as a function within the organisation that simply 'talks at' customers through advertising or selling or tried to persuade customers to buy things that they do not require.

1.4 Marketing myths

If marketers are adopting a true market orientation and are seeking to satisfy customers needs, then there should be no place for the more unscrupulous marketing activities which have been detrimental to the reputation of the business discipline. Over a decade ago, UK and US based university lecturers and authors Dibb, Simkin, Pride and Ferrell (1997) surveyed students views about typical marketing myths, large proportions agreed or strongly agreed with the following:

Myth	% either strongly agreeing or agreeing
Marketing depends on advertising	61%
Dealers profits significantly increase prices customers pay	53%
Marketing is selling	48%
Marketers persuade	46%
Strategic planning is nothing to do with marketing	38%

Source: based on findings from Dibb, Simkin, Pride & Ferrell (1997) Marketing, Third European Edition, Houghton Miffin

Unfortunately, the same response is just as likely today if a similar survey were to be conducted because it does take a significant time for reputations to change. You may want to take a quick 'straw poll' to establish if these views are typical of your own friends, colleagues and family. Complete the worksheet activity below.

WORKSHEET ACTIVITY 1

1 Discuss the statements in the table below to colleagues, friends and family.

2 Keep a tally of those who agree with the statement

3 Think about the likely background and experiences of everyone you have spoken with.

4 Are there likely to be any reasons for differences in opinions or the strengths of opinion?

5 Once you have completed your discussions, to what extent do you agree or disagree with the comments, do you think that marketing has changed at all since Dibb et al's findings were published?

Statement	Tally	% of total	Your thoughts and comments
Marketing depends on advertising			
Dealers profits significantly increase prices customers pay			
Marketing is selling			
Marketers persuade			
Strategic planning is nothing to do with marketing			

You will find an activity debrief at the end of this chapter.

By now, you should have more of an idea what the term marketing refers to and in particular what it is not limited to. We now should look at what it is that marketers actually do. Some people question whether there is an actual role for marketing if being customer orientated means that everyone within the organisation should put the customer at the centre of what they do, is there actually a role for market

2 The role of marketing

Not only is marketing a philosophy (being customer-centric) but it also is a function with priority tasks to action in order to fulfil the role of marketing as a 'management process' , these include:

- Identifying customer needs and wants
- Satisfying customers
- Identifying market opportunities
- Targeting the 'right' customers
- Staying ahead in dynamic markets
- Knowing and pre-empting competitors
- Using resources effectively
- Enhancing profitability

To achieve this range of activities, marketing is broken down into four manageable stages: analysis; planning; implementation and control (Kotler, 1994). The diagram below, outlines these four stages and adds details about exactly what each of these stages will involve and the inputs that are required in terms of the actual marketing activities that will need to take place.

Each of these phases will be covered in detail in later chapters of the study workbook and so you should not worry at this point about each of the specific elements. The main point you should take from here is an awareness of the wide range of activities which are included within the marketing remit.

On the right hand side of the diagram you will see that the inputs which are needed at each stage include, marketing research and management information, marketing planning and actual operational marketing activities which includes day to

day activities. The list of day to day activities will be enormous and dependent on the actual job role of the individual marketing team members but it could include anything from day to day sales forecasting, writing press releases, booking ad space, dealing with customer complaints, monitoring a customer web forum or working with a design agency to ensure the exact colour specification for artwork. Marketing research enables marketers to make decisions more easily and is an activity that may be ongoing in many organisations to help with

MARKETING AT WORK

application

Imagine you are working for a manufacturer of cooking sauces. You would be using marketing information in a number of ways throughout the marketing planning cycle. The table below outlines typical marketing research projects that may be used over a typical year.

Phase	Example research	Purpose of research
Marketing planning for the next period	Study into home cooking trends Environmental impact of use of glass jars Observation reports on competitor activity	Analysis of customer need for cooking sauces Marketing environment analysis of 'green issues' likely to impact the company Competitor analysis
Preparation of strategy	Internal research into future factory capacity Customers perception of the pricing levels of cooking sauces New product ideas generation Retailers preference for alternative jar sizes Cost of alternative promotional methods	Analysis of the availability of internal resources To assist the pricing strategy To assist the new product development programme To assist with distribution objectives To assist the promotional strategy
Implementing marketing plans	Product taste test Customer perception of advertising message Website monitoring Staff awareness and perception of marketing activities	Developing product Advertising creation Web development Encourage cross functional interest in customer wellbeing
Control and evaluation of marketing	Sales figure tracking Customer satisfaction responses Advertising awareness	Review sales against marketing activity and forecasts Overall satisfaction measurement Review media, message and timing decisions for advertising

At the analysis phase, marketers concentrate on identifying customers needs and wants and deciding whether the organisation is able to satisfy these in the future. Market trends, competitor activity and factors that are outside of the organisations control but are operating within the business environment are all analysed at this stage. The planning phase then tackles the design of the marketing strategy. It is imperative that this strategy is consistent with the overall business objectives and will place customer satisfaction at the centre. At this point, based on the findings from the analysis phase, the market needs to be separated into more defined groups. This is referred to as market segmentation. The organisation then selects the group which is profitable and the organisation is able to meet their needs. This is referred to as targeting. The final stage is to position the organisations offering to appeal to that segment of the market by implementing an appropriate marketing plan. The process is shown in the following diagram.

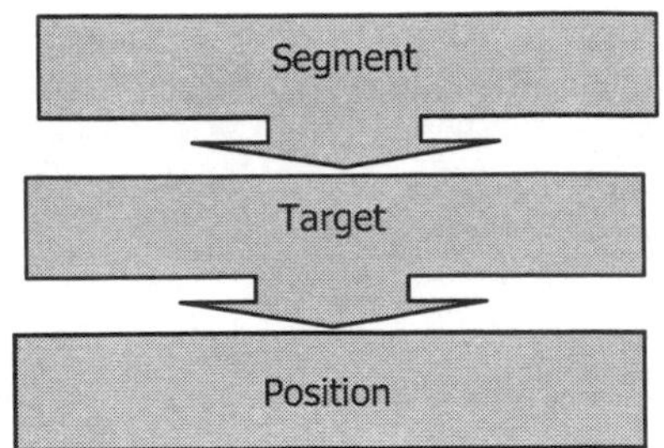

MARKETING AT WORK

application 

Not all TV viewers will want to watch the same programmes. We can split audiences into groups who have similar tastes and viewing preferences for between the different genre such as drama, sport, reality shows or documentaries. This is a form of market segmentation.

A TV production company would then select the audience that they are able to meet their needs, for example Ragdoll specialises in producing programmes aimed at children. This is targeting.

The production company would then put together a marketing plan which would help to achieve marketing objectives and meet those viewers needs. They would use a combination of marketing variables and create what is summarised as the marketing mix to help satisfy customers . This stage is positioning.

In order to put the marketing strategy into operation, marketers then compile a marketing plan which outlines the range of tactics which should be utilised. To simplify this, McGreggor (1960) summarised a 'marketing mix' to be planned , commonly known as the 4P's which stand for: Product; Price; Place and Promotion. These four variables are at the heart of all aspects of marketing. They have been supplemented by three extra service marketing variables: People, Process and Physical Evidence. The complete marketing mix can be illustrated as follows

The extended marketing mix

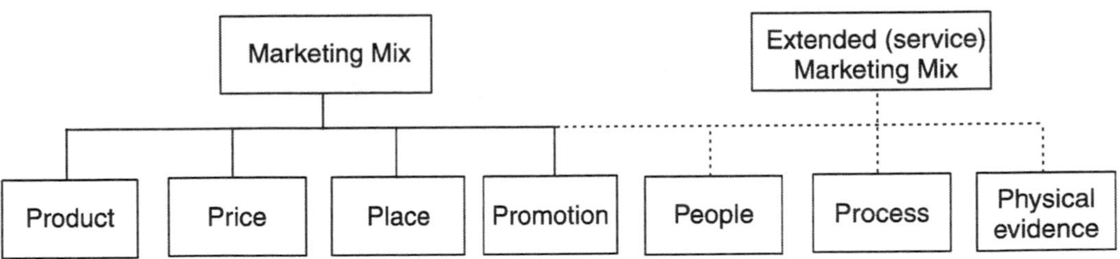

Marketing uses the marketing mix to satisfy needs and create 'value' for customers.

4 Ps	How marketing creates value
Product	Marketing undertakes various kinds of product and market research about customers' needs and wants. This generates ideas for **product improvements** and **new products**, either extending the existing product range, or meeting a previously unrecognised need. This adds value to the *business* (by enhancing its offering) and adds value for *customers* (by meeting their needs and preferences).
Price	Some products are valued because they are cheap (low-cost phone calls), some because they are expensive (designer-label clothes). Marketing adds value for the *business* by researching how buyers **perceive prices** for different goods and enabling the organisation to **target** its goods or services appropriately. Price decisions add value for *customers* by offering value for money, rewards for bulk or repeat purchases, esteem value and so on.
Place	More usually called **distribution** or **logistics** in modern management-speak. Marketing adds value for the *business* by getting goods and services to market reliably and efficiently. It adds value for *customers* by creating a comfortable and convenient place to buy, in the case of a supermarket or restaurant. Or it invents

4 Ps	How marketing creates value
	new ways of displaying goods and getting them into people's homes, in the case of e-commerce sites such as Amazon.com.
Promotion	Also called **marketing communications**, this includes a vast array of techniques, from media advertising to personal selling (the sales force) to direct mail to public relations. Promotion adds value to the *business* by securing demand for its offering, building customer loyalty, promoting a positive image (for its brands and for the organisation as an employer). It adds value for *customers* by making sure that they can make well-informed **buying decisions**, are rewarded for their loyalty and are able to feel good about their purchases.

To build an appropriate marketing mix, we are reminded of the inputs which are needed at each stage of the marketing process. These are, marketing research and management information, marketing planning and actual operational marketing activities which include day to day activities. The list of day to day activities will be enormous and dependent on the actual job role of the individual marketing team members but it could include anything from day to day sales forecasting, writing press releases, booking ad space, dealing with customer complaints, monitoring a customer web forum or working with a design agency to ensure the exact colour specification for artwork. The list of actual marketing job roles continues to grow and a number of levels of seniority can exist within a large marketing department. Typically, marketers are recruited into either 'agency' or 'client-side' roles.

WORKSHEET ACTIVITY 2

application

Think about your own organisation and try to answer the questions below.

- Does your organisation have a specific marketing department or individuals dedicated to marketing functions?

- What are the typical job titles of marketing based personnel?

- If there is no marketing department, who is responsible for the planning of the marketing mix?

- How closely do those responsible for marketing work with other specific departments or individuals?

- How are marketers generally regarded within your organisation?

The CIM have two publications which may help you to put the actual working role of marketing into context:

1 *Marketing Job Description Guide- This outlines the roles and responsibilities of individuals with a wide range of marketing positions.*

2 *Professional Marketing Standards- This outlines the competencies that marketers should demonstrate at each level of seniority within an organisation.*

You will not be expected to know these documents by heart but it would give you better insight into the marketing function in general. ■

From completing worksheet activity 2, you may have noticed that the marketing department may work closely with others or that there is a certain amount of conflict between this function and others. Because of the need to put customer satisfaction at the core of the business objectives, marketing tends to become involved with most business functions.

3 Marketing as a cross functional activity

In order to combine the efforts within the organisation. Market-orientated companies need proper co-ordination between market needs, production decisions and financial well-being. That requires good communication between the marketing function and people responsible for development, design and manufacturing, and finance.

However, that does not mean that the marketing department can impose their will on all other departments. Relationships with other departments should be developed and managed to ensure all departments are working towards the same overall goal.

Although every organisation is different, common patterns appear in the structure of organisations.

- Marketing departments have often evolved from sales departments. In traditional sales or production orientated organisations, marketplace issues were the responsibility of a sales director reporting to senior management.
- When the need for a market orientated approach became apparent, a marketing director appeared in parallel to the sales director, but each had separate functional departments.
- With fuller recognition of the marketing approach to business, sales and marketing may become a single department, with sales as a sub-group within marketing (as opposed to marketing being a sub-group within sales).

Marketing managers have to take responsibility for planning, resource allocation, monitoring and controlling the marketing effort, but it can also be claimed (and often is, by marketing managers!) that marketing involves every facet of the organisation's operations. If the philosophy of a market orientation is regarded as a prerequisite for success, the marketing department naturally becomes the main co-ordinator.

3.1 Conflicts with other departments

Care should be taken not to understate the role of finance, production, personnel and other business functions, as this may cause resentment and lack of co-operation. To reduce the potential for conflict, senior management should ensure that departmental heads have clear instructions as to the organisation's priorities.

The table below shows the types of decision typically taken by a marketing department. However, bear in mind that in the truly market-oriented organisation, marketing is not an activity that can be pigeon-holed as the responsibility of the marketing department. All of the company's activities must be co-ordinated around the needs of the customer. When you look at the typical objectives

Other departments	Their emphasis	Emphasis of marketing
Engineering	Long design lead time	Short design lead time
	Functional features	Sales features
	Few models with standard components	Many models with custom components
Purchasing	Standard parts	Non-standard parts
	Price of material	Quality of material
	Economic lot sizes	Large lot sizes to avoid stockouts
	Purchasing at infrequent intervals	Immediate purchasing for customer needs
Production	Long order lead times and inflexible production schedules	Short order lead times and flexible schedules to meet emergency orders
	Long runs with few models	Short runs with many models
	No model changes	Frequent model changes
	Standard orders	Custom orders
	Ease of fabrication	Aesthetic appearance
	Average quality control	Tight quality control
Inventory	Narrow product line	Broad product line
management	Economic levels of stock	Large levels of stock
Finance	Strict rationales for spending	Intuitive arguments for spending
	Hard and fast budgets	Flexible budgets to meet changing needs
	Pricing to cover costs	Pricing to further market development
Accounting	Standard transactions	Special terms and discounts
	Few reports	Many reports
Credit	Full financial disclosures by customers	Minimum credit examination of customers
	Lower credit risks	Medium credit risks
	Tough credit terms	Easy credit terms
	Tough collection procedures	Easy collection procedures

An article in Marketing magazine in January 2008 outlined a research report titled 'Marketing 3D' by consultancy Deloitte on the role of marketing. The article is titled 'Marketing 2008 – a discipline in crisis' was published in the 16th January edition, pages 26 – 28. As CIM studying members you can access this article using your CIM login details on the CIM's website. It is worth reading because it looks at the perceptions of marketers by senior board members. This will give you an indication of how the discipline of marketing still has a misunderstood role within many large organisations. ■

3.2 Key departments

When we look again at the central role of marketing as being to satisfy customers and to maintain positive relationships with customers in the long term, there are some departments that marketing will need to work closely alongside.

The table below shows these key departments and some of the shared goals

Department	Common goals with marketing
Research and development	• New product development • Product modifications • Innovation
Human resources	• Staff training to encourage a positive customer focus • Articulate a shared vision • Communicate ideas to staff • Implement internal marketing
Production, operations and logistics	• Ensure product quality • Meet customer demand efficiently • Ensure product availability • Efficient delivery of product
IT	• Effective corporate website • Implementing marketers design of online corporate messages • E-commerce functionality • Supplier and key customer access to extranet and intranet
Customer service	• Correcting customer problems • Increasing levels of customer satisfaction

4 Internal and external marketing

Up to this point, we have focused almost entirely on customers and stakeholders who are external to the organisation. It should however be apparent that marketers will also have a range of internal stakeholders in the form of the job functions who each have their own individual needs and wants. Internal marketing is the term used to describe marketing within the firm. Internal marketing suggests that all employees should treat each other as if they are each other's customers (Hill & O'Sullivan, 2004). Think about your own job role, how dependent are you on others to be able to carry out your work effectively. The answer is probably quite a lot, and even as a customer you may have experienced times when you have tried to contact a firm when you have a problem only to be told by the individual you speak to that they cannot resolve your issue until someone else within the organisation completes another part of a task. A sales person for example will have customers who are external to the organisation but they will also have sales order processors who will need accurate information to ensure products are dispatched properly, individuals within this team will therefore be internal customers.

WORKSHEET ACTIVITY 3

application

- List your own internal customers and their specific needs and wants

Internal Customer	Needs and wants

- How do the needs and wants differ between the various internal customers?

- What makes working with internal customers challenging?

- Do these internal customers also view you as a customer of theirs?

Although different individuals within the organisation will have varying degrees of 'front –line' customer contact, given that the overall objective of all employees should be to ultimately meet customer needs, consideration of internal marketing is essential. Many organisations also encourage all non customer facing staff to meet customers at some point so they are better able to understand their needs and appreciate the importance of their role in contributing to overall customer satisfaction.

Typical groups of staff were categorised by Blythe (2006) according to their level of contact with customers. These are shown in the table below along with example roles.

Front line staff (frequent contact)	**Second line staff** (occasional contact)	**Backstage staff** (virtually no contact)
Drivers	Financial controllers	Factory workers
Receptionists	Warehouse staff	Office based staff
Credit controllers	Administrators	Engineers
Salespeople		Research and development people
Canteen staff		
Doormen		
Telephonists		
Telephonists		

Hill and O'Sullivan (2004) chapters 1 & 2 will provide more detail about the definition and evolution of marketing as well as it's practice in the real world. Try not to get too theoretical at this stage as the CIM require that you have a more broad appreciation of the definition of marketing for the Introductory Certificate. You will not need to study the historical evolution of marketing in any great depth. Differences between product and services marketing which are covered in depth in chapter 2 will be referred to later in this study workbook.

Blythe (2006) Chapter 3 provides an excellent overview of internal marketing. ■

Learning objective review

Learning objectives	Covered
1 Define marketing as an exchange process	☑ Alternative definitions of marketing ☑ Marketing is a mutually perceived exchange ☑ A number of myths surround marketing
2 Explain the role of marketing	☑ Typical marketing roles ☑ Customer satisfaction is key ☑ What is a market
3 Describe concepts of analysis and planning and marketing's involvement	☑ The marketing process of analysis, planning, implementation and control ☑ Market segmentation ☑ The Marketing Mix
4 Identify the role of marketing in achieving customer satisfaction and retention	☑ Putting customer satisfaction at the heart of the heart of the business
5 Discuss marketing as a cross functional activity	☑ Links with IT, HR, customer service, operations, production ☑ Conflict between departments often arise
6 Recognise the key internal functional relationships that are important to the marketing function.	☑ Interdependency of departments
7 Define internal marketing	☑ Marketing within the organisation ☑ All internal employees regarded as customers of one another
8 State the difference in needs between internal and external customers	☑ Worksheet activity relevant to your own organisation.

Quick quiz

1 Which of the following statements represents a fair view of the term marketing?

A Marketing concentrates on selling more products

B Marketing is about meeting customer needs profitably

C Marketing is about creating advertising

2 Internal customers are:

A Employees of the organisation

B All stakeholders

C Customers who have lots on interaction with the organisation

3 The process of marketing is split into the following stages:

A Planning, analysis, implementation and control

B Analysis, planning implementation and control

C Planning, analysis, control, implementation

4 Which of the following roles is not a role that HR department would perform in collaboration with the marketing department?

A Articulate a shared vision

B Brief advertising agencies

C Communicate ideas to staff

5 The extended marketing mix is abbreviated to:

A The 4P's

B The 5M's

C The 7P's

6 Place refers to:

A Where customers can find out more about a product or service

B Where the product or service is available to purchase and how it is delivered to the customer.

C The location the product will be used

7 Promotion refers to:

A A range of methods designed to raise awareness of a product or service

B Special price offers

C Just how the product is advertised

8 A market is:

A A place where products are distributed

B All the potential customers sharing a particular need or wants who might be willing and able to engage in exchange

C A category of products

1 B- - look at the definition at the beginning of the chapter.

2 A- Employees are important as they need to 'believe' in the product or service and understand the value of customer service.

3 C- See section 2

4 B- Briefing agencies would normally only involve the marketing department

5 C- The 7 P's are product, price, place, promotion, people, process, physical evidence

6 B- Place represents logistics and distribution

7 A- Promotion involves far more than just advertising, there is a wide range of promotional tools availible

8 B- See section 1

Worksheet activity 1

Statement	Comment
Marketing depends on advertising	Advertising is only a small element of marketing. It sits within the category of Promotion in the Marketing Mix Framework. This is one of the more visible elements of marketing and therefore is often thought of as 'marketing' per se.
Dealers profits significantly increase prices customers pay	Although there are some dealers who do apply large margins which pushes up the cost of products and services, a marketer would ensure that there is some value attached to the increased price. For example, you should also get some additional service from using the dealer. In many markets (especially since the increased use of e-commerce) customers sometimes have the opportunity to deal directly with manufacturers and avoiding additional costs eg holidays eg Portland Direct, computer manufacturers such as Dell.
Marketing is selling	Similar to advertising, Sales promotion is just one function of marketing. True market orientation means that customer needs are taken into account which negates the need for the stereotypical 'pushy' sales person.
Marketers persuade	The connotation here is that it marketing is a manipulative practice. Marketers look to meet needs, not to persuade customers that needs exist when they don't because there is no long term benefit in taking this approach.
Strategic planning is nothing to do with marketing	As customer orientation is as much a philosophy as a function, then it needs to be integrated strategically thorough out the organisation.

Worksheet activity 2

It is likely that you will have a large list of marketing roles if you work for a large organisation and maybe no specific marketing specialist if you work for a very small organisation. Either way, you are likely to find that no matter which end of the spectrum your company falls into, there will be common tasks that need to be completed. In a large number of organisations, unfortunately these tasks are still viewed as the central role of marketing rather than the philosophical aspect of the customer being at the centre and marketing is a way to co-ordinate this effort. More recently, there have been calls to

define marketing roles more clearly so that the function and the philosophy are separated into two distinct issues, this may lead to the reference to both rather than just one by organisations.

Worksheet activity 3

Although it will depend on the size and nature of your organisation, you are likely to have a significant list of internal customers. It is important that you try to establish what the main needs are for each of these internal stakeholders because you will then be able to better meet their needs.

References

Baker, M. (1992) Marketing Strategy and Management Second Edition, Macmillan. London.

BBC 4 (2007) 'The Edwardian Larder' BBC 4, First Aired Monday 11 June 2007 10.50pm-11.50pm

Blythe, J. (2006) Principles and Practice of Marketing, Thompson, London.

Gronroos, C (1990) Services Management and Marketing, Lexington Books, Lexington MA.

Hill, L. And O'Sullivan, T. (2004) Foundation Marketing 3rd Edition, Prentice Hall, London.

Jardine, R (2007) Interview sourced from, http://www.bbc.co.uk/bbcfour/documentaries/features/edwardian-larder.shtml [Accessed 18.12.07]

Kotler, P. (1994) Marketing Management: Analysis, Planning, Implementation and Control, Eighth Edition, Prentice Hall, New Jersey.

Marketing (2008)'New Campaign: Fanta Still' Published 30.01.08,pg 2, Marketing, Haymarket Publishing, London.

The Times (2008)a 'Is Diet Coke Uncool?' Published 31.01.08, The Times Online, London [Accessed 31.01.08]

Chapter 2

The Marketing Environment

Topic list

1 Macro and micro marketing environments

2 PESTEL factors

3 The micro environment

4 Monitoring the marketing environment

Introduction

This chapter looks at the first stage of the Marketing Process, the Marketing Environment. If you remember, in chapter 1 we outlined how the marketing process begins with analysis of the marketing environment before moving on plan, implement and control marketing variables known as the Marketing Mix. The first section of this chapter starts by looking at what is defined as the marketing environment. Differences between macro and micro marketing environments are outlined.

In the second section we break down the acronym PESTEL which is used by marketers to remember the range of variables operating within the macro environment. PESTEL stands for Political; Economic; Social; Technological; Environmental (or ecological) and; Legal. The implications of each of these factors are discussed in terms of the implications for marketers.

The third section focuses on the internal and micro environments. Finally, the fourth section outlines the different methods that marketers use in order to monitor their overall environment before we move on to consider how much control an organisation may have over the different aspects of over its environment.

Syllabus linked learning objectives

By the end of the chapter you will be able to:

	Learning objectives	Syllabus link
1	Discuss why an appreciation of the marketing environment is required	2.1
2	Distinguish between internal, micro and macro environments	2.2
3	Explain the elements of PESTEL	2.2
4	Identify key stakeholder characteristics in relation to the micro- market	2.3
5	Explain market analysis and monitoring	2.4
6	Identify controllable from non-controllable environmental factors	2.1

1 Macro and micro marketing environments

A marketing environment represents the world that the organisation exists within and the related factors which will determine its success . Obviously this is very broad and so marketers split their 'environments' into different levels in order to make it easier to understand the complex situations.

KEY CONCEPT

concept

The term marketing environment is often defined as;

'the external factors which affect a company's planning and performance, and are beyond its control'

CIM (2008) Online Knowledge Hub, Marketing Glossary

1.1 Levels of a Marketing Environment

The marketing environment is often defined into different levels. Initially internal and external environments are distinguished.

(a) The Internal environment is the environment ***within*** the organisation.

(b) The external environment includes all those forces and events ***outside*** the organisation which directly impact its activities.

Next we think specifically about the external environment and differentiate micro and macro environments

(c) Micro environment is the ***closest*** external environment where changes and events here ***directly impact*** the organisation eg. competitor activities.

(d) The Macro environment is again external but ***beyond the immediate*** environment .This environment can have major impacts on the organisation eg. political changes .

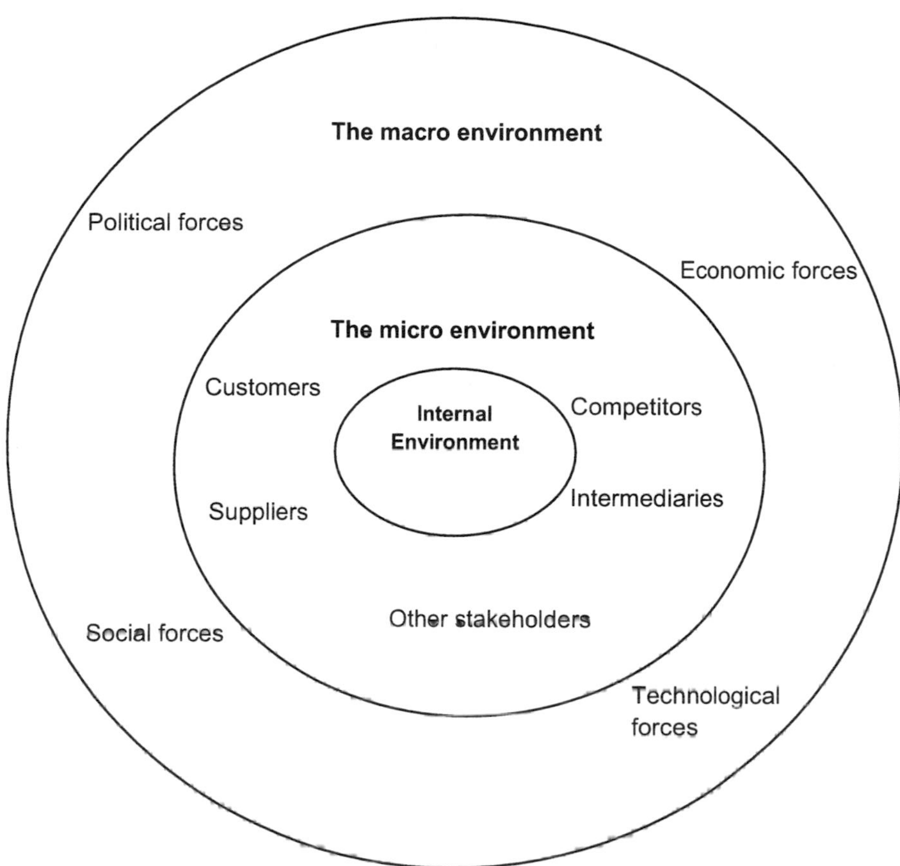

Source: Adapted from Palmer, A. And Hartley, B.(2006) The Business Environment 5th Edition, McGraw Hill

EXAM TIP

concept

It is highly likely that within the online test, you will be asked to identify whether an environmental factor is a macro or a micro force. To remember these quickly within the exam, make sure that you are familiar with your own organisation's (or one you are familiar with) macro and micro forces.

An organisation exists within society as a whole: Changes in the external environment will form the basis for building marketing plans. Careful monitoring of the external environment will help an organisation to identify opportunities and threats and be proactive rather than reactive in the face of change.

The organisation will have different levels of control of the various forces within its marketing environment, it is likely that there will be more control of the internal environment and less control over the external environments. It is equally important for the marketer to fully understand both micro and macro in order to adjust their actions to enable them to best meet the needs of all stakeholders.

1.2 The need for a Marketing Audit

In order to meet customers changing needs, it is important to fully understand how their needs are changing, whether these changes are short-term issues or longer lasting. To continue to be able to offer profitable goods and services, the marketer must be able to anticipate how customer needs and behaviour is likely to change in both the short and the long term. There are many examples of where organisations have not effectively evaluated the factors likely to impact their market and have therefore experienced a decline in business. The retailer Marks and Spenser for example suffered considerably because they failed to notice improvements that competitors were making to the quality of their offerings and didn't make similar improvements to their own clothing lines (Palmer and Hartley, 2006).

MARKETING AT WORK

application

Bingo Club's in Ireland had failed to recognise the impact that the smoking ban would have when it came into effect. By the time the ban later entered the UK in July 2007, the large bingo organisations were well prepared with new outside smoking areas and 'break time' electronic game consoles along with much improved online bingo offerings to appeal to their 60% of players who were also smokers.

To be effective, marketing should be well planned, ideally using the defined process as shown in the next diagram. Within the overall marketing planning process; identifying 'Where we are now ?' involves a thorough marketing audit.

KEY CONCEPT

concept

The marketing audit is often also referred to as the situation analysis.

The audit helps to make sense of the environment the organisation is currently operating within. Analysis requires a thorough study of the broad trends within the economy and society, as well as a detailed analysis of markets, consumers and competitors.

MARKETING AT WORK

application

The global recession has had a major effect on nearly all organisations and although it is difficult to predict which will survive, those who have kept abreast of the developments within their marketing environments are more likely to survive if they have used the information they have gathered to adapt their strategies accordingly. Those who are not aware of the changes in their market will only be able to react to the ever rapid changes. Although this is equally true in boom periods, in periods of economic downturn effects of unanticipated industry changes and consumer behaviour are magnified and lead to faster detrimental consequences.

Completing an audit within the marketing planning process helps to ensure that the markets the organisation is currently targeting with the range of products or services tailored to meet customers' needs will need to be modified in the short, medium or long-term future. It also serves to justify and identify whether marketing decisions about the targeted segments and marketing mix which is used are appropriate in light of the market forces in place both now and in the future. For example, a cosmetics company which began trading in 1940 would have found that it was preferable to test their cosmetics extensively on animals so that consumers were assured of their 'safety'. Compare that requirement to today's environment. Although consumers insist upon 'safe' products, the last twenty years has seen a move towards products which have not been tested on animals because consumers prefer products which do not use animal experimentation. The company may therefore find it more appropriate to change their manufacturing processes, ingredients and communications messages and move towards a 'cruelty free' range.

The marketing audit involves three main stages:

1. **PESTEL analysis** is used to describe the relevant factors and trends in the external environment. Marketers investigate the political, economic, social, technological, ecological and legislative factors (PESTEL analysis is covered in detail in section 2).

2. **Formal marketing research** is used to generate information from market research, product research, competitor analysis, customer research. Although it is mostly used to gain information about the external environments, sometimes where necessary research may be conducted internally to identify where changes should be made within the organisation and how it organises it's marketing activities. Staff surveys for example may help here.

3. **Internal audits** are used to identify how the business operates. Overall, how the organisation puts together it's product/service offering and whether the capabilities, structure, resources are appropriate to meet the needs of customers are audited.

The Government website www.statistics.gov.uk is very useful in looking at trends in the UK. You will find this very helpful when you research the marketing environment for a UK based organisation. It is worth spending time 'browsing' the site to see what information you may be able to use.

For global trend insights the United States CIA website has a world facts book with key statistics on all nations and some links to country specific information :https://www.cia.gov/library/publications/the-world-factbook/geos/au.html. ■

MARKETING AT WORK

application

Cruise line Royal Caribbean restructured its UK sales team into separate brand focussed teams for Celebrity cruises and Azamara brands. The purpose of this move was to be able to capitalise further on the UK and Irish markets which would require more specialist sales agents.

Source: Marketing Week, 21.2.08

It is assumed that this would have been planned following an extensive internal audit. Sometimes audits are conducted by external consultants in order for an impartial view to be taken, these however are expensive and therefore will not be appropriate for smaller organisations.

2 PESTEL factors

Within the Macro environment, there are a number of factors which are generally beyond the control of the organisation but will play a huge role in determining the long-term success of its marketing strategy.

concept

PESTEL is sometimes shortened to PEST. PEST analysis looks at the Political, Economic, Social and Technological factors affecting the organisation. PESTEL highlights the need to differentiate ecological and legislative forces.

The external environment can be described in terms of four key components: Political/legal, Economic, Social/cultural, and Technological (**PEST factors**). A more complete version of this model is PESTEL Socio-cultural, Technological, Economic, Ecological, Political and Legal. Sometimes STEEPLE is also used as an alternative and this includes the concept of Ethical factors. The following diagram shows STEEPLE factors.

The total environment

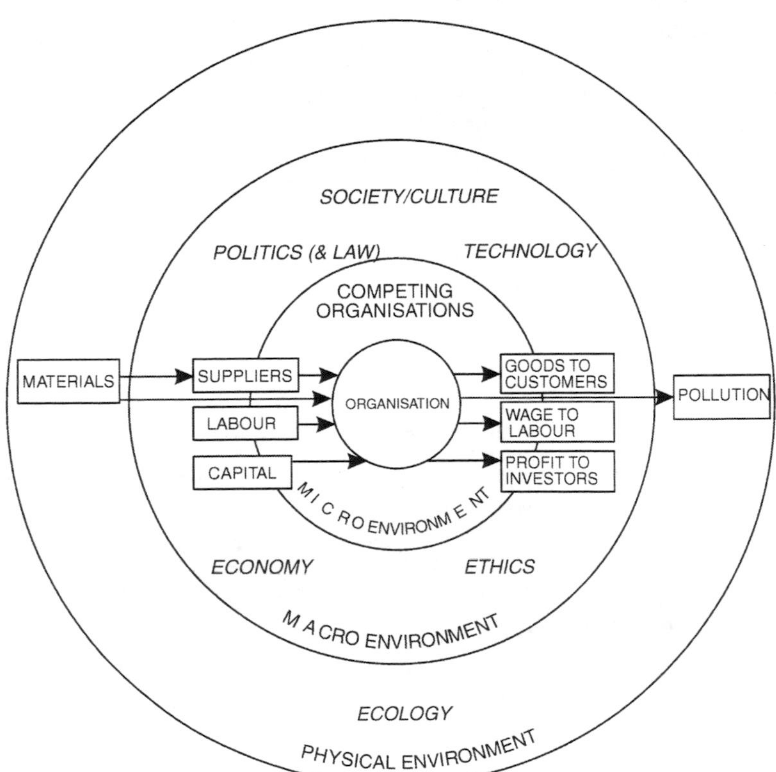

2.1 The political environment

This involves the interaction between organisations and **government** or regulatory bodies. The political environment can be one of the most unpredictable for the marketer (Palmer and Hartley, 2006). Central and local government and any related bodies or departments will influence marketing plans considerably. Change in the political environment can lead to a number changes for marketers. Typically a change in government can make considerable changes e general laws (Blythe, 2006) In the relatively recent past opening times of shops, the weights and measures that products can be sold in, the times at which alcohol can be sold have all been changed by governments and will have had an impact on many individual organisations.

WORKSHEET ACTIVITY 1

application

List as many types of businesses that you can which will have been affected by the government decision to ban smoking in public places from July 2007.

Palmer and Hartley (2006) p.4 discussed several ways in which the political environment can impact business strategy and operations.

Palmer and Hartley's (2006) political impacts can be summarised as:

1. **Political stability** affects the attractiveness of a national market eg reluctance of international business to invest in certain developing countries due to political instability.
2. Governments **pass legislation** which both directly and indirectly impacts the organisation eg anti-competitive practices legislation, patent legislation, consumer protection legislation.
3. Governments see **organisations as vehicles for social change** through their roles as employers eg minimum wages and holidays legislation.
4. Governments are responsible for **protecting the public interest** at large and therefore imposes standards and regulations to safeguard safety eg food standards, smoking ban.
5. The **economy is influenced by government** policy eg government intervention in money markets by buying and selling currency, levels of taxation and inflationary controls .
6. At both central and local levels is a **major consumer of goods and services** in its own right eg 40% of the UK's GDP is accounted for by government spending on schools, hospitals, public services etc.
7. Government **policies influence social and cultural values** eg. Smoking ban, anti pollution policies , nutrition, education.

Political systems within UK markets can be categorised into central, regional, local and European Union:

- Central government consists of Parliament, the Cabinet, ministers, civil servants and political advisors, not all of whom are elected.

- Regional government eg. Scottish Parliament, National Assembly for Wales, Northern Ireland Assembly and Greater London Authority
- Local government eg County, Town and district Councils are responsible for social services, education and local services.
- European Union coordinates business law throughout the member states in order to ensure a fair competitive environment.

The government overall will influence organisations in a number of ways as shown in the following diagram.

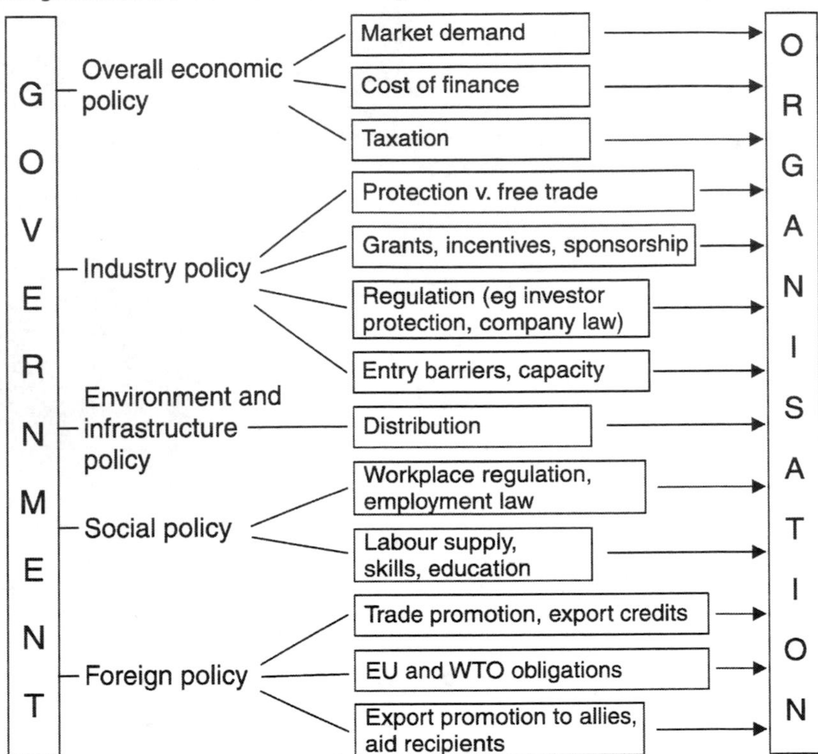

MARKETING AT WORK

application

Different councils throughout the UK have adopted alternative refuse collection policies. In some area, household waste is only collected once a fortnight. In these areas, many small businesses such as wheelie bin cleaners have grown or diversified into offering additional waste collection services so that residents can opt to still have their waste collected on a weekly basis. Other services which have grown at this time have included bin washing, recyclable materials sorting and collection and specialist business refuse collection arrangements. The impact of local government policies therefore can therefore influence both large and small business decisions.

2.2 The economic environment

Developments within **the economy** – which are likely to have an impact on businesses either directly, or as a result of their impact on consumer spending – are critical to business. The economic environment is basically about the level of demand within the economy. Key aspects of the economic environment include inflation, unemployment, economic growth, consumer income, interest rates and currency fluctuations (in international trade).

2.2.1 Business Cycles

The economy generally goes through cycles and fluctuations. Most national economies follow the boom and bust economic cycle (Blythe, 2006). Economic growth is good for business prosperity. In times of growth, organisations will invest more

heavily in product development, make improvements to production processes and employ higher numbers of staff. At this time consumer confidence will be higher because they will have a higher level of spending power. Although the actual definition of a recession varies by country, within the UK the term is refers to a two or more consecutive quarters when the economy ceases to grow (Pym, 2008). During this time output shrinks and consumer confidence is dented leading to a reduction in demand. Reduced demand results in a drop in business expenditure and job cuts which in turn reduced consumer demand further.

MARKETING AT WORK

application

In the latter part of 2007 and into 2008 the UK press reported heavily on 'the credit crunch'. The situation was underpinned by several threatening economic factors:

- A slow down in the property market with improvements not expected until 2012
- Strong inflationary pressures being seen as a result in high prices of oil, food and exchange rates
- High levels of personal dept compared to the rest of Europe and an increasing level of National dept with the Government accruing a debt of 5% GDP
- The Credit Crunch brought about initially from bad debt within the US mortgage market began to turn into a banking crisis and many international banks searched for alternative sources of credit to 'prop up' losses.

Warnings to 'tighten their belts' and prepare for a recession were issued to consumers by financial pundits throughout the UK media. By the end of 2008 the UK high street began to look very different with many well known retailers falling into trouble and ceasing to trade. Woolworths and MFI were amongst the first to close in early January 2009. Within manufacturing food, electronics and car manufacturers were quickly hit by the global downturn. Within the marketing sector, advertising and PR agencies began to make redundancies across the globe.

Sources: Finance Markets (2008), The Economist (2007)

2.2.2 Industry impacts

There will be some industries which will be impacted more than others by economic changes. In general luxury and non essential items will be most heavily affected by a downturn in economic conditions. Staple products such as basic foods will continue to be demanded but even within the food industry, markets change significantly. In the last major UK recession during the early 1990's; grocery retailers launched large numbers of basic, 'value' ranges of everyday food and household products. The era of the 3 pence tin of beans was born. When the economic situation improved and consumers moved into a period of relative affluence, luxury ranges such as Tesco's Finest and Sainsbury's Taste the Difference ranges gradually developed. With the full ranges in place by the 2008 downturn, retailers began demonstrating to consumers how they may switch to cheaper alternatives when selecting products in online stores.

2.2.3 Key economic indicators

Some key economic indicators and factors exist that businesses should be aware of, these are shown in the table below. The table shows at the most simplistic level why these are relevant to marketers:

Economic factor	Relevant because...
Interest rates The price of money	• Impact borrowing power of businesses and consumers with higher interest rates making loans more expensive • Impact on household disposable income as a result of mortgage rates and interest earned on savings • Saving levels are an indicator or consumer confidence in their job security and value of assets. When confidence is low, saving is more likely.
Exchange rates The price of a currency expressed in terms of another country	• The relative price of imported goods are affected • How expensive and thus appealing domestic goods are to foreign countries (export)
Gross National Product The sum of all incomes as a result of economic activity plus the net property income from abroad	• The level of wealth or income within a country including monies earned overseas • Indicates the general level of wealth within a nation • Demonstrates the likely purchasing power within a country and the economic position
Taxation Government income through direct taxation of incomes and indirect taxation of products and services.	• Impacts the spending power in particular market segments • Can impact consumer confidence and thus spending • Impacts business policies and employment strategy • Some businesses in specialised areas may have a larger tax burden eg wine importers
Inflation An increase in prices	• Increasing prices which reduces purchasing power • Once inflation increases, **expectation inflation** occurs. Regardless of whether the inflationary factors still exist, inflation is *expected* which leads to increase in wages and prices to protect future income levels.

2.3 The social/cultural environment

The social and cultural environment is quite often one of the main areas that marketers draw inspiration for their segmentation, targeting and positioning strategies. Blythe (2006) identified four categories that these forces can be grouped into:

1. **Demographic forces** eg the structure of the population in terms of age, income, ethnicity and gender
2. **Culture** eg beliefs, values, behaviours and customs
3. **Social responsibility and ethics** eg these are derived partly from culture. They can have implications for marketers in terms of how society responds to marketing initiatives
4. **Consumerism** eg there has been a shift in power away from companies and to consumers. Consumers are increasingly savvy when it comes to marketing initiatives, how to obtain the best 'deals' and their purchase rights.

Many countries are undergoing a rapidly accelerating **demographic change** and changing **attitudes and perceptions**. Developed countries tend to have ageing populations, which in turn has many implications for marketers and recruiters. The changing role of women may also affect the marketer. Cultural values and norms also influence buyer behaviour and tastes in different national/ethnic contexts, creating particular challenges for international marketing.

2.3.1 UK social changes

Within the UK society has changed considerably over the last twenty years. All of Blythe's (2006) categories of social forces have changed. It is too simplistic to suggest that society has changed to for the UK of today for just a couple of reasons. In reality, there have been many interrelated changes which have a combined effect in carving our current society. A small selection of these changes include:

- An increased multi cultural mix within the population
- Rapid technological developments changing communication patterns eg social networking, mobile telecoms etc
- Changing working patterns with an increased service industry and reduction in manufacturing, more flexible hours
- Increased labour mobility, short term working contracts and an increase in small business start ups
- A 24/7 culture
- Increasing varied family structures and roles

MARKETING AT WORK

The National Centre for Social Research launched their 24th British Social Attitudes Report on , Wednesday 23 January 2008. The report was launched with a press release which outlined some major changes within the social environment in the last twenty years. Extracts from the press release are shown below.

Press Release from National Centre for Social Research

The report describes the state of public attitudes towards: relationships and parenting; cohabitation; gender roles; national identity; working in the public sector; prejudice; car use and the environment; newspapers; political participation; party policies; and poverty. Among the findings:

Views on family life have become more liberal
70% of people think there is nothing wrong with sex before marriage, up from 48% in 1984.
Only 28% of people think married couples make better parents than unmarried ones.
Only 17% of men think that a 'man's job' is to earn money, while a woman should stay at home, down from 32% in 1989.

But we do not always practise what we preach, and are confused about the legal implications of new family forms
When it comes to doing household chores, our behaviour has not changed as much as our attitudes.
77% of people in couples say that the woman usually does the laundry, little changed since 1994.
There is widespread confusion about what protection cohabiting couples have under the law, with 51% of people thinking (incorrectly) that there is such a thing as 'common law marriage'.

There is widespread concern about the environment and inequality
80% of people think that current levels of car use are having a serious impact on climate change. And 45% of drivers are both willing and able to reduce their car use.

But pockets of selfishness and self-interest remain
23% of people think everyone should be able to use their cars as much as they like, even if it damages the environment.
People are less sympathetic towards the poor. 35% think government should spend more money on welfare benefits for the poor, down from 55% in 1986.

WORKSHEET ACTIVITY 2

application

Suggest at least three industries that will be impacted either in a positive or a negative way as a result of the changes in British society as identified by the British Social Attitudes Report. Outline why they will be impacted.

1

2

3

You will find that social influences are highly varied and their impact will differ considerably for within different industries. If we take one indicator within societies food consumption we can outline the complexities that result. Between 1992 and 2004 'out of home' food consumption doubled and the amount of money spent on eating out was higher than that spent food eaten at home (Government Statistics, 2006). A number of cultural and social issues may have contributed to this change including:

- **Busier lifestyles**
  Fewer people have time to make lunches or eat breakfast at home therefore there has been a growth in the ready-made sandwich sector and the breakfast bar industry developed. In turn these would have has an adverse impact on sliced bread, cold meats and other sandwich filling products because more people are buying lunch rather that making lunch. The breakfast cereal manufacturers have had to develop breakfast bar products to avoid consumers reaching for alternatives such as chocolate bars (as appeared to be a threat at one time).

- **An increased propensity for dining out as a social activity**
  The popularity of dining out as a social activity has grown within the UK. Always a popular activity within the rest of Europe, dining out with the French, Spanish and Italians being renowned for socialising, taking long lunches and extended dinners. In these cultures eating out is not regarded a luxury as it once was within the UK but part of the fabric of life.

Managed pub operators Mitchells and Butler (2008), identified several additional demographic reasons why social food consumption out of home has increased as part of their justification for providing food within their pubs, these were:

- an increased number of working women
- more single person households
- increasingly active retired people

The situation for the overall food industry is increasingly complex if we factor in other current issues relating to UK food consumption such as: rapid food price increases (Wallop, 2007); government concern about obesity levels (Department for Health, 2008) and social changes in terms of the pressure to move towards healthier and more natural food choices.

MARKETING AT WORK

application

The concern within many Western societies about the 'couch potato' lifestyles adopted by young people as a result of computer games may have been the reason behind Nintendo's strategy to develop more fitness based products which encourage players to move. The Nintendo Wii initially featured movable controls, this was later followed by the Wii Balance Board. The wireless 'step' requires players to actively move in order to play fitness based games or take part in fitness training style sessions. The board enables users to measure their body mass index and other health related tests. This is an

important change in the nature of the product in ensuring the long term needs of the market are met. Without the more active dimension to the product, Nintendo would have risked groups of consumers moving away from the concept of computer games because of adverse publicity and changing social attitudes. Now they are directly tackled the 'active issue' and are could be perceived as acting in a more socially responsible way.

WORKSHEET ACTIVITY 3

evaluation

Consider at least five social changes that are likely to impact your organisation over the next five years.

1

2

3

4

5

2.3.2 International differences

Society varies considerably between cultures and marketers need to be aware that as borders open differences in social perspectives remain intact. The term psychic distance is used to refer to socio-cultural differences between a home country and host country (Jobber, 2007). Language, cultural norms, behaviours, customs, values and attitudes all need consideration.

MARKETING AT WORK

application

Think about grocery shopping habits and how these vary between cultures. Not only do differences in choice of food types occur but also (among others):

- **Time** of the day and **frequency** of visits (eg daily weekly or monthly shopping). For example, in Canada monthly shopping is the norm whilst in the UK a 'weekly shop' is commonplace with' top up' shops in between for *essentials*.
- The **distribution outlet or method** used to purchase groceries eg internet food shopping, local markets, supermarkets, small local shop, individual specialist stores (butchers, bakers etc) hypermarkets, door to door delivery vans will all differ culturally according to their prevalence within society.
- **Who** shops for groceries may also vary. Increasingly in some Western societies, men are shopping in increasing numbers. In some parts of the world however children may find that shopping for the family is one of their responsibilities.

As a collective group of indicators, shopping habits may be one factor which provides a lot of information for marketers when considering cultural and lifestyle differences.

2.3.3 Societal marketing

Societal marketing considers the needs of society and consumers wider interests (Jobber, 2007). For example, the long term needs of society and consumers may be at odds with the short term profit motives for some organisations. Organisations who forsake their own short term profitable opportunities for the sake of social wellbeing are not necessarily doing this for short term positive PR but are considering the longer term societal needs by adopting societal marketing principles.

KEY CONCEPT

concept

Societal marketing is sometimes linked to a related term 'cause-related' marketing.

Cause-related marketing involves forming partnerships with charities. Many organisations publicly work with charities and promote their causes eg Tesco computers for schools vouchers

2.4 The technological environment

The nature and rate of change in technology affects the way an organisation undertakes its business. Many of the products in common use today such as the television, frozen foods, dishwashers, microwaves were not even thought about a 100 years ago (Blythe, 2006). **Technological change** has been more apparent and ever faster in recent years, most notably in computing and telecommunications (or ICT), but also in the biological sciences. This creates new product potential, faster working, improved internal and external communications– as well as new marketing tools.

MARKETING AT WORK

application

US scientists began working on a new material nicknamed 'frozen smoke' in 1931. It wasn't until 2007 that Aerogel (as it is now formally branded) was dubbed the miracle material for the future. Aerogel has a wide range of uses such as insulation, bomb-proofing, protecting from extreme heat, specialist filtration and being ultra absorbent. The low density material is thought to have numerous product applications. Product possibilities are numerous and first uses in consumer products include next generation strengthened tennis rackets, jewellery, winter clothing and house insulation. Industrial products include space suits which protect astronauts to 130 °c and absorption products for mopping up ecological pollution and disasters such as oil spills.

Racket manufacturer Dunlop have already created a range of more powerful tennis and squash rackets. Hugo Boss sold a range of lightweight winter jackets which were insulated with Aerogel. Unfortunately the product in this instance was not a success in the UK because consumers complained that they were too warm.

Adapted and based on Taher, A. (2007).

Awareness of technological developments can help an organisation in a number of ways. Some examples (some of which will probably be superseded before this book is published due to the nature of technology) are outlined in the following table.

Potential benefit of technological development	Examples
Cut costs	New ingredients may be developed that are more cost effective. Mars controversially changed their ingredients for the Mars bar in 2007 to cut costs. The decision was withdrawn in this instance because the new cheaper ingredient contained animal products which upset vegetarians.
Brand new products	Almost any 'brand new to the world' new product would have been influenced by technological capabilities. Some famous examples include Dyson vacuum cleaners, squirty cream, I Pods.
Improved products	Either due to new features or improved quality, many product developments will have a technological dimension. Deodorant containing ingredients which do not leave white marks on clothing for example.
Production efficiency	Toyota made use of tool technology to revamp their factory which meant they were able to dramatically cut production times. Introducing self scanning devises into supermarkets has led to the reduced need for checkout staff and faster exits for consumers.
Increase brand reputation	Sometimes making use of the most modern technology in a visible manner can help build a reputation for being cutting edge. Hairdressers who invest in the latest drying equipment, have LCD screens at each ergonomically designed chair to demonstrate style and use the most advanced hair care products could possibly gain a reputation for keeping up with current trends. This is a positive attribute within this competitive Industry because of the related ideas that staff may be better trained etc.
Improved communications	Mobile, wireless, fast communication is commonplace and part of everyday business. The ability to conference call, text, webchat, video conference and even participate in virtual world meetings are making it unnecessary for time consuming travel for formal meetings in some instances. Technology has to some extent also had an adverse effect on good quality communications particularly with email becoming overused and conversations which could resolve issues possibly more effectively becoming rare.
New promotional opportunities	Orange were able to use mobile phone technology effectively to launch their Orange Wednesday where 2 for 1 cinema tickets are sent as a code to customers mobile phones. The ability to print coupons at store checkouts for products which are likely to be of interest to consumers because of the items they have just scanned.
New distribution/ sales opportunities	Mars was the first FMCG company to sell products via the social networking website Facebook. Adapting the idea of 'poking' friends' in other words sending a message/ picture) to them online.

Understanding technology from the perspective of what the organisation can use it for is essential however it is also important to think about it from the perspective of how your customers and the rest of society are responding to technological developments. Changes in technology are likely to lead to significant cultural and lifestyle changes which in turn will eventually impact other PESTEL factors and impact your market. When digital cameras became mainstream and overtook the market for film based products many high street retailers who had previously offered film development services gradually changed to offering printing booths designed for consumers to download and print out the shots they wanted. Printer manufacturers began to develop smaller printers designed specifically to be used to print 8x4 sized photos and print straight from the camera. Next, online sites and sites of high street retailers began to offer the opportunity for creating bound albums which consumers designed online and were then developed. This example will no doubt continue to change and evolve over time, the point is that when a large technological change happens, many smaller steps which have far wider implications for industries and society as a whole tend to follow.

EXAM TIP

concept

Often students think only about the IT aspect of technology and forget other scientific developments that can help to improve packaging, ingredients, manufacturing processes etc. Don't forget that at one time the development of the wheel was a major technological advancement and the world did exist (albeit at a slower pace) before computers!

WORKSHEET ACTIVITY 4

evaluation

List the technological changes that have had an impact on your organisation over the last five years. What proportion of these would you say are computer or 'gadget' based?

2.5 The ecological or 'green' environment

Issues relating to the natural environment have already had a considerable impact on marketing policies and this influence is expected to increase in the future. In the past there has been a tendency to regard marketing, and business activities in general, as incompatible with 'green' principles, but it is now recognised that the two can be complementary.

The focus on 'green' ecological and ethical issues has become so intense in recent years that some of the marketing press began to use the term 'greenwash' to suggest that some companies are merely jumping on an environmental bandwagon because they think that it will win them favour in the eyes of consumers (Aitken, 2007).

The Guardian ran an article entitled 'Wiping out Greenwash' on Monday 19th November 2007. The article looked at how some organisations were making small environmental moves but with a hidden agenda to generate an improved reputation. The article includes a number of examples of good and bad green initiatives including M&S's positive 'Look behind the label' and 'Plan A' campaigns and Ariels campaign to encourage people to reduce their washing temperatures.

The web link to the article is:
http://www.guardian.co.uk/media/2007/nov/19/mondaymediasection.climatechange ■

Much of the concern about companies' social responsibilities focuses on their attitude towards environmental concerns of the public. The environment has come to people's attention for a number of reasons.

(a) The entry into decision-making or political roles of the generation which grew up in the 1960s, where ecological issues became aired for the first time, has affected the political climate. Global environmental concerns now feature heavily within politics.

(b) The growth in prosperity after World War II has encouraged people to feel that **quality of life**, as opposed to material production and consumption, is no longer a luxury.

(c) **Expansion of media coverage** (eg of famines) and wider discussion of long-term environmental trends (eg the impact of global warming on the weather) has fuelled public anxiety. This has been particularly true in relation to third world issues such as rain forest destruction and drought. The concert Live 8 held throughout the world in the summer of 2007 and similar initiatives work not only to raise immediate cash but to increase the profile of the cause through PR and media support.

(d) Some **notable disasters** (eg Chernobyl, oil slicks caused by the Exxon Valdez accident and the Gulf War) have aroused public attention.

(e) **Greater scientific knowledge** is available about the effect of productive activity on the environment. For example, it has only recently been possible to measure the hole in the ozone layer and assess its causes.

(f) **Longer-term cultural shifts** against the ideals of science and rationality have encouraged the idealisation of a 'natural' way of life. (Appeals to nature are common in advertising.)

It is possible to identify several ways in which the public concern with environmental issues will impinge on business.

- Consumer demand for products which appear to be **environmentally friendly**
- Demand for **less pollution** from industry
- **Greater regulation** by government
- Demand that businesses be charged with the **external cost** of their activities
- Possible requirements to conduct **ecological** (or environmental) **audits**
- Opportunities to develop products and technologies which are **ecologically friendly** (eg vegetable fuel sources)

Areas which seem to cause most concern and are therefore essential for marketers to consider are:

- Packaging
- Waste
- Sustainability
- Climate change

Although these concepts are interrelated, we will deal with them in turn.

2.5.1 Packaging

Many products have been criticised either for unnecessary packaging or for using materials which are not environmentally friendly. In the 1980's and early 1990's when consumer concern about Cluro fluro carbons (CFC's) intensified many aerosol based products such as hairspray, deodorant and polishes changed to non-aerosol based. Cosmetics frequently use more packaging than strictly necessary apparently because consumers subconsciously like to see a larger box for the amount of money that they spend. This was a strategy that The Body Shop initially entered into the market trying to combat and encouraged consumers to return their old bottles to be refilled. It is not just grocery and other FMCG items where packaging is a problem. Printer ink cartridges for example are also frequently returned for refilling or recycling.

MARKETING AT WORK

application

For the Easter 2008 season, Cadbury removed outer boxes from their smaller size Easter eggs. Eggs were wrapped only in foil which meant that the Easter product range used 75% less plastic and 60% less cardboard. 2000 trees were expected to be saved as a result and helped towards Cadbury's goal to reduce their environmental footprint by 50%.

(BBC, 2008)

Sensible disposal of packaging and the ability to recycle should also be considered. For decades snack foods have shown logos or have requested in writing that consumers dispose of their packaging in a bin. Nowadays they are likely to contain information about the type of recycling bin to use whether this is glass, plastic or cardboard. TetraPak is an example of packaging material which was used extensively because of its strength. TetraPak however is losing favour because it cannot be recycled easily as it mixes plastic, metal and cardboard.

2.5.1 Waste

Waste, rubbish or garbage is of concern for the following reasons;

1. The difficulty associated with its disposal eg rapidly filling landfill sites, problems associated with burning waste.
2. It is a resource that has taken a large amount of materials and energy to initially produce.
3. It is a resource that could be re-used for another purpose.

(Waste Watch, 2008)

There are a number of pressure groups such as Waste Watch who advocate the need to *reduce* the amount of waste we are creating in the first instance, *re-use* any waste for another purpose and *recycle* wherever possible. Waste comes in many forms and is not only an environmental but an economic issue for organisations. Waste Watch estimate that 4.5% of annual turnover is lost each year in avoidable waste. Within the workplace, waste can take the form of:

- **physical solid waste** – general manufacturing waste is increasingly re-used to create other products through recycling. Marks and Spenser for example launched a range of clothing which was manufactured using recycled plastic bottles .
- **gasses-** CO2 and other emissions. The brewery Adnams re-uses the steam used within their factories during the production process of an 'environmentally friendly' beer.
- **water** – both clean and dirty water needs to be carefully managed to avoid excessive use and encourage responsible discharge. Anglian Water builds a snowman out of fat which has been released into the dirty water system to demonstrate the amount of oils clogging up the pipe work from an average house.

MARKETING AT WORK

application

The consumer climate change group Together was launched in 2007 to help households reduce the waste (CO2 in particular). Tony Blair, Al Gore and partners B&Q, M&S, Tesco, O2, BSkyB, Barclaycard and British Gas endorse the group which runs promotional campaigns, conducts research and educates sector leaders alongside the international charity The Climate Group. Together only grant partner status to organisations who:

- Make significant contributions to CO2 reduction themselves and encourage their customers to also do so.
- Only launch new products which make a measurable reduction in waste levels.
- Provide Together with live data to help them calculate the reduction of CO2 they are facilitating.

An April Fools day viral marketing campaign used a spoof character Dan Power to encourage consumers to be wasteful. The campaign directed people to his MySpace and Facebook sites which gave tips about how to waste energy including leaving lights on, filling kettles to the brim and driving unnecessarily.

The campaign was created because Together identified although a growing proportion of the population were committed to becoming more environmentally friendly, 26% of people would only do so if green messages were more fun, warmer and humorous. It was hoped that the exaggerated Dan Power would evoke a response of 'what an idiot'.

(Sandison, 2008, Together.com, http://www.energywastingday.com)

As the global trend towards becoming more ecologically aware and less wasteful, organisations will be defined by their actions in this area. Internally staff will become aware of their own and the organisations efforts, suppliers may be selected according to their green credentials and consumers will become increasingly aware of the companies who are making attempts to become less wasteful. Simple initiatives such as encouraging paper recycling, using more ecological building materials for new offices, turning off lights are all small but significant changes you may have seen happening within your

own organisation. Many organisations are pledging to become carbon neutral within a particular time period, you may find it useful to find out the policy within your own organisation.

2.5.2 Sustainability

Sustainability involves developing strategies so that the company only uses resources at a rate which allows them to be replenished (in order to ensure that they will continue to be available). At the same time emissions of waste are confined to levels which do not exceed the capacity of the environment to absorb them. In relation to the development of the world's resources, policies based on sustainability seek to:

- Pursue equity in the distribution of resources
- Maintain the integrity of the world's ecosystems
- Increase the capacity of human populations for self-reliance

2.5.3 Climate change

Climate change is high on the agenda for governments and despite conflicting reports and disparate views about the extent and effects of climate change, it will remain one of the key priority areas for the foreseeable future. Scientists predict that warming of the earth's atmosphere will lead to food shortages, disease, extreme weather and oceans rising. Overall not a great picture. Although scientific knowledge is not exact in this area and there are extremes of opinion. Some for example believe that there is no problem at all, others speculate that climate change will result in the end of human life. It would be a foolhardy organisation however that doesn't take the issue seriously because of the amount of negative PR and possibly legislative action they may incur.

The Climate Group is an international body looking into the effects of climate change . You will find a large amount of information about the effects of climate change. Their website is www.theclimategroup.org.

2.6 The legal environment

Generally you can to some extent argue that *all* legislation will have an impact on the marketing environment because it will always effect one or more groups within a society. At the same time, to look at every single piece of legislation which operates within society and think about how it effects an individual organisations marketing plans is unrealistic and not needed. There are however some key pieces of legislation that all marketers should be aware of and then it is their responsibility to keep abreast of the specific laws and regulations that have a direct impact on their own industry.

KEY CONCEPT

concept)

The legal environment consists of **legislation** (made by act of parliament), **case law** (precedents developed by the courts) and **quasi-laws**, such as government-sponsored codes of conduct and rules developed by trade associations. European Union countries also face an increasing body of legislation from the European Commission.

MARKETING AT WORK

application

Generally, within practice, individual organisations will have a range of sources to help them work their way through the legislation that they need to comply with and changes that may occur. Large multinational organisations are likely to have teams of in-house lawyers who can advise on different aspects of the law. If in-house lawyers are not employed, these organisations and perhaps smaller businesses will employ retained solicitors from some of the major law firms.

Trade associations and professional bodies will also play a role in educating organisations in the role of the laws and their potential impact. It is one of the key reasons that organisations become members of such bodies. Associations and professional bodies also play a role in lobbying for changes in the law as well as developing their own mandatory codes of conduct to facilitate self regulation within industries.

The Melton Mowbray Pork Pie Association successfully worked for ten years to gain the EU legal protection of ' Protected Geographical Indication' which was awarded in April 2008. EU law states that only Melton Mowbray pork pies which are made in Melton Mowbray to the required recipe and process can be branded as Melton Mowbray. 34 other British regional foods including Scottish farmed salmon and Whitstable oysters also have their reputation protected by this law (Alleyn, 2008).

In the UK, one of the major changes in legislation to effect marketers has been the changes in the law relating to advertising to children. From 1st April 2007,ads targeted at children for food products which contained high levels of fats, sugars and salt were banned. Marketers were made aware of this from a range of sources including the Advertising Association, the Advertising Standards authority, The Food Standards authority and the related food trade associations.

The CIM identified that young marketers are not as familiar with laws effecting their industries as they should be. For example, the 2012 Olympic games is considered to be a major opportunity that many UK marketers will be taking advantage of. In a CIM Marketing Trends survey a staggering 90% of marketers had no understanding of the 2006 Games act which stipulates strict rules relating to the use of the Olympic logo and terminology surrounding the games (CIM, Marketing Trends Survey 2007) .

2.6.1 Consumer protection legislation.

There is a considerable about of consumer protection legislation which marketers need to comply with. A selection of these are outlined in the table below.

Table 1 Legislation to protect consumers

Law	Generally covers
Consumer protection Act	Compensation can be claimed if a product or service is responsible for death or injury
Data Protection Act	Protects the rights of individuals with regard to their personal data held by organisations
Consumer Credit Act	Protects consumers as credit providers must be licensed, consumers should be given a seven day 'cooling off' period. APR should be clearly stated. Credit is only given to those over 18.
Fair Trading Act	Led to the development of a Consumer Protection Advisory Committee and Director General of Fair trading. Regulates trading so that consumers rights are protected
Food Act	The entire food chain is included within the act which enforces food safety standards
Medicines Act	A system of licensing for all human and animal medicines laid down within this act
Prices Act	Directs how prices should be displayed
Sale of Goods Act	All goods sold by a trader must be 'fit for purpose'; of satisfactory quality and; as described
Sunday Trading Act	Stipulates times and nature of Sunday trading
Supply of Goods and Services Act	All products must be of satisfactory quality
Trade Descriptions Act	False of misleading information must not be given about products or services
Unfair Contract Terms Act	Consumers can challenge contracts they have entered into if they are unfair
Weights and Measures Act	Regulates the use of weights and measures and is enforced by Trading Standards officers

(Hill & O'Sullivan, 2004; OPSI, 2008; Statutelaw.gov.uk, 2008)

EXAM TIP

concept 

The syllabus requires that you are familiar with the first two important laws listed above, The Data Protection Act and The Sale of Goods Act.

2.6.2 The Data Protection Act

KEY CONCEPT

concept 

Data protection legislation protects the rights of individuals about whom personal data is held by organisations (data users). It is underpinned by The Data Protection Act (1998) which came into force on 1st March 2000.

Especially with the advent of computer records systems, fears have arisen with regard to:

- access to personal information by unauthorised parties
- the likelihood that an individual could be harmed by the existence of data which was inaccurate, misleading or sensitive (eg medical details)
- the possibility that personal information could be used for purposes other than those for which it was requested and disclosed.

The Data Protection Act 1998 (and the related Employment Practices Code) address these concerns. The legislation is an attempt to protect:

- **Individuals** (not corporate bodies)
- in regard to the gathering, storage and use of **personal data** (information about a living individual, including facts and expressions of opinion)
- which are **processed** (mechanically or manually) so that records can be systematically used to access data about the individual
- by **data controllers**: organisations or individuals who control the contents and use of files of personal data.

Data controllers and computer bureaux have to register with the Data Protection Commissioner. They must limit their use of personal data to the uses registered, and must abide by Data Protection Principles.

DATA PROTECTION PRINCIPLES

(1) The information to be contained in personal data shall be obtained, and personal data shall be processed, fairly and lawfully. (In particular, information must not be obtained by deception.)

(2) Personal data shall be held only for one or more specified (registered) and lawful purposes.

(3) Personal data shall be adequate, relevant and not excessive in relations to its purpose or purposes.

(4) Personal data shall be accurate and, where necessary, kept up to date. ('Accurate' means correct and not misleading as to any matter of *fact*. An *opinion* cannot be challenged.)

(5) Personal data shall not be kept for longer than is necessary for its purpose or purposes.

(6) An individual shall be entitled:

   (i) to be informed by any data controller whether he/she holds personal data of which that individual is the subject

   (ii) to be informed of the purpose or purposes for which personal data is held

(iii) to have access to any such data held by a data controller and

(iv) where appropriate, to have such data corrected or erased.

(7) Appropriate security measures shall be taken against unauthorised access to, or alteration, disclosure or destruction of, personal data and against accidental loss or destruction of personal data. The prime responsibility for creating and putting into practice a security policy rests with the data controller.

(8) Data may not be exported outside the European Economic Area, except to countries where the rights of data subjects can be adequately protected.

EXAM TIP

concept

It is well worth trying to remember the eight principles of The Data Protection Act because they are the type of topic which examiners like to test in online multiple choice examinations .

Benefits of improved data protection

The Information Commissioner (www.ico.gov.uk) suggests that following the Employment Practices DP Code will not only help employers to comply with the Data Protection Act, but will:

- Increase trust in the workplace: there will be transparency about information held on individuals, thus helping to create an open atmosphere where workers have trust and confidence in employment practices.
- Encourage good housekeeping: following the Code encourages organisations to dispose of out-of-date information, freeing up both physical and computerised filing systems and making valuable information easier to find.
- Protect organisations from legal action: adhering to the Code will help employers to protect themselves from challenges against their data protection practices.
- Encourage workers to treat customers' personal data with respect: the Code is intended to be consistent with other legislation such as the Human Rights Act 1998 and the Regulation of Investigatory Powers Act 2000 (RIPA).
- Assist global businesses to adopt policies and practices which are consistent with similar legislation in other countries.
- Help to prevent the illicit use of information by workers: informing them of the principles of data protection should discourage them from misusing information held by the organisation.

MARKETING AT WORK

application

The use of laptop computers to hold personal information about customers and members of staff has led to a number of prosecutions using The Data Protection Act during 2008. Skipton Financial Services were found by the Information Commissioners Office to be in breach of the DPA when an unencrypted laptop was stolen which contained the personal details of 114,000 of the companies customers. Marks and Spenser were also found to be in breach of the act in a similar incident when a stolen unencrypted laptop contained the details of 26,000 employees.

(http://www.ico.gov.uk/about_us/news_and_views/press_releases.aspx)

2.6.3 The Sale of Goods Act

When a consumer buys goods from a trader, they are entering a contact with them. As a result, if anything is faulty with the product the consumer has the right to take up the issue with the retailer. This is an important distinction because it has implications for manufacturers, retailers and consumers.

KEY CONCEPT

The Sale of Goods Act 1979 (as amended) stipulates that all goods sold by a trader must be:

- as described
- of satisfactory quality and not damaged (unless the fault is pointed out at the time of purchase)
- fit for purpose

There are a number of guides written for consumers about their rights and general consumer protection issues. The Office of Fair trading have a leaflet which looks at shoppers rights which can be downloaded from: http://www.oft.gov.uk/shared_oft/consumer_leaflets/general/CDSR1.pdf

Trading Standards have produced some guidance for traders which are quite detailed whilst remaining readable. They can be found at the following web link:

http://www.tradingstandards.gov.uk/cgi-bin/bglitem1.cgi?file=BADV073-1011.txt&msg=br

The CIM have written a basic guide to the law for marketers , this provides a range of sources of legal information and can be downloaded from:

http://www.cim.co.uk/MediaStore/FactFiles/Marketing%20law.pdf

(These sources have been used to put together the materials used within this section)

The Contract

The Sale of Goods Act is based within contract law and states that when a trader offers a service or item for sale they are at the first stage in making a contract by offering consumers an ' **invitation to treat'**. The consumer will then make an **offer** to purchase. At this point the trader is under no obligation to accept the offer.

Think about the following two scenarios:

Scenario 1 Chocolate bar purchase

A consumer goes into a newsagent and picks up a chocolate bar. They then take the chocolate to the counter and ask to pay for it. By placing the chocolate on the shelf with a corresponding price, the newsagent is offering an invitation to treat. The consumer by picking up the chocolate bar and taking it to the sales counter is then making an offer to purchase. Ordinarily, you would not think about this as the point at which a contract is made because the sales person would normally take the money quickly and the consumer would then leave the shop. By taking the money, the trader is completing the contract. The trader could technically still refuse to accept the consumers money in this scenario thereby not accepting the offer to purchase.

Scenario 2 House purchase

A person makes an offer to buy a house for a particular sum of money. The current house owner (now within the role as a trader) refuses to accept the offer because the price offered is not high enough. This scenario is quite typical and highlights the point that because an offer if made, the trader is at no point under obligation to accept the offer. It is only once formal contracts are exchanged that in this purchase the trader is obliged to sell or else they would be in **breach of the contract**.

Acceptance of the offer is assumed once the product has been kept for a 'reasonable' amount of time (changes according to the nature of the product), the customer tells the trader that they formally accept the goods, alteration of the goods or using the goods after complaining.

Six months from the time of the purchase is often deemed to be an acceptable period. Any problems with products within six months are assumed to have existed at the time of purchase unless the trader can prove otherwise.

Terms and remedies for a breach of contract

- **A change of mind**

  If a consumer changes their mind about a product they are technically in breach of contract unless they have made a purchase online, through home shopping or a salesperson in their home where this does not automatically apply.

  If in the case of a service booked the customer does not show up, the service provider is entitled to

- **Not as described**

  If a product or service is not as described for example, if orange juice states 100% freshly squeezed juice, then it cannot be made from a concentrate and added water because it would not be 'as described'.

- **Satisfactory quality**

  This refers to the finish, appearance, safety, durability and freedom from defects in products and within services that the service has been conducted with reasonable care.

- **Fit for purpose**

  When products are obviously designed to a specific purpose or a consumer outlines their intended purpose, the trader should ensure that the product or service could be put to that use. If a consumer on the other hand purchased a car and wished to use it as a boat, then they could not hold the car dealer to account for this because it is not the intended obvious purpose for a car. If on the other hand they visited a dealer and requested a car that they could use as a boat, if they were sold an ordinary car then they could claim that the dealer was in breach of contract.

  Remedies for a breach of contract include refund or repair entitlements and sometimes compensation.

  Exclusions apply with regard to complaints when consumers have damaged goods themselves, when they have bought a product for a purpose that they have not specified to the trader and it is outside the normal product usage, faults brought to the attention of the consumer before the sale and fair wear and tear.

Implications of the Sale of Goods Act

Although it is not the most dynamic of environmental factors because it does not change frequently, the Sale of Goods act can have major implications for customer service levels.

Offering customers 'no questions asked' money back returns for example is a significant goodwill gesture and often used as a retailers strategy to encourage relationships customers. Training sales and customer service staff in customer rights is another important service strategy.

Implications also exist for manufacturers. Although the Sale of Goods Act from a consumers perspective rests with the retailer, a manufacturer of products which are regularly faulty or breach the act in other ways is not likely to continue to be stocked by retailers. The retailer as the customer of the manufacturer will also have rights but will not appreciate complaints from their own valued customers.

WORKSHEET ACTIVITY 5

evaluation

Think about the impact of legal issues for your organisation. What special working practices or considerations does your organisation make.

2.6.4 Voluntary regulation

One way to minimise problems from governmental and legal intervention by companies is to participate in social and commercial good **citizenship**, complying with **best practice** and be responsive to **ethical concerns**. Often what is considered good practice at present is likely to acquire some regulatory force in the future, so proactive organisations are only pre-empting measures. They may also be responding proactively to a genuine environment threat or opportunity (eg by voluntarily reducing waste emissions or seeking fuel efficiencies). Voluntary regulation often allows businesses to adopt more cost-effective and realistic approaches than may be imposed on them. In addition, compliance with voluntary codes, particularly those relating to best practice or relations with consumers, can be marketed positively, enhancing the organisation's image.

MARKETING AT WORK

application

- In the UK, **junk food ads** are banned from being shown during programmes aimed at kids aged four to nine. From 1 January 2008, the restrictions will be extended to TV shows aimed at children up to 15, as well as any TV shows watched by a large number of kids.
- A May 2007 online survey showed that 89% of respondents in Australia would support similar restrictions (rather than voluntary self-regulation) in Australia.
- In April 2007, the Malaysian advertising industry moved towards self-regulation of fast-food advertising by presenting a proposed framework to government, including a cap on ads targeting children under the age of 10.

Some governments are more 'interventionist' than others: the UK government has historically preferred non-intervention and encouraged voluntary self-regulation. However, under EU influence, previously unregulated areas have come under regulation: one recent example is the outlawing of age discrimination, which used to be subject to self-regulation. This is partly because voluntary codes of practice are only 'recommendations' and cannot be effectively enforced if organisations choose to ignore them.

2.7 Fuzzy boundaries

An important issue to remember is that often it can be very difficult to separate marketing environmental forces into an individual category. For example the boundary between political, legal and economic issues are often fuzzy, changes in technology can often then lead to knock on social changes. The result of the linkages between concepts id that they are often interrelated as changes in one area can impact the others.

WORKSHEET ACTIVITY 6

evaluation

Read the following hypothetical scenario.

In the British milk market there has been an increased consumption of milk and milk based drinks. Within the last year, the following features have occurred:

1. The press reported a number of reports outlining the health benefits associated with milk.
2. The EU has significantly increased the subsidies offered to farmers producing milk which has meant that it is a good business option.
3. Supermarkets have focussed on the recent health benefits associated with milk and as part of social responsibility initiatives have decided to pass price reductions onto consumers and contribute to the health awareness campaigns

4 The Government has decided to increase the age that school children are entitled to free milk to drink in schools to 13 years.

5 News that milk is the main drink consumed at mealtimes within Scandinavian countries has been widely reported and discussed within the broadsheet press and topical news programmes

6 A new method of producing UHT milk which tastes like fresh milk has been developed

7 A push for the reduction on the use of fridges within supermarkets has become a major campaign for an leading group of ecologists.

8 New laws have been enforced to ban the promotion of food and drink considered to be high in salts, fats and sugars.

Tasks

a. Which PESTEL factors are the biggest force within the market?

b. What changes may result within the market as a result of these PESTEL factors?

WORKSHEET ACTIVITY 7

application

Now that you have fully covered the Macro Environment, it would be a good idea for you to identify the PESTEL factors which are impacting your own organisation (or one that you are familiar with). Next, think about what action the organisation will have to take as a consequence.

Company:
Industry:

PESTEL Factor	Important issues	What changes will be needed as a result?
Political		
Economic		
Social		
Technological		
Ecological		
Legal		

3 The Micro Environment

An organisation's micro-environment consists of itself and its current and potential customers, suppliers and intermediaries. The competition also has a key influence on the micro-environment.

KEY CONCEPT

concept

The **micro-environment** comprises all those individuals and organisations that affect the operations of a business on a day-to-day basis.

The following groups are important influences on how successful a business is:

- Customers
- Suppliers
- Distributors
- Competitors
- Employees
- Shareholders

The diagram below shows the relationships between these groups.

Elements of the micro-environment

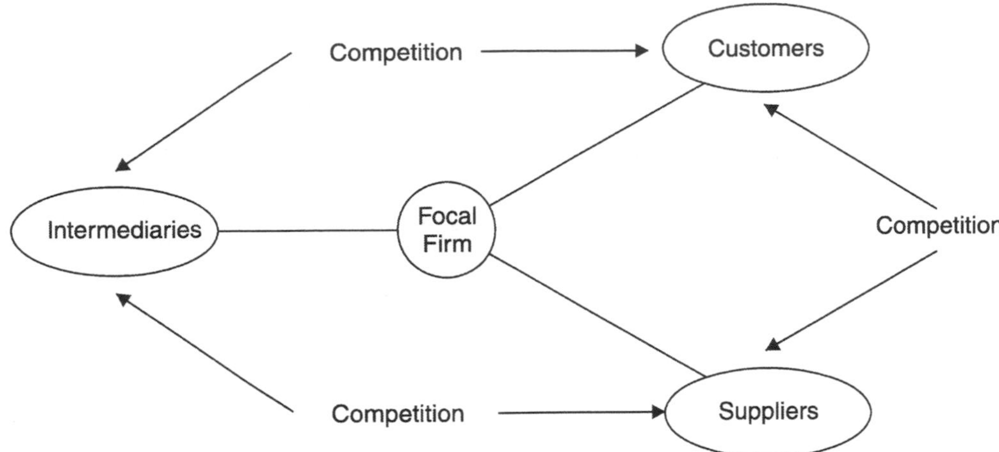

The diagram shows that the micro-environment comprises not just those firms that an organisation **actually** does business with. It also includes those firms and individuals that an organisation could **potentially** do business with.

Therefore it includes not just our current customers, but potential customers who may currently be served by another organisation. Thus, an important element in understanding the micro-environment is **competition** between organisations.

- To get **customers**
- To obtain **supplies**
- To get access to the best **intermediaries (also known as distributors)**

In assessing competition, the various factors can be considered under these basic headings.

- **Who are** the **competitors**; how strong are they?
- What are the **characteristics** of the markets they compete in?
- What are the **environmental influences** on the market?
- How can the organisation maintain a **competitive advantage**?

3.1 Customers

Customers are clearly of vital importance to the organisation because without them the company would cease to exist. The nature of these customers will differ according to the type of organisation you are. A charity for example will have a number of customers some of whom you may not automatically think of as a customer. Those who provide donations and those who actually are in receipt of the charities work will be customers. Those in receipt of the charitable work will be the primary customer. The charity exists in the first place to meet their needs. The people who donate to the charity will also have needs and expectations to be met by the charity. For example they may want to be confident that their money is being put to good use. They will also have their own private reasons for helping that charity and these will have to be Barnardo's for instance will have different groups of customers, regular donators, corporate donators, ad hoc givers of money and perhaps even those who form a internal role of being volunteers. The children who Banardo's support and those that they educate are primary customers .

Customers differ considerably in the types of products they demand. It is impossible for marketers to design products and services that meet the needs of everyone. If we look at cars for example, people vary according to whether they prefer saloons or hatchbacks, like four wheel or two wheel drive, performance or economy. This is even before we get into details such as colours, interiors, prestige of marques etc. Overall because we as consumers will differ on many dimensions because we are individuals, marketers must select groups of consumers with specific sets of needs and focus on satisfying those groups. In the case of the motor industry, larger manufacturers such as Ford, Toyota, Vauxhall tend to produce different models so that they have a vehicle to suit many tastes. Manufacturers such as Rolls Royce, Aston Martin however tend to

focus on prestige models and manufacturers like Kia at the economy end of the market. The process of splitting a market according to differing needs is known as market segmentation. Markets are usually segmented according to specific characteristics where consumers are similar for example by lifestyle, their values, demographics (age, gender etc) or geographic location.

EXAM TIP

concept

You are not expected to know a lot about market segmentation at Introductory Certificate level but you are expected to appreciate that consumers needs differ.

3.2 Suppliers

Suppliers are important because they will help the organisation to create the product or service to meet their customers needs. The reputation of suppliers is important also because when associations are made between organisations any indiscretions may also impact the organisation.

Suppliers will differ in importance to the organisation. This importance will depend on how important their product is to the business, how many suppliers there are within the industry and whether the company would be able to switch suppliers easily or not. If you think about a stationery supplier for example, it probably wouldn't be that difficult to switch if a better price, superior products or better service levels where available elsewhere. A specialist supplier of a particular favouring to be used within a confectionery product where consumer taste tests had shown that this is the preferred flavour, it would be quite difficult to find an alternative supplier able to provide exactly the same item.

MARKETING AT WORK

application

Co-op are highly selective with their choice of suppliers because they are keen to protect their reputation of being an ethical organisation. The company sources coffee, bananas and chocolate under a fair trade initiative so that they only buy directly from

3.3 Competitors

Competitors will need to be watched in order to assess their overall effect on the market. Five key questions should be addressed when assessing how much impact competitors will have.

1. Who are we competing against?
2. What could be their objectives?
3. What strategies are they using (and are they successful)?
4. What are their strengths and weaknesses?
5. How are they likely to react (to us and changes in the marketing environment)?

Even if you are the only supplier within a market, you should never assume that you have no competition. Gas and electricity companies for years made this mistake and as such thought that their customers would never go elsewhere. Once competition within these industries was opened up, there was a flurry or customer switching.

3.4 Shareholders

Shareholders are owners of business and as such will require a return on their investment. The key needs of the shareholders are that the value of their shares increases in the long run and that they are adequately rewarded for the risks they take. Profits can lead to dividends which are paid to shareholders.

Shareholders tend to be made of different groups. For companies listed on the stock exchange, large corporate shareholders such as pension fund companies may be a powerful shareholder. Employees are also sometimes shareholders as well as small private investors. The primary objectives of each of these groups are often very different. Employees may place job security or personal wellbeing in the workplace above profit whilst a strategy which leads to redundancies but will increase the share price in the long run will be preferable for large corporate investors.

3.5 Distributors

Distributors are organisations which buy a manufacturers goods and sell them to customers. Car dealers for example are distributors as are the major grocery retailers such as Tesco. When products are sold is important in not only making sure that they are available to customers but also that the correct level of customer service and advice is available for your product. Major cosmetics houses for example will only allow certain department stores and high street retailers to sell their brands because they wish to protect their reputations as high quality products. Personal sales assistants at beauty counters are required to advise customers and to ensure that they select the exact product to best meet their needs. The nature of the distribution channel will have an effect in the perception of the brand and is something that many organisations have fought to control over the years. With the advent of online retailing, the number of distributors increased dramatically but so did the level of control. Dell computers will only ever sell their products through their own online site in order to avoid problems with distributors. Smaller organisations often do not have this option as they may not have the sales staff, packing and other infrastructure needed to only sell direct.

3.6 Employees

Employees are the lifeblood of any organisation. At the end of the day, the organisation is only as good as the people working for it. Customer facing staff can make or break a relationship with customers but equally those who work in the background are important to the long term success of the organisation. Whether an employee is the managing director or the person watering the plants they have a role to play and need to appreciate the importance of their role.

Blythe (2006) points out:

"*everyone goes home at the end of the day and talks to family and friends about the firm, and as such everyone in the firm bears some responsibility for the corporate image and for marketing*" p. 709.

The roles, responsibilities, concerns, views, ideas and contributions of employees is therefore an important aspect in understanding your micro environment.

4 Monitoring the Marketing Environment

To fully appreciate what is going on within both the macro and micro environments, marketers need to continuously be aware of changes. It is too large a job to at the end of a year pull some information together. There is no such thing as a quick marketing audit. Companies who collect and review information on a regular basis in a co-ordinated way are the best placed to understand their market and respond quickly to any changes.

To begin to apprreciate your marketing environment, at the very least you should be reading the quality national press on a regular basis. Keeping a scrapbook either in paper form or electronically is a useful activity. Marketing specific publications such as Marketing, Marketing Week and Campaign, along with any relevant trade specific publications eg The Grocer for the food industy, will provide a large proportion of the information you wil need. ■

Information will come from a range of sources including internally held records and reports and an extensive array of external parties. We differentiate information which already exists (secondary information) from information which is collected completely from scratch for the specific purposes of addressing a question. For example, if a local hairdresser wanted to find out whether clients are likely to demand chemical or na

4.1 Secondary information

The majority of work investigating the marketing environment will come from secondary desk research.

KEY CONCEPT

concept

Secondary data is data which has already been gathered and assembled for other purposes or general reference.

Desk research involves collecting data from internal and external sources. The sources of secondary data for marketing will vary according to the needs of the organisation.

(a) **Records inside the firm**, gathered by another department or section for its own purposes.

- Data about sales volumes, analysed by sales area, salesman, quantity, price, profitability, distribution outlet, customer etc
- Customer database interrogation
- Data about marketing itself, such as promotion and brand data
- Employee satisfaction surveys and appraisals
- Competitor assessments
- All cost and management accounting data
- Marketing Information Systems, which model and analyse marketing data to support decisions

(b) **Published information** from external sources

- Publications of market research agencies, such as the ACNielsen
- Government statistics
- Publications of trade associations (often a valuable source of under-used information within all kinds of industries)
- Professional journals

(c) The **government**: a major source of information about industry, population and social trends. See the website of the Office for National Statistics (www.statistic.gov.uk) where you can feely view and download a wealth of economic and social data. For national equivalents (outside the UK), go to: www.wto.org.

(d) **Non-government sources**, including:

- The **national press** (*Financial Times* etc) and financial and **professional magazines** (*Marketing, The Economist* etc) and journals (and their websites)
- Companies and other organisations specialising in the provision of **business information** (eg Reuters, LexisNexis, Datamonitor) on a subscription basis, and **specialist research** organisations who analyse certain markets and publish and sell the results (eg Mintel, Euromonitor)
- **Professional institutions** (eg Chartered Institute of Marketing, Chartered Management Institute, Institute of Practitioners in Advertising)
- **Trade sources** such as the Association of British Insurers (ABI), or the Society of Motor Manufacturers and Trades (SMMT)

WORKSHEET ACTIVITY 8

application

Make a list of all the secondary data sources you would use to research the industry/ company you work in.

4.2 Primary information

Occasionally primary research will be used to better understand the environmental factors because there is no information that already exists or it may be expensive to buy a particular marker report.

KEY CONCEPT

concept

Primary research is research designed and conducted from scratch to gather information about a specific issue.

Surveys, focus groups, interviews and observation are examples of methods that can be used to understand the key environmental forces.

4.3 Level of environmental control

Part of the reason for monitoring the external environment is to consider the areas that as an organisation you have control over and those that you don't. If you are in control of environmental impacts you are in a better position to limit or diminish and negative consequences and to maximise and positive effects. For example, Automed is a hypothetical small repair garage based in Cartown with just three branches within a thirty mile area. Prowhich is well managed will be able to control issued relating to their own internal staff. The garage will be in a position to adjust their staffing levels, manage skill levels through training and development programmes and manage the customer experience when dealing with staff through training in customer care. They will on the other hand not be in any way able to control the

Generally speaking, you are more likely to be able to control *some* of the components of your micro environment than the macro environment. It will also depend on the nature, size and scope of your organisation.

WORKSHEET ACTIVITY 9

Think an organisation, how much control does the organisation have over each of the elements within their marketing environments? For each aspect shown on the , identify whether there is very little control, a moderate amount of control or a lot of control. Try to make a note why you have come to that decision.

Try to think about why this is the case, are there any similarities or differences within the levels of marketing environment?

Aspect of the marketing environment	Level of control (Little, moderate or high)	Possible reason / rationale
Internal Environment		
• Other departments		
• Staff		
Micro Environment		
• Customers		
• Competitors		
• Intermediaries		
• Suppliers		
• Other stakeholders		
Macro Environment		
• Political forces		
• Economic forces		
• Social forces		
• Technological forces		
• Natural environment		
• Legal forces		

Hill & O'Sullivan (2004) Introductory Marketing. Chapter 3 of this text covers the Marketing Environment. The chapter takes you through the Two famous marketing case studies are covered. Case study 3.4 refers to the legal battle between jeans manufacturer and Levi Strauss and Tesco in the late 90's/early 2000's. The second famous example is case study 3.5 which reviews the anti-Nestle campaign which has been running since 1973 due to their distribution of infant formula in less developed countries. Both of these cases are worth reading because of their notoriety but you should also try to think of more recent examples of companies impacted by different factors in their marketing environment.

You should also ensure that you are able to remember alternative methods of reviewing the marketing environment, this is not covered within Hill & O'Sullivan's chapter 3

Learning objective review

Learning objectives	Covered
1 Discuss why an appreciation of the marketing environment is required	☑ Aid the marketing planning process ☑ To justify and identify whether marketing decisions with regards to the targeting segment, marketing mix employed are appropriate in light of the market forces in place both now and in the future
2 Distinguish between internal, micro and macro environments	☑ Internal = employees, functional departments ☑ Micro = customers, competitors, intermediaries, suppliers, other stakeholders ☑ Macro = political, legal, technological, social
3 Explain the elements of PESTEL	☑ Political ☑ Economic ☑ Social/ cultural ☑ Technological ☑ Environmental (green/ecological) ☑ Legislative
4 Identify key stakeholder characteristics in relation to the micro-market	☑ Stakeholders ☑ Customers ☑ Shareholders ☑ Competitors ☑ Suppliers ☑ Distributors
5 Explain market analysis and monitoring	☑ The Marketing Audit ☑ Market Scanning ☑ Secondary Research
6 Identify controllable from non-controllable environmental factors	☑ The level of control will be dependent on the industry and nature of the organisation. ☑ The closer to the organisation the factor is, the greater the control. ☑ Internal environments are the most likely to be controllable ☑ Macro forces are the least controllable

Quick quiz

1 What does PESTEL stand for?

A Public, environmental, social, technological, ethical, legal

B Political, economic, social, technological, ecological, legal

C Political, economic, service, technological, environmental, legislation

2 Which of the following is not a macro factor?

A customer factors

B political factors

C social factors

3 Which is not a piece of consumer protection legislation?

A The Data Protection Act

B The Sale of Goods Act

C Neither

4 When should the organisation ideally collect information to assess their marketing environment?

A Annually as part of the marketing planning process

B Bi-annually

C Continuously

5 Which is not a piece of secondary research?

A sales records

B a survey conducted especially to find out about customers changing lifestyles

C newspaper reports

6 Which of the following is true of the Data Protection Act?

A Individuals are protected

B Corporate bodies are protected

C Both are protected

7 The Sale of Goods Act states that if a product is faulty the consumer has the right to discuss the matter with;

A The manufacturer

B The trader

C The trade association

8 Technology refers to which of the options below?

A IT developments, improved ingredients, quality developments

B Increased use of IT by consumers

C Both of the above

Quiz answers

1	B	Political, economic, social, technological, ecological, legal
2	A	Customers are part of the micro environment.
3	C	Neither is NOT a piece of consumer protection legislation because both seek to preserve consumer rights
4	C	Because it is a large job it is best to keep up to date with what is going on in the marketing environment in an organised manner continuously.
5	B	A survey of this nature would be a primary piece of research to investigate a social factor.
6	A	Individuals are protected and corporate bodies have to abide by the act
7	B	The trader needs to comply with the act, other legislation will impact the manufacturer
8	C	Technology relates to both of these

Activity debriefs

Worksheet activity 1

You should have a large list of industries which have been directly impacted by the government's decision to ban smoking in public places in the UK. Although the tobacco industry and pubs and clubs are the most obvious to be impacted by this ban, you should have identified a much larger range of industries. Smoking cessation products such as nicotine patches, shed and shelter , awning and patio heater manufacturers are some of those to benefit from a positive impact of the ban. Dry cleaners conversely have reported an adverse effect on sales as customers do not need to remove the smell of tobacco from their clothing.

Worksheet activity 2

There would be many industries impacted by the outlined changes in British social attitudes, these are examples of just a few and you are likely to have a range of different examples:

- The Cleaning products industry - it is still likely that products will be targeted at women rather than men
- The Childcare industry - is likely to continue to grow given the number of working parents
- The food industry – may way continue to expand lines of convenience foods or 'easy to prepare'

Worksheet activity 3

You were asked to name at least five social changes that are likely to impact your organisation over the next five years. Your answer here will be unique to your industry but you should have included issues related to demographic composition within your industry, lifestyle changes which will impact you because of consumer and customer changes as will changes in working patterns and norms.

Even if you are a business to business organisation, you will impacted indirectly by social changes because of the knock on effects that your customers will pass on. The type of promotional activities you can use may for example be impacted, in the 1980's highly indulgent corporate entertaining was a major tool for many business to business organisations, as the more thrifty 1990's emerged the perception of organisations adopting this a sales technique was seen to be inappropriate in some industries.

Worksheet activity 4

You will probably find that unless you have recently introduced a new computerised system (which is often involves a huge *amount of upheaval) the majority of the developments will actually not be to do with IT at all.*

Worksheet activity 5

You should at the very least have identified some of the data protection issues outlined within this area of PESTEL because these will affect all organisations. Look again at the specific guidelines and outline what information you handle and therefore what you can and can't do with it.

Worksheet activity 6

1 Press reports of health benefits (social).

2 EU subsidies (political/ economic).

3 Supermarkets price reductions (economic)

4 Government free milk to drink in schools to 13 years (political).

5 Milk is the main drink consumed at mealtimes within Scandinavia (social)

6 UHT milk developments (technological)

7 Reduction on the use of fridges (ecological)

8 New laws (legal).

Worksheet activity 7

You should have put together as detailed PESTEL analysis as possible. Try to add in as many factors and you can.

Worksheet activity 8

You are likely to have not very much control over competitors. Depending on the nature of your industry and where you sell your products will determine power over distributors. If you are a service organisation or charity you will not have obvious distributors anyway. Employee control should be relatively high but could depend on factors such as the management style used within your organisation, whether your industry is unionised or not. With customers, even if you are in a monopoly situation (you are the only supplier) you will have little control because you should be trying to identify and meet their needs which you cannot control. Shareholders may not have much power individually but collectively you will not have much control.

References

Aitken, L. (2007) '*Wiping out Greenwash*' The Guardian, Monday 19th November 2007, London.

Alleyn, R. (2008) '*Melton Mowbray pork pies fight Euro elite after 10 year battle*' The Telegraph, London.

Anon (2006) '*Spending on eating out overtakes meals at home*' Government News Release available online at http://www.statistics.gov.uk/pdfdir/ioa0806.pdf [accessed 23.1.08].

BBC (2008) '*Cadbury Eco Easter Egg unveilled*' BBC News 24 available from [http://news.bbc.co.uk/1/hi/england/west_midlands/7251243.stm[accessed 21.2.08.

Blythe, J. (2006) Principles and Practice of Marketing, Thompson, London.

CIM (2007) '*Marketing Trends Survey 2007*, Chartered Institute of Marketing, Cookham, Berkshire.

Department for Health (2008) 'Healthy Weight, Healthy Lives A cross government strategy for England' available online from: http://www.dh.gov.uk/en/Publicationsandstatistics/Publications/PublicationsPolicyAndGuidance/DH_082378 [accessed 12.3.08].

Financial Markets (2008) '*Threats to the UK economy in 2008*' available from http://www.financemarkets.co.uk/2007/12/23/threats-for-the-uk-economy-in-2008/ accessed 2.2.08]

Hill, L. And O'Sullivan, T. (2004) Foundation Marketing 3rd Edition, Prentice Hall, London.

Information Commissioners Office (2008) Press Releases available from [http://www.ico.gov.uk/about_us/news_and_views/press_releases.aspx] accessed 3.4.08

Jobber, D. (2007) Principles and Practice of Marketing. 5th Edition, McGraw Hill education, Maidenhead, Berks.

Marketing Week (2008) '*Royal Caribbean re jigs sales team*' Marketing Week 21.2.08, Centaur Publishing, London.

Mitchells and Butlers (2008) ' *Eating Out*' Online report available from; http://www.mbplc.com/index.asp?pageid=412 [accessed 23.1.08]

Palmer, A. And Hartley, B.(2006) The Business Environment 5th Edition, McGraw Hill

Pym, H (2008) ' The UK is on recession watch' available from [http://news.bbc.co.uk/1/hi/business/7686117.stm] accessed 10.11.08.

Sandison, N (2008) '*Together Creates Energy Wasting Day Viral as April Fool*' Marketing, 26th March 2008, London.

Taher, A (2007) 'Scientists hail 'frozen smoke' as material that will change the world' The Times, 19th August 2007, London.

The British Social Attitudes 24th Report is published available from http://www.policyhub.gov.uk/news_item/british_social_attitudes08.asp accessed 14.3.08

The Economist (2007) '*Postcards from the ledge*', 19.12.07, London.

Wallop, H. (2007) ' *Fastest rise in food prices for 14 years*' The Telegraph, 14.11.07, London.

Waste Watch (2008) 'Waste Watch Home page' available from [http://www.wastewatch.org.uk] accessed 14.3.08.

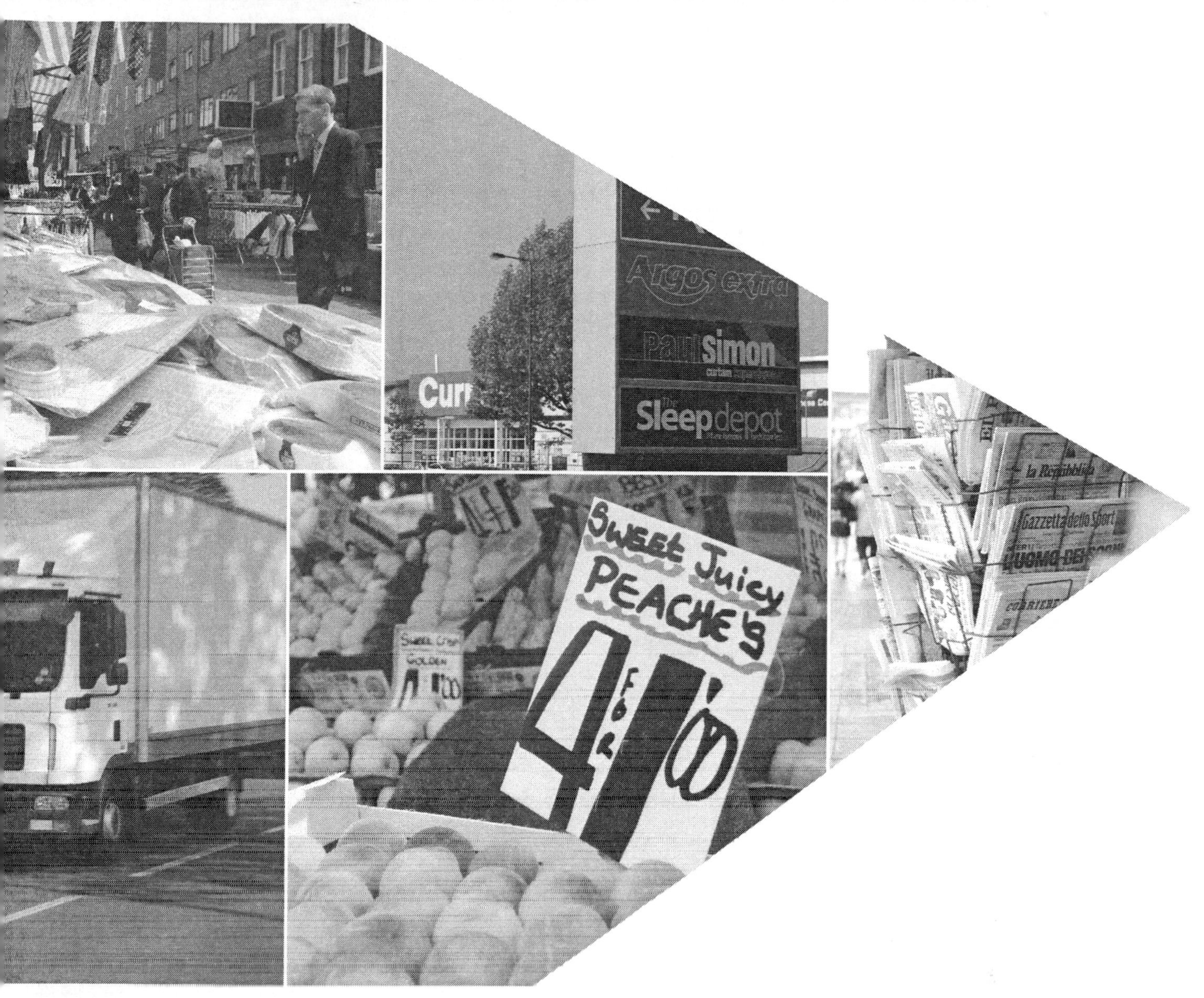

Chapter 3
The Marketing Mix

Topic list

1 An overview of the marketing mix
2 Product
3 Price
4 Place
5 Promotion
6 People
7 Process
8 Physical evidence

Introduction

Within this chapter we look at a central marketing concept- the marketing mix. Essentially the marketing mix is the toolbox that the marketer has to enable them to build products to meet the needs of different customers. To make it easier to remember, the marketing mix is also known as the 7P's. Each P stands for a component (or tool) of the marketing mix, they are; product, price, place, promotion, people, process and physical evidence. We briefly mentioned the marketing mix in chapter 1. This chapter takes each of the 7 P's in turn and considers why it is important and how it can be used to meet customer needs and wants.

The marketing mix elements are often described as **'the controllables'(Kotler, 1994)**, to distinguish elements that an organisation can influence from those that are beyond its control. **'Uncontrollables'** include competitor's actions, government policy, general economic conditions and the other factors within both the micro and macro marketing environments as discussed in chapter 2.

Syllabus linked learning objectives

By the end of the chapter you will be able to:

Learning objectives	Syllabus link
1 Explain the importance of the marketing mix	3.1
2 Outline the components of product, price, place, promotion, people, process and physical evidence.	3.1
3 Appreciate the linkages between each of the 7P's	3.1

1 An Overview of the Marketing Mix

The original marketing mix had just four elements; product , price, place and promotion. You will find therefore that some marketing textbooks that you come across will still refer to the 4P's as they commonly became known. As services marketing began to develop it was recognised that the original 4P's did not fully explain all the issues that a services marketer needed to consider. The marketing mix was extended to 7P's (Bitner & Boom, 1981) in order to better reflect services marketing. Some texts refer to the 7P's as the Extended Marketing Mix.

KEY CONCEPT

concept

The examiners for this qualification have specifically stated that they will test on the Extended Marketing Mix (7p's) and NOT the original marketing mix (4P's).

The newest additional P's are a bit of a stretch on the P theme. **People** mainly refers to employees. **Process** refers to the way that services are delivered using user-friendly systems for buying and selling. **Physical evidence** refers to intangible aspects such as the look and feel of the organisation and brand through things like their buildings, livery, uniforms, letterhead etc. It is useful to remember them by their P acronyms because they help to be more memorable.

Marketing mix variables are highly interactive. A highly co-ordinated approach is needed for the most effective results. As we start to go through each of the P's you should begin to see that changes in one are likely to have a profound effect upon what we can do with the others. For example, a biscuit which is produced using the most cost effective ingredients and processes is unlikely to be a sales success story if it is priced at a premium. Equally given the properties of the product, it

would obviously fail if it was advertised only in a magazine aimed at diabetics and sold mainly though sales at slimming classes! Clearly, we have a case for careful coordination and complementary marketing mixes.

1.1 The 4C's

The 7Ps can be balanced by customer-focused equivalents: Choice, Cost, Convenience and Communication.

At some time in your marketing studies you will probably start thinking that the 4 Ps are rather old hat. That may be true – and two of them don't really begin with P anyway! – it is useful however because it is easy to remember. The remaining three P's (even bigger stretches of the letter P!) of the extended marketing mix are actually preferred by the CIM and so you should not forget these.

Other formulations of the marketing mix have been proposed by various writers. Ace (2001) argues that the 'Ps' of the extended marketing mix still have a producer or service provider focus. She suggests four **customer-focused** 'C' equivalents.

Producer/provider focused activity	Customer/consumer focused activity
Product Plan product/service mix	**Choice** Consider how customers make choices: differentiate and inform to support the purchase decision
Price Consider all elements of the price mix	**Cost** Consider how customers perceive value for money
Place Manage distribution channels	**Convenience** Consider what customers find convenient: they may not like the channels (for example Internet) that are most 'efficient'
Promotion Persuade customers that the product meets their needs	**Communication** Enter into dialogue with customers; inform and support their decision-making: they are increasingly aware that promotion is being used to persuade or manipulate

WORKSHEET ACTIVITY 1

application

To get into the habit of applying marketing terms, think of **two** purchases that you have made fairly recently and describe them in terms of the 7 Ps Take one FMCG product (Fast moving consumer good eg food, make-up, newspaper), and your most recent consumer durable purchase (eg TV, a business suit, etc)

Marketing mix	FMCG purchase:	Consumer durable purchase:
Product		
Price		
Place		
Promotion		
People		
Process		
Physical evidence		

You may have found Activity 1 fairly tricky for the 'extended' marketing mix elements. If you did, try to repeat the exercise but this time in relation to a service you have used recently. You will find that the 'people', 'process' and 'physical evidence' elements are much easier.

MARKETING AT WORK

application

If you think about the times you may visit a hairdresser or barber, it is easy to identify the extended marketing mix elements.

People – Many people tend to select where they have their hair cut according to the skills of the hair stylists. These skills can be a mixture of hair styling and interpersonal skills.

Process- Increasingly hair salons are adapting the ways they can encourage customers to use the salon. For example they sometime offer online appointment booking or walk in 'no appointment' needed services.

Physical Evidence- The look, design, location and overall ambiance of the salon are considered as the 'physical evidence' aspect of the salon. Additional elements include any uniforms used by staff, the quality of towels used etc.

WORKSHEET ACTIVITY 2

application

Repeat the exercise shown in Activity 1 using the same items purchased but this time use the 4C's.

4C	FMCG purchase:	Consumer durable purchase:
Choice		
Cost		
Convenience		
Communication		

2 Product

2.1 What is a product?

Those unfamiliar with marketing probably think of a 'product' as a physical object. However, in marketing the term must be understood in a broader sense.

KEY CONCEPT

concept

A **product** is a 'package' of something that satisfies a set of wants that customers have. When you buy a set of wine glasses, for example, you are buying them because you want to drink wine and you prefer not to do so straight from the bottle. You may also want to impress your dinner guests with your taste, and choose to do so by possessing a particularly fine set of wine glasses.

The package of benefits includes:

(a) A **physical aspect**, which relates to the components, materials and specifications (colour, size etc.) of the product: for example, a size 12 pullover made of 100% pure wool in a natural colour

(b) A **functional aspect**, which is a statement of how a product performs and for what purpose it is likely to be bought: the wool pullover may give warmth and comfort

(c) A **symbolic aspect**, which represents the qualities the product suggests to, or confers upon, the buyer: the '100% pure wool' label may represent quality, status or ecology (as a natural rather than synthetic product).

The overall package for the marketer includes:

- Product specifications and materials
- Product design or styling
- Product functions and benefits
- Product packaging
- The range of products in a 'line', and additions to or deletions from it.

A product 'package' satisfies customer needs because of both tangible and intangible attributes:

(a) Tangible attributes

Availability and delivery

Performance

Price

Design

(b) Intangible attributes

Image

Perceived value

These attributes are interlinked. A product has a tangible price, but for your money you obtain the value that you perceive the product to have. You may get satisfaction from paying a very high price for your wine glasses, because this says something about your status in life.

2.2 Features and benefits

Marketers need recognise the difference between **features** and **benefits**. This is important because customers look for solutions to their needs. It is not important to them necessarily *how* these needs are met so long as they are. As such customers buy benefits rather than the specific feature of a product or service.

2.3 The total product

The total product represents both the tangible and intangible elements . of the 'package'. The following diagram outlines the different levels of a product.

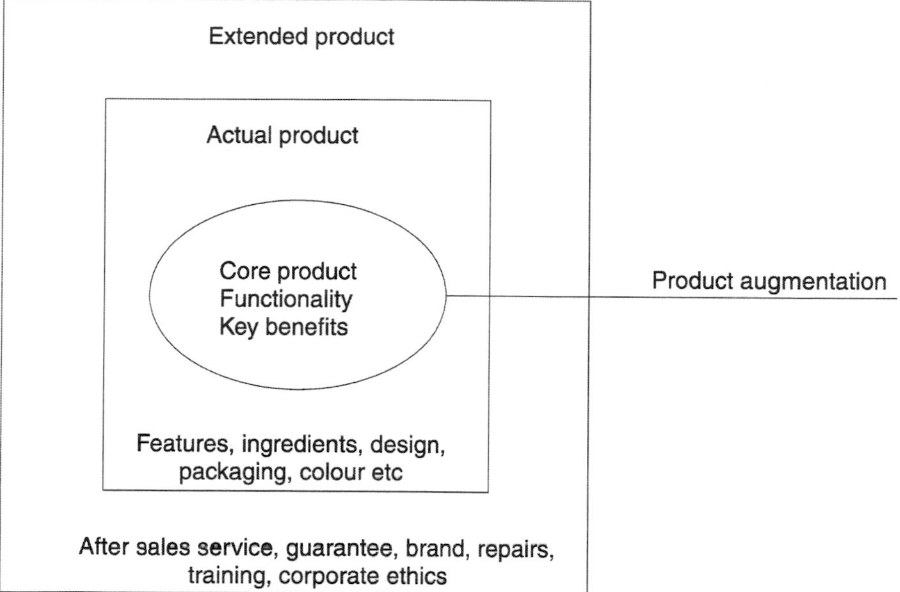

The concept of a **'total product'** is built up from various 'layers'. The **core product** is associated with what the product is designed *to do*. The **actual product** represents the improvements made to the basic core and these generally add different benefits provided by the product. The extended product are the additional elements which build trust and the reputation associated with the product.

Think about your brand of toothbrush as you follow this example which helps to explain how these product layers are built up.

Colgate manufacture a wide range of different toothbrushes including children's character versions and adult manual and battery operated brushes. Within their core adult manual range, there are currently six different models, all with differing product **features**. Toothbrushes generally are designed simply to clean teeth and the different features such as curved bristles, bendy heads etc. The consumer **need** is to ensure that they maintain oral health and hygiene. To the consumer the need for oral health are obvious (very few individuals actually wanting to loose their teeth or gain a reputation for having bad breath!).

In consumer behavioural terms there is a multitude of purchase risks associated with buying a relatively inexpensive everyday product. The reason Colgate produce a range of toothbrushes is that they are building a range of alternative 'total products' to meet the needs of different target consumers. Consumers who want to minimise their risk of bad breath would be most likely to choose the Colgate 360° because of the added *features* such as a tongue scrapper, raised, cupped and rounded bristles at different points in the brush head. Those consumers with sensitive teeth would opt for the Colgate sensitive version due to the product features associated with being gentle to the teeth and gums.

If you think about a basic complementary toothbrush you may have been given at a hotel or on an airplane, they generally are a plain, straight piece of plastic with hard and straight nylon bristles. In other words they have minimal product features. This type of product will help you to clean your teeth but it is generally accepted that as they are designed for emergency uses to be used a couple of times and then disposed with. Essentially it is a **'core product'**.

If you now think of a slightly upgraded version of a toothbrush, perhaps a retailer own brand basic version which is coloured, and has an angled neck and possibly rounded bristles. This toothbrush has distinct advantages because the colour makes it more aesthetically pleasing and additional features of the angled handle would mean that it is more comfortable to use and easier to reach back teeth. This product is 'augmented' by the additional features and represents the **'actual product'**.

Next think of a premium brand of toothbrush such as those in the Colgate range. The brand is recognised as highly credible by consumers and is one of the key players in the market. The brand is synonymous with professionalism due to years of work by Colgate-Palmolive in ensuring the endorsement of the brand by dental practitioners, well designed and informative packaging, promotional activity, in-store presence and the use of guarantees, an educationally based website and customer information help-lines. The contribution of all these augmented elements represents the **'extended product'** and benefits the consumers by providing confidence in the product they have purchased.

2.4 New Product Development

New product development is important for maintaining customer satisfaction through change; refreshing or extending the product range; and adapting to environmental opportunities and threats. These will all contribute towards the success of a company's long-term business strategy.

New products may be genuinely innovative, but 'newness' may also mean 'adapted', 'repackaged' or 'introduced' in a new market.

What is a new product?

- One that opens up an entirely new market
- One that replaces an existing product
- One that broadens significantly the market for an existing product

An old product can be new if:

- It is introduced to a new market
- It is packaged in a different way
- A different marketing approach is used
- A mix variable is changed – for example, a new price is set, or a new distribution channel is used

"There is a strong positive relationship between a firm's innovative activities and its ability to survive and prosper, so many companies place a strong emphasis on developing new products to replace those which become obsolete, or which are superseded by competitors' offerings." Blythe, J. (2006) p126

2.4.1 Product extension

KEY CONCEPT concept

Product extension involves adding new products to add to the company's existing lines. 25% of new product launches are extensions (Jobber, 2007).

Adding additions to existing lines is appealing to marketers because they benefit from the existing brand recognition and associations from day one. As such, product and brand extension is regarded as one of the least risky ways to launch a new product. Many industries use this form of NPD, it is particularly obvious within the confectionary market for example.

MARKETING AT WORK application

As a 74 year old established brand Kit Kat has seen many product extensions over the years and particularly since the mid 1990's. Product extensions are not necessarily the best approach as Kit Kat found out to its cost. During the mid 2000's, Kit Kat had an excessive product line. As more product extensions hit the shelves, sales actually declined.

Variants included their traditional two and four finger biscuits but at various times also included chunky, white, lemon, low carb, dark and peanut butter chunky.

Another completely different industry which heavily relies on product extension is the Hollywood film industry. Given the cost of production and promoting movies, Hollywood has developed a culture of producing sequels to blockbuster movies which are virtually guaranteed large audiences.

2.4.2 Product modification

A significant proportion of the work of NPD teams is not designing completely 'new to the world' products but modifying and making product improvements to existing products.

MARKETING AT WORK

application

Think about the number of times you shop for groceries and notice an 'on pack flash' (a highlighted section on the packaging) which reads along the lines of ' New' or 'Improved recipe'.

The purpose of these modifications can be for a number of reasons including:

- Modernising to keep abreast of market developments

2.4.3 The NPD Process

New products should only be taken to advanced development if there is evidence of:

- **Adequate demand**
- Compatibility with existing **marketing ability**
- Compatibility with existing **production ability**

The stages of new product (or service) development are as follows.

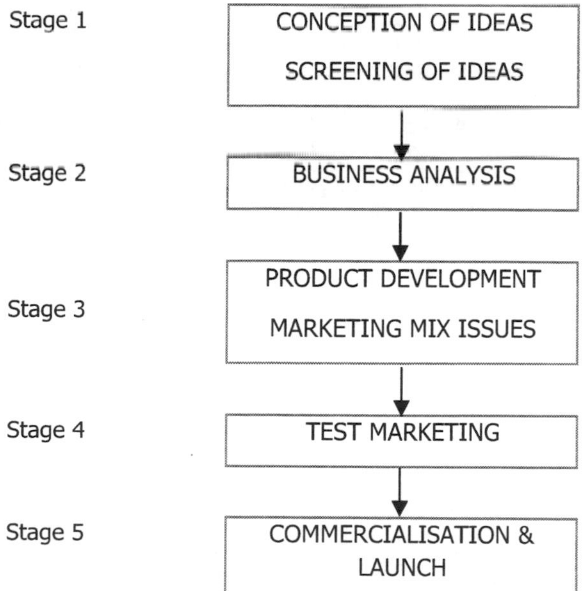

The mortality rate of new products is very high. To reduce the risk of failure new product ideas must be screened. Only the best will make it to the next development stage.

2.4.4 Conception and screening of ideas

The **concept** for the new product could be **tested on potential customers** to obtain their reactions. Some caution does however need to be exercised when interpreting the results.

- When innovative new designs are tested on potential customers it is often found that they are conditioned by traditional designs and are dismissive of new design ideas.
- However, testers may say they like the new concept at the testing stage, but when the new product is launched it is not successful because people continue to buy old favourites.

2.4.5 Business analysis

A thorough business analysis is required for each product idea, projecting future sales and revenues, giving a description of the product so as to provide costs of production, providing estimates of sales promotion and advertising costs, the resources required, profits and return on investment. Other factors such as the product life cycle, legal restrictions, competitors' reactions among others, must also be evaluated. Products which pass the business evaluation will be developed. A timetable and a budget of resources required and of cost must be prepared, so that management control can be applied to the development project.

2.4.6 Product development

Money is invested to produce a working **prototype** of the product, which can be tried by customers. This stage ensures that the product can be produced in sufficient quantities at the right price. The form which the product **test** takes will depend very much on the type of product concerned. The test should replicate reality as closely as possible.

- If the product is used in the home, a sample of respondents should be given the product to use at home.
- If the product is chosen from amongst competitors in a retail outlet (as with chocolate bars), then the product test needs to rate response against competitive products.
- If inherent product quality is an important attribute of the product, then a 'blind' test could be used.
- An industrial product could be used for a trial period by a customer in a realistic setting.

The marketing mix for the product will need to be planned at this stage.

2.4.7 Test marketing

The purpose of **test marketing** is to obtain information about how consumers react to the product. Will they buy it, and if so, will they buy it again? With this information an estimate of total market demand for the product can be made.

A market test involves implementing marketing plans in selected areas which are thought to be 'representative' of the total market. In the selected areas, the firm will attempt to distribute the product through the same types of sales outlets it plans to use in the full market launch, and also to use the intended advertising and promotion plans.

3 Price

KEY CONCEPT

concept

Price can be defined as a measure of the value exchanged by the buyer for the value offered by the seller.

Pricing decisions are important to the firm. This may be stating the obvious, but it is worth making it clear that pricing is very important as it is the only element of the marketing mix which generates income, revenue and profits, rather than creating costs.

All profit organisations, and many non-profit ones, face the task of pricing their products or services. Price can go by many names: fares, fees, rent, assessments among others.

Price was once the single most important decision made by the sales department. In those production-oriented times, price was viewed as the major factor in satisfying customer needs, and a price change was the usual reaction to competitor activity.

Today, though, marketing managers view price as just one of the factors involved in customer satisfaction. In fact it is sometimes suggested that marketing aims to make price relatively unimportant to the consumers' decision making process. There is certainly some truth in this view. The other elements of the marketing mix are concerned with adding value to the product and tailoring it to the consumers' needs, to ensure that the choice between two products is not simply based on their different prices.

However, the role of price in the marketing mix is still significant, and should not be underestimated. It contributes towards the organisation's business and financial objectives in the following ways.

- Pricing is the only element of the mix which generates revenue rather than creating costs.
- It also has an important role as a competitive tool to differentiate a product and organisation, and thereby exploit market opportunities.
- Pricing must be consistent with other elements of the marketing mix, since it contributes to the overall image created for the product.

MARKETING AT WORK

application

The failed fashion retailer Morgan which was reported as bankrupt in December 2008 targeted women aged 18 to 35, competing in the UK with rival high-street brands such as Topshop, H&M, Primark and New Look.

Morgan stuck to its traditional fashion model, stocking just two collections a year, and while the price of fashion in the UK has steadily been getting lower, it struggled to keep pace due to its inflexible pricing model. One commentator says:

"*The key problem for Morgan is a lack of clear brand positioning. The high-street fashion market in the UK is brutally competitive; consumer expectations are high and retailers require a tightly run operation to meet those expectations and still turn a profit.*

Shoppers want to see the very latest fashions in-store and online, at extremely keen prices. Premium pricing can be an option, but consumers want value for money, and product quality and brand values must support this.

As women happily mix Primark shoes with a Prada top, there must be clarity in consumer minds about what the brand is offering. Morgan's pricing is mid-point and its image is indistinct."

www.brandrepublic.com – accessed 14 May 2008, Bawden (2008)

3.1 Influences on pricing decisions

Pricing decisions are affected by a range of factors, both internal (to the organisation) and external (in the competitive environment).

Internal factors	External factors
• **Marketing objectives**: profit maximisation; market share leadership; brand targeting and positioning	• **Competition:** the extent of competition in the market; whether there is non-price competition; competitor pricing and promotions.
• **Marketing mix strategy**: factoring in the cost/ price implications of quality, distribution, brand differentiation	• **Demand**: the sensitivity of customer demand for the product to change in price (elasticity of demand) in the given market.
• **Costs**: at least setting the lowest viable price at which the company can afford to sell the product.	• **Customer perceptions** of price and what it means for quality and value
• **Price-setting methodologies**: negotiated by sales force; set by management	• **Suppliers and intermediaries**: impacting on costs; reacting to price decisions to protect their own margins.
• **Product portfolio strategies**: launch/new-product incentive pricing; 'loss leaders' to support the product range	• **PEST factors**: economic factors determining affordability; government price watchdogs; social responsibility dictating affordability; changing perceptions of 'value'; technology lowering costs.

3.2 Business objectives

Pricing decisions are guided by one or other of two business objectives.

Maximise profits	Maintain or increase market share
Charge as **high** a price as possible. This depends on how good your product is and how much demand is affected by higher prices.	Charge a **lower** price than competitors, or the **same** price. You would do this if you want to hold on to existing customers and/or attract new ones.

Either approach may be used in specifying pricing objectives, and they may appear in combination. It is important that pricing objectives are consistent with overall **corporate objectives**: you might not want to raise prices, for example, if the corporate objective is to be an accessible, ethical low-cost provider of essential services.

3.3 Competition

Prices may be set on the basis of what competitors are charging, rather than on the basis of cost or demand. This sometimes results in '**going rate**' pricing. Some form of average level of price becomes the norm, including standard price differentials between brands.

3.3.1 Price as a competitive tool

In established industries dominated by a few major firms, it is generally accepted that a price initiative by one firm will be countered by a price reaction by competitors. Consequently, in industries such as breakfast cereals (dominated in Britain by Kellogg's, Nabisco and Quaker) or canned soups (Heinz, Crosse & Blackwell and Campbell's) a certain **price stability** might be expected without too many competitive price initiatives. A firm may respond to **competitor price cuts** in a number of ways.

- **Maintain existing prices**, if the expectation is that only a small market share would be lost, so that it is more profitable to keep prices at their existing level. Eventually, the rival firm may drop out of the market or be forced to raise its prices.
- **Maintain prices but respond with a non-price counter-attack**. This is a more positive response, because the firm will be securing or justifying its price differential with enhanced product quality, improved back-up services or other augmented features.
- **Reduce prices**, to protect the firm's market share. The main beneficiary from the price reduction will be the consumer.
- **Raise prices and respond with a non-price counter-attack**. The extra revenue from the higher prices might be used to finance the promotion of product improvements, which in turn would justify the price rise to customers.

3.4 Customer expectation

Customers often use price as an indicator of quality (Jobber, 2007). Premium hair salons are used as an example by Blythe (2006) to demonstrate how customers use price to assess the quality of a service. Customers are often wiling to pay significantly higher prices for salons that are perceived as being higher quality because there is an expectation that their service experience will be significantly better due to better trained stylists and luxurious salons.

WORKSHEET ACTIVITY 3

application

Go to an online review site and look up reviews of well known hair salons within your country. Within the UK market there are several review sites which refer to celebrity hairdresser salons. A search on Google using the term ' *hairdresser reviews*' should provide a number of options for you to choose between.

4 Place

"... people can only buy products that are available and easily obtained". Blythe, J. (2006)

KEY CONCEPT

Place is concerned with the selection of distribution channels used to deliver goods to the consumer. The 'place' element of the marketing mix is really concerned with the processes by which the product reaches the consumer in a convenient way. Other terms for 'place' include distribution, delivery systems or channels.

The importance of place within the marketing mix should not be underestimated. If you get it right for your market it can be a crucial source of competitive advantage. Marketing effort will be futile if the product is not actually in the right place at the right time so that the customer has the choice of buying your product, not your competitors'.

The choice of a particular distribution policy, such as whether or not to use wholesalers or retailers, may result in the company delegating at least part of its marketing function to others. We look at factors governing such a decision in section 3.

In setting up a channel of distribution, the supplier has to take several factors into account.

- Customers
- Nature of the goods or services
- Distributor characteristics
- Competitors' channel choice
- The costs associated with available channels
- The supplier's own characteristics

4.1 The supply chain and intermediaries

There are a variety of types of intermediary and several may intervene before a product gets from the original provider and the final buyer.

The diagram that follows shows the range of options for intermediaries.

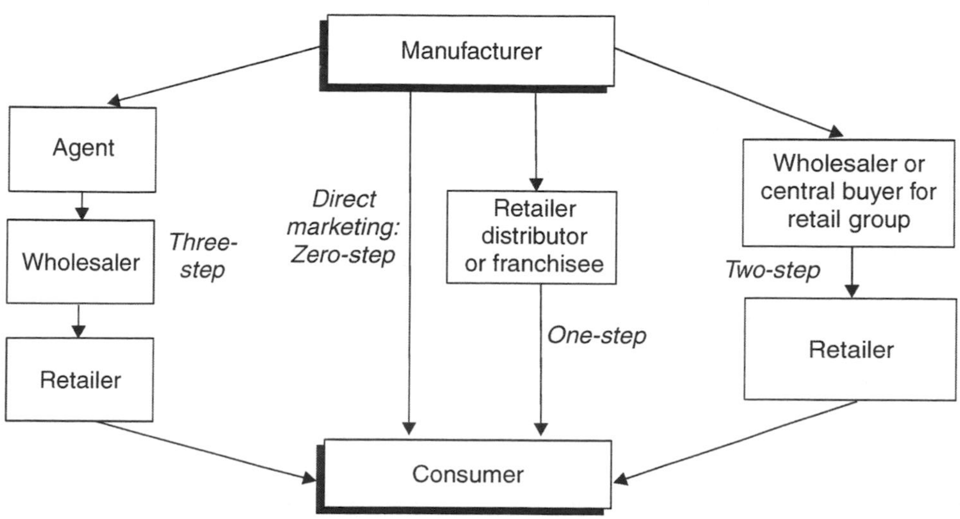

The choice of intermediaries used will depend on the 'fit' between the product and brand strategy and the strategy of the intermediary.

MARKETING AT WORK

There are many examples of products which have been sold through the wrong intermediary which has lead to either a lack of sales or the devaluing of a brand. The legal case between Tesco and Levi is a particularly well known example of a premium brand taking legal action to prevent a retailer distributing a premium brand.

The growth of e-tailing has led to an increase in 'disintermediation' (or in plain English- cutting out intermediaries to sell direct). Dell for example always sold directly to consumers rather than through an intermediary.

Veterinary medicines which were only available through veterinary surgeries such as high strength worming and flea treatments which do not require a prescription are now available through online veterinary pharmacies. Some such websites can even take prescriptions written by vets in order to dispense any animal medicine.

4.2 Maximising Accessibility

One of the main aims for a marketer is to maximise the opportunities for customers to be able to purchase goods and services. The nature of the product will determine what this actually means in practice. For grocery products for example this will include trying to gain listings in as many grocery retailers ad possible such as supermarkets, convenience stores and online grocery retailers. The marketer will also try to gain the best on-shelf positions within these retailers in order to be highly visible and maximise the opportunities from this distributor.

WORKSHEET ACTIVITY 4

application

Think about the education sector for a moment and specifically the market for CIM qualifications.

a. Who are the supply chain members for CIM qualifications?

b. Now think about your own organisation (or one you are familiar with)- who are the supply chain members?

5 Promotion

The word 'promotion' implies that the seller is doing all the talking, yet in a market-orientated business there is a two-way dialogue, where the buyer's response is as important as the seller's message. The term 'marketing communications' more fully represents the role of the promotional P of the marketing mix. Another source of confusion is also sometimes made with the concept of a 'price promotion' where a product is sold at a discounted rate.

Overall, the role of promotion is to raise awareness of goods and services and illicit a response from the target market. Promotional activities are often classified as **above-the-line** and **below-the-line**.

KEY CONCEPTS

application

Above-the-line promotion is advertising placed in paid-for media, such as the press, radio, TV, cinema and outdoor/transport poster sites. The 'line' is one in an advertising agency's accounts, above which are shown its earnings on a commission basis, from the buying of media space for clients.

Below-the-line promotion is a blanket term for a range of non-commissionable marketing communication activities. (Agency earnings on a fee basis are shown below the 'line' in their accounts.) More specifically, it refers to activities such as direct mail, sales promotions, sponsorship and exhibitions or trade shows.

In order to be most effective, the promotional tools selected should:

- Project the image of the organisation which the marketer wishes to reflect
- Communicate a message which will raise awareness, increase sales, evoke an attitude, instil familiarity, build a relationship with customers (or a combination of all or some of these)
- Illicit some form of behavioural or attitude change in those the organisation is targeting.

Generally, the most successful marketing communications involve utilising a number of different communications methods commonly known as the promotional mix in a co-ordinated manner.

5.1 Promotional mix

The basic **promotional mix** consists of advertising, sales promotion, personal selling and PR, but more promotional methods are appearing all the time, particularly with the development of information and communication technologies. The following diagram indicates the extensive range of tools that can be used to communicate with a customer or potential customer.

The marketing communications mix

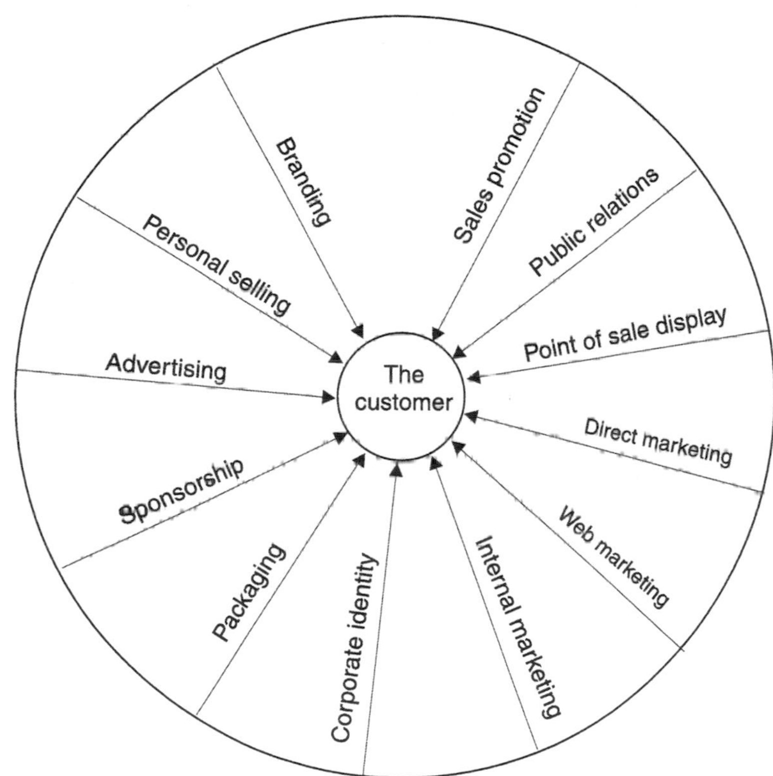

5.2 Advertising

KEY CONCEPT

Concept

Advertising is 'any paid form of non-personal presentation and promotion of ideas, goods or services by an identifiable sponsor'. (American Marketing Association)

Why advertise?

- To promote **sales**
- To create an **image**
- To support **sales staff**
- To offset **competitor advertising**
- To **remind and reassure**

Advertising can take many forms and uses a number of mediums including online media, press, broadcast (TV, radio etc) billboards, leaflet drops and point of sale displays. Increasingly sophisticated methods of advertising are opening up to marketers. Often the most inventive forms of advertising are also the most interesting and evoke a massive public response – there are whole books dedicated to effective campaigns. The increased use of online media and particularly social networking in recent years has meant that many campaigns are launched online first and are circulated via social networks.

MARKETING AT WORK

application

Cadbury have made viral marketing work particularly effectively for them in recent years. First there was the drumming gorilla campaign which caused significant interest before being aired as a TV. Next came their ad featuring children with what appeared to be dancing eyebrows. These campaigns worked well because they were first featured on social networking platforms such as You Tube and circulated amongst friends because they were funny. By the time the ads hit paid for TV broadcasts they have already received significant press coverage and therefore maximised their exposure.

5.3 Sales promotion

Sales promotion techniques add value to a product in order to achieve a specific marketing objective.

KEY CONCEPT

concept

The Institute of Sales Promotion (ISP) defines **sales promotion** as 'a range of tactical marketing techniques, designed within a strategic marketing framework, to add value to a product or service, in order to achieve a specific sales and marketing objective'.

Sales promotion activity is typically aimed at increasing short-term sales volume, by encouraging first time, repeat or multiple purchase within a stated time frame ('offer closes on such-and-such a date'). It seeks to do this by adding value to the product or service: consumers are offered something extra – or the chance to obtain something extra – if they purchase, purchase more or purchase again. The following diagram shows commonly used consumer sales promotion tools.

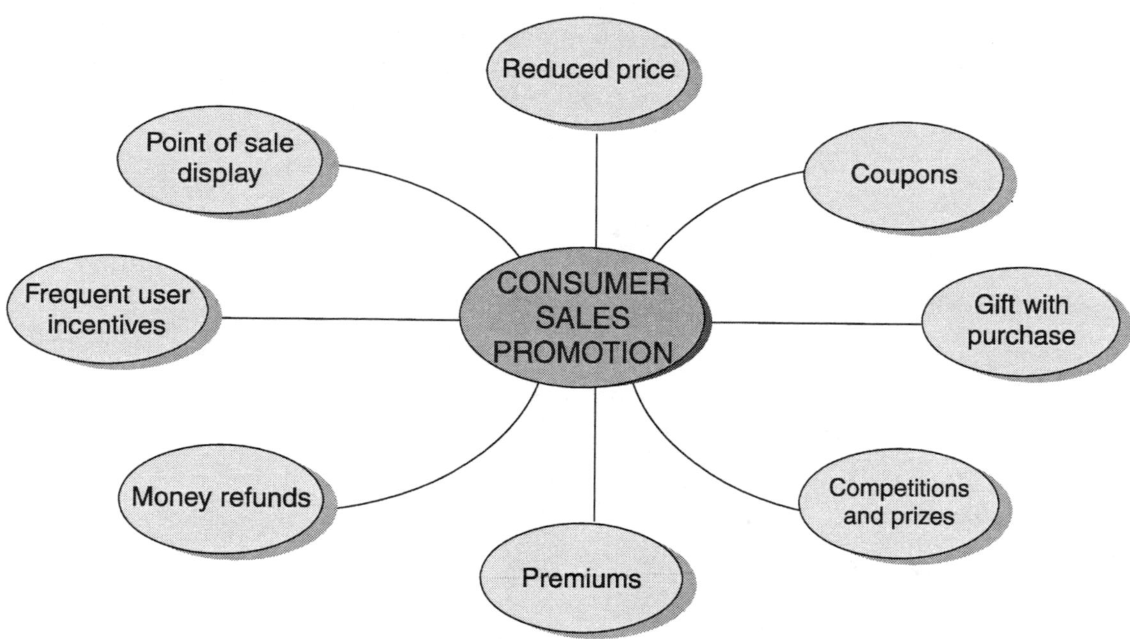

5.4 Public relations

Public relations aims to enhance goodwill towards an organisation from its publics.

KEY CONCEPT

concept

The Institute of Public Relations has defined **public relations** as 'the planned and sustained effort to establish and maintain goodwill and mutual understanding between an organisation and its publics'.

This is an important discipline, because although it may not directly stimulate sales, the organisation's image is an important factor in whether it attracts and retains employees, whether consumers buy its products/services, whether the community supports or resists its presence and activities and whether the media reports positively on its operations.

An organisation can be either reactive or proactive in its management of relationships with the public.

- **Reactive public relations** is primarily concerned with the communication of what has happened and responding to factors affecting the organisation. It is primarily defensive.
- In contrast, **proactive public relations** practitioners have a much wider role and thus have a far greater influence on overall organisational strategy. The scope of the PR function is much wider, encompassing communications activities in their entirety.

Typical PR activities involve maintaining strong media and press relations, managing events and ensuring consistent corporate communications messages are maintained.

5.5 Direct marketing

KEY CONCEPT

Concept

Direct marketing creates and develops a direct relationship between the consumer and the company on an individual basis.

(a) The Institute of Direct Marketing in the UK defines direct marketing as 'The planned recording, analysis and tracking of customer behaviour to develop relational marketing strategies'.

(b) The Direct Marketing Association in the US defines direct marketing as 'An interactive system of marketing which uses one or more advertising media to effect a measurable response and/or transaction at any location'.

Direct marketing involves use of a wide variety of media to communicate directly with the target market and to elicit a measurable response.

5.5.1 Features of direct marketing

It is worth studying these definitions and noting some key words and phrases.

- **Response**. Direct marketing is about getting people to respond by post, telephone, e-mail or web form to invitations and offers.
- **Interactive**. The process is two-way, involving the supplier and the customer.
- **Relationship**. Direct marketing is in many instances part of an on-going process of communicating with and selling to the same customer.
- **Recording and analysis**. Response data are collected and analysed so that the most cost-effective procedures may be arrived at.

Direct marketing helps create and develop **direct one-to-one relationships** between the company and each of its prospects and customers. This is a form of **direct supply**, because it removes all channel intermediaries apart from the advertising medium and the delivery medium: there are no resellers. This allows the company to retain control over where and how its products are promoted, and to reach and develop business contacts efficiently.

5.5.2 Tools of direct marketing

Direct marketing is the fastest growing sector of promotional activity. It now embraces a range of techniques, some traditional – and some based upon new technologies.

- **Direct mail** (DM): a personally addressed 'written offering' (letter and/or sales literature) with some form of response mechanism, sent to existing customers from an in-house database or mailing list.
- **E-mail**: messages sent via the Internet from an e-mail database of customers. E-mails can offer routine information, updates and information about new products: e-mail addresses can be gathered together via enquiries and contact permissions at the company's website.
- **Mobile phone text messaging (SMS)**. Messages can be sent via mobile phone to a captive audience, catching them wherever they are. This form of marketing is still in its infancy, but with the proliferation of mobile phone usage it is likely to be very significant, at least in terms of numbers reached. It is also becoming increasingly sophisticated, with '3G' (third-generation) mobile phone technology. SMS marketing is governed by the Mobile Marketing Association in the UK.
- **Direct response advertising** as described at paragraph 2.1 above.
- **Mail order**. Mail order brochures typically contain a selection of items also available in a shop or trade outlet, which can be ordered via an order form included with the brochure and delivered to the customer. Mail order extends the reach of a retail business to more (and more geographically dispersed) customers.
- **Catalogue marketing** is similar to mail order, but involves a complete catalogue of the products of the firm, which typically would not have retail outlets at all. Electronic catalogues can also be downloaded on the internet, with the option of transferring to the website for transaction processing, and on CD-ROM.
- **Call centres** and **telemarketing**. A call centre is a telephone service (in-house or outsourced by the marketing organisation) responding to or making telephone calls. This is a cost-effective way of providing a professionally trained response to customer callers and enquirers, for the purposes of sales, customer service, customer care or a contact point for direct response advertising.

5.6 E-communications

E marketing has been the most significant development in marketing communications in recent years although it merely is a new medium which has become available, the same 'rules' of marketing and communications still apply- albeit at a possibly faster pace.

Key issues for e-communications include:

- the ability to **optimise the visits to websites** (search engine optimisation)
- the need to be more than an online brochure with the opportunity for **real interaction** with customers
- a consideration of the role of the **networking opportunities** online and the increased propensity for customers to **review** every aspect of a good or service and self broadcast this – the role of word of mouth has therefore become intensified

5.7 Personal selling

Personal selling encompasses a wide variety of tasks including prospecting, information gathering and communicating as well as actually selling.

KEY CONCEPT

concept

Personal selling is the presentation of products and persuasive communication to potential clients by sales staff employed by the supplying organisation. It is the most direct and longest established means of promotion within the promotional mix.

Personal selling, or sales force activity, must be undertaken within the context of the organisation's overall marketing strategy. For example, if the organisation pursues a **'pull'** strategy, relying on massive consumer advertising to draw customers to ask for the brands, then the role of the sales force may primarily be servicing, ensuring that retailers carry sufficient stock, allocate adequate shelf space for display and co-operate in sales promotion programmes.

Conversely, with a '**push**' strategy, the organisation will rely primarily on the sales force to persuade marketing intermediaries to buy the product. The following model demonstrated the tasks involved with personal selling.

Elements and tasks of personal selling

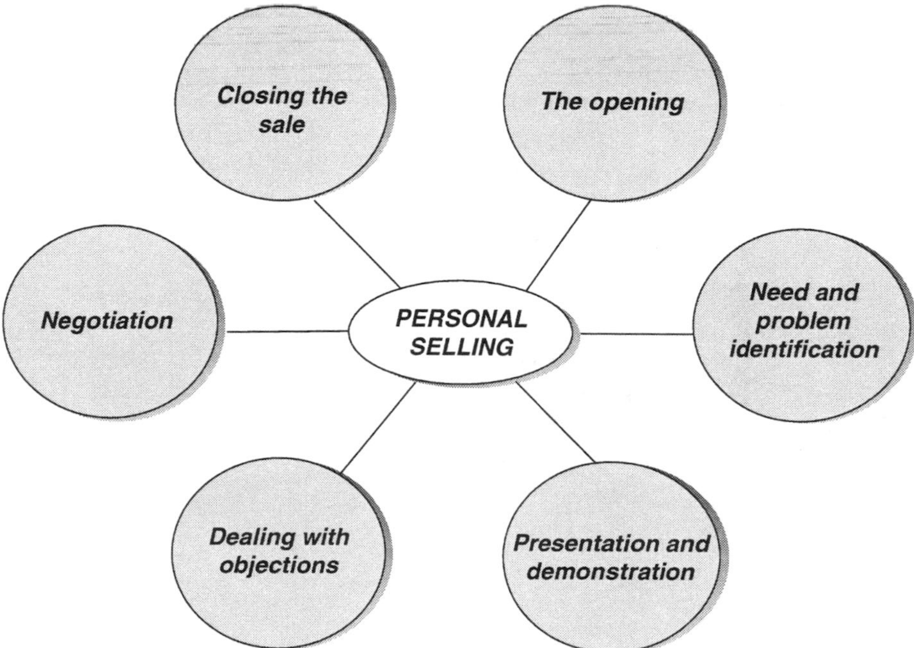

6 People

The higher the level of customer contact involved in the delivery of a product or service, the more crucial is the role of people. In many cases the delivery and the physical presence of the staff involved are completely inseparable. This is why the term 'people' was specifically added in order to reflect services marketing more fully.

In some cases, the physical presence of people actually performing the job is a vital aspect of customer satisfaction. Think of counter staff in a bank, or waiting staff in a restaurant, or builders who leave your house tidier than they found it. The people involved are performing or 'producing' the service, selling the service and also liaising with the customer to promote the service, gather information and respond to customer needs.

Organisations need to take measures to institute a customer orientation in all sectors of activity. People issues will include the following.

- Appearance
- Attitude
- Commitment (including quality/customer)
- Behaviour
- Professionalism
- Skills/competence
- Discretion/confidentiality
- Integrity/ethics

Managers must promote values of customer service in order to create a culture of customer service. This may entail any or all of the following.

- **Job design** to give people the authority they need to meet customer needs
- Careful policies of **recruitment and selection**
- Programmes of **training and development** to ensure that staff have both technical competence and 'people skills'
- Standardised **rules and practices**, to ensure consistent basic levels of service
- Effective programmes of **staff motivation and reward**, creating commitment to the organisation, quality and customers
- Effective **communication** of quality, service and customer care values

For members of the organisation who are not in customer-facing roles their value to the overall marketing proposition should not be underestimated. Recognising that in order to provide a high quality offering needs to be at the centre of every functional department.

7 Process

The term process within the marketing mix essentially is concerned with the delivery process of the customer proposition- in other words, what processes and procedures are in place to get the value proposition to the customer. You may think that his sounds very much like 'place' but it does not refer to this exactly (although in some examples there will be overlap) rather it refers to policies and procedures along with the customer service elements.

If you think about the processes associated with a trip to the dentist. The dentist will have a particular method for you to book your appointment- there may be an online booking facility for example, telephone bookings or practice of making your next check up appointment at each visit. Your practice may have a procedure or routine that you also go through when you arrive at the surgery, for example, there may be a specific queuing system in place and some method of dealing with latecomers. The complete process of delivering a quality service is sometimes referred to as end-to end customer service and encompasses every aspect of the service encounter from start to finish.

KEY CONCEPT

Process involves the ways in which marketing tasks are achieved. They include all administrative, ordering and customer service features.

- Procedures
- Policies
- Automation of processes (eg online or by automated telephony)
- Information flow to service units/customers
- Capacity levels, for continuous performance
- Speed/timing of service
- Queuing/accessibility arrangements

MARKETING AT WORK

application

Efficient processes can become a marketing advantage in their own right. For example, computer company Dell's success is due as much to the remarkable efficiency of its ordering and customer information system as it is to the quality and manufacturing efficiency of its production system. The company's marketing line is 'Easy as Dell', which refers to the process and sums up Dell's competitive advantage in a nutshell. Take a look, even if you don't want to buy a computer: **www.dell.com**.

The level and quality of service which is available to the customer is especially sensitive. Process issues include the following.

- **Capacity utilisation:** matching resource/staff utilisation to anticipated demand, to avoid delays, bottlenecks and waste.
- **Managing customer contacts and expectations**: keeping people realistically informed and empowering staff to respond to changing needs.

8 Physical Evidence

"Physical evidence gives the consumer something to refer to and to show other people if necessary. Since service products are usually intangible, the consumer of (say) an insurance policy will need some written evidence of its existence in order to feel confident in the product". Blythe, J. (2006)

You receive monthly bank statements – but all they are, really, is reassurance in tangible form that the bank still has your money. The following are other examples of items of physical evidence that the marketer can use in the marketing mix.

Environment of service delivery

- Colours
- Layout
- Staff uniforms
- Noise levels
- Smells
- Ambience
- Website design

Facilities

- Vehicles/aeroplanes
- Equipment/tools

Tangible evidence of purchase

- Labels and other printed information
- Tickets, vouchers and purchase confirmations
- Logos and other visible evidence of brand identity
- Packaging

The layout, décor and 'branding' of a bank or travel agency, for example, are likely to be an important part of the customer's experience of receiving services which are otherwise intangible. Likewise, the appearance, user-friendliness and branding of a company's website can give a visible and 'interactive' aspect to the encounter.

A service can be presented in tangible (and promotional) physical form: consider how travel tickets are presented in branded envelopes (or more sophisticated document wallets), with vouchers for added services, information leaflets and other added value elements – despite the fact that all the customer has purchased is the promise of a future benefit.

Note that physical evidences can be used as a **marketing communications** tool and helps to project a particular corporate image through staff livery uniforms and logos. Promotional messages printed on vouchers/ envelopes/receipts are all promotional opportunities which provide additional physical evidence.

Learning objective review

Learning objectives	Covered
1 Explain the importance of the marketing mix	☑ 7 P's ☑ Highly interactive and interdependent ☑ The sum of 'things' for the marketer to organise
2 Outline the components of product, price, place, promotion, people, process and physical evidence.	☑ Product- the ☑ Price- generates revenue ☑ Place- distribution strategy ☑ Promotion –activities to raise awareness ☑ People- customer facing and co-ordinated effort by all employees to meet customer needs ☑ Process – processes associated with purchase and delivery of products and services ☑ Physical evidence- environment, corporate image
3 Appreciate the linkages between each of the 7P's	☑ Required for a co-ordinated, consistent marketing strategy ☑ Essential for success

Quick quiz

1 The extended marketing mix includes

A Product, price, place, promotion

B Product, people, price, process, place, physical evidence, promotion

C Product, people, price, project, place, physical evidence, promotion

2 From a marketers perspective products are:

A just tangible goods

B a definitive physical object

C a 'package' that satisfies needs and wants

3 Which statement is not true?

A price is a revenue generating tool

B price should always match competitor pricing

C price often indicates a level of quality to customers

4 Place refers to:

A The location where a product is sold

B The country where a product is made

C The entire distribution network and supply chain for an organisation

5 Which of the following is not a promotional tool

A Advertising

B Customer service

C Public relations

6 People are important because

A They help to build relationships with the organisations customers

B Trade unions require them to be treated fairly

C They are paid

7 Process refers to:

A Procedures, customer service and support and processes to build a quality offering

B Manufacturing processes

C Rules for staff

8 Physical evidence is important because:

A A positive image is portrayed

B not applicable as it is not important

C It enables intangible services to be seen as more tangible

1	B	Option A is the original 4 P's, Option B may be cited in a different order but contains the correct 7P's
2	C	Both goods and services are 'packages' designed to satisfy needs and wants
3	B	Competitors pricing is not always matched
4	C	The entire process of getting the product or service to the customer
5	B	Customer service
6	A	Customers build relationships with staff within the organisation
7	A	Processes include marketing processes to help the transaction and are not limited to manufacturing processes or simply rules for staff.
8	C	Physical evidence includes corporate image, ambiance and environment which help to make services more tangible.

Worksheet activity 1

Your answer will of course depend on your purchase. A typical example of an answer to this activity is shown below. Remember that the more detail you add to your descriptions and the harder you try to describe the marketing mix, the more sense it will make to you. Once you fully understand the concept you will be more likely to remember it in the exam.

Marketing mix	FMCG purchase: Jam	Consumer durable purchase: Breadmaker
Product	Retailer own luxury brand. A premium 'conserve' Standard jar size with a conventional opening	A retailer own brand – kitchen appliance
Price	Mid price level. Priced to complete with the mid level branded jams.	Discounted promotional price. Lowest priced model within the category.
Place	Supermarket retailer- in store. The product can also be purchased online for home delivery.	Bought online
Promotion	A larger size shelf label (shelf barker) to draw attention used in store.	Promoted online using a pop up advert
People	Not so relevant directly from a consumer perspective however there will be significant relevance of people within the supply chain.	A courier was used for delivery. They were polite and efficient when delivering the package.

Process	This was purchased in a store and the only personnel who were encountered were check out staff.	The website was easy to use, secure in terms of payment method and delivery was made on the expected day.
Physical evidence	An attractively designed jar demonstrating a premium product. Labels appear to be of good quality with embossed text.	The product was nicely packaged. The website looked a bit amateurish which lead me to question whether the intended product would actually arrive. The delivery paperwork was all

You may have found that the final three P's- people, process and physical evidence have been more difficult to complete. If you were to complete the activity again but this time using a service, you will find it considerably easier.

Worksheet activity 2

This again will depend on the products you have chosen. Generally, you will find that many of the issues you thought about in activity 1 will also be relevant for this activity.

Worksheet activity 3

You are likely to have found that many of the reviews will refer to the higher price that the salons charge and point to the fact that their expectations prior to their visit had been raised as a result. Those customers who after their visit report a positive outcome are likely to use phrases like ' it was worth the higher price'. Those who had a negative experience are likely to focus heavily on the high price within their review.

Worksheet activity 4

a. The CIM are in effect the 'manufacturer' or 'producer' of the qualification. At one point, students were able to work directly with the CIM register to self study alone for qualifications. Now students are required to study through a study centre. The study centre is in effect an Intermediary. Alternative 'products' are available through some intermediaries such as a distance learning product, classroom based product etc.

b. This will depend on your organisation.

References

Bawden, T (2008) *'French Fashion Retailer Morgan files for bankruptcy'* The Times, 31st December, London.

Bitner & Booms (1981) '*Marketing Strategies and organisational structures*' in Marketing of Services American Marketing Association, Chicago.

Blythe, J. (2006) Principles and Practice of Marketing, Thompson, London, .

Hill, L. And O'Sullivan, T. (2004) Foundation Marketing 3rd Edition, Prentice Hall, London.

Jobber, D. (2007) Principles and Practice of Marketing 5th edition, McGraw Hill, London.

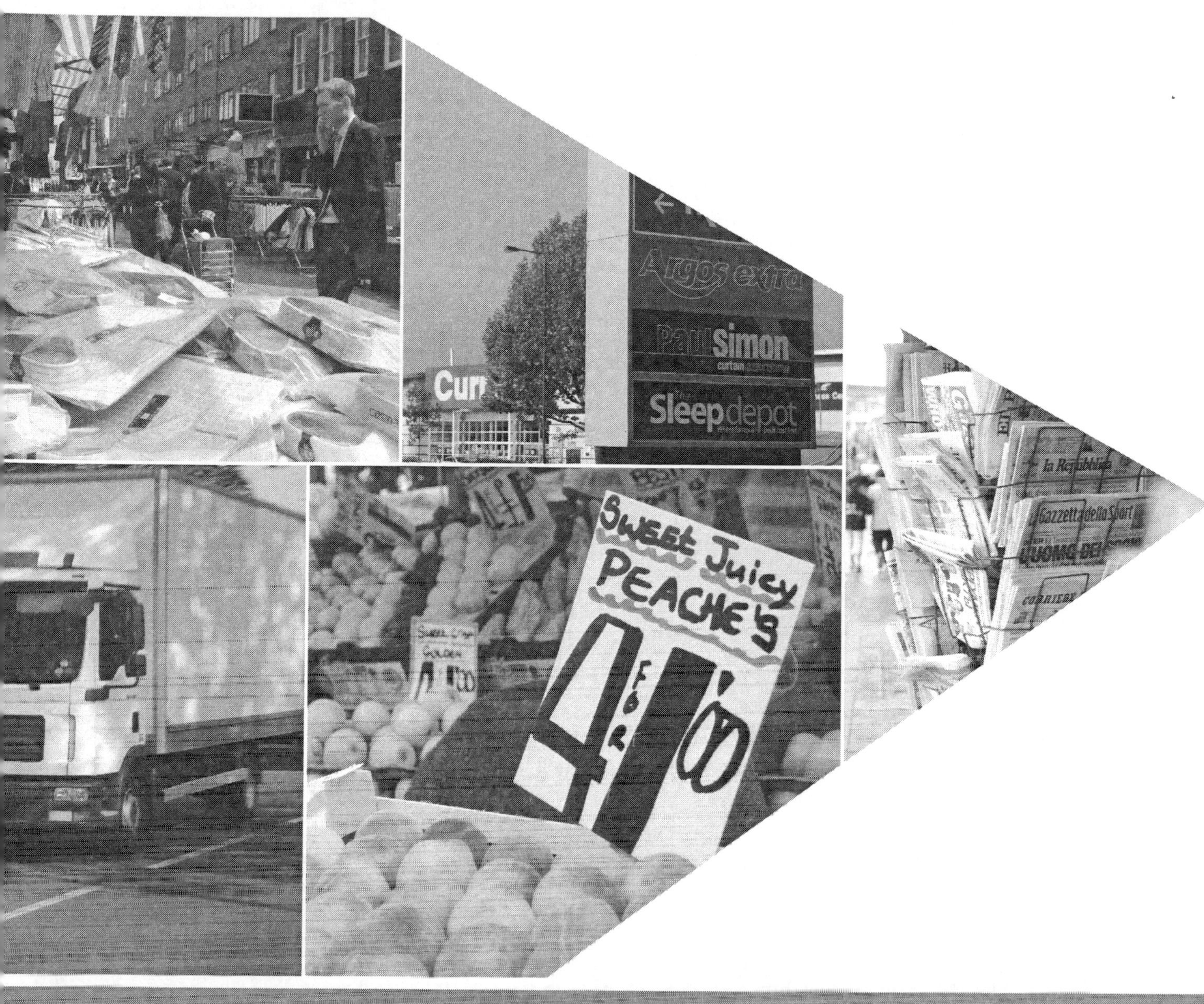

Chapter 4

Marketing in Different Contexts

Topic list

1 Influences on buying behaviour
2 Decision making processes
3 Decision making units
4 Types of markets

Introduction

In this chapter we are going to consider the differences in the characteristics of various types of marketing context and see what impact these differences may have on marketing mix decisions. Imagine buying a car for yourself. As a consumer faced with this purchase scenario you are likely to behave very differently than if you were purchasing a van to use for work. Although they are both vehicles (and as an individual you may have specific attributes you look for in a vehicle), the criteria that you either overtly or subconsciously apply will differ because of the roles of other people you involve in the decision making, the usage requirements and your attitude to risk in making purchases. As requirements and behaviours differ in different purchase contexts, marketers need to adapt their entire marketing mix so that they are able to fulfil customer needs. The chapter begins by explaining the nature of buyer behaviour before looking at decision making units. A range of 'markets' or contexts are then considered in terms of how marketers can adapt their marketing mixes.

Syllabus linked learning objectives

By the end of the chapter you will be able to:

Learning objectives	Syllabus link
1 Describe ways in which customers and consumers make buying decisions	4.1
2 Explain how the marketing mix is used in different markets	4.2

1 Influences on buying behaviour

Dibb (1996) suggest that the study of buying behaviour is important for a number of reasons.

(a) The buyer's reaction to the organisation's marketing strategy has a major impact on the **survival and success** of the organisation.

(b) If organisations are truly to implement the marketing concept, they must examine the main influences on what, where, when and how customers buy. Only in this way will they be able to devise a **marketing mix** that satisfies the needs of customers.

(c) By gaining a better understanding of the factors influencing their customers and how their customers will respond, organisations will be better able to plan effective **marketing communications** and activities.

However, it is important to note that not all consumers behave in the same way. Decision making and purchase patterns vary considerably within markets or product categories, between individuals – and even within individuals according to circumstances and over time! You must begin to recognise this complexity and aim to adapt marketing communications to the needs of different **target audiences**.

We also need to consider the titles we use when discussing 'customers'.

1 As a **customer**, we would engage in a purchase transaction with a supplier of goods. In a domestic context, these would be for our own or our family's consumption.

2 As a **client** we would be availing ourselves of a range of professional services such as accountants, solicitors etc.

3 As a **professional**, we would be exercising special skills in purchasing, often in large quantities and/or expending millions of pounds, as a part of our job on behalf of an organisation. For example, media buyers are professionals who purchase advertising space.

4 As a **consumer**, we are the end user of the product. A consumer may not be a customer and vice-versa. We do not necessarily take direct part in the purchase but, because we use up the product and gain some satisfaction or benefit from it, we may influence its purchase and/or its re-purchase. We are the end-user of the products.

5 When we are part of a group combining our influences we are known as a **Decision Making Unit** (DMU), for example children influencing the purchase of breakfast cereals; the adults in a family choosing a new carpet; or a group of colleagues of differing disciplines in an organisation. The latter DMU may have a very formal structure and the former have very little.

KEY CONCEPT

concept

Key elements of buyer behaviour include: stakeholders in the purchase decision (the decision making unit); and the process by which information is used to make purchase decisions (the decision making process). These differ in consumer and organisational contexts.

The variables in buying behaviour are wide ranging and complex. However, they can be broadly categorised as:

- **Stakeholders** and **participants** in the buying decision
- The **decision making processes** by which information is used to solve problems, make choices and reach the decision to purchase
- Various **factors and characteristics** which influence buyers' perceptions, judgements, choices and decisions

We will look at each of these in turn, in relation to both **consumer buying behaviour** and **organisational buyer behaviour**.

KEY CONCEPT

concept

Consumer buyer behaviour refers to the buying behaviour of final consumers, those individuals and households who buy goods and services for personal consumption. (Kotler *et al* 1999)

Organisational buyer behaviour refers to the buying behaviour of organisations which buy goods and services to use in the production of other products and services that are sold, rented or supplied to others.

Most large organisations sell, one way or another, to other organisations. Some sell products and services predominantly to other businesses or government bodies. Some supply raw materials, components and machinery to manufacturers of those products. However, even companies that produce consumer goods and services may sell their products to other businesses (wholesalers and retailers) who serve the consumer market or institutions (such as schools, hospitals, nursing homes and prisons) which pass them on to the end users in their care.

1.1 Consumer buyer behaviour

The 'core' process of consumer buying behaviour will be influenced by a number of outside variables. These variables have been classified by Wilson and Gilligan (1997), as follows:

- Cultural
- Social
- Personal
- Psychological

Each factor will be considered in more detail separately, but it is essential to remember that they are not **mutually exclusive**. Marketers must have a clear understanding of how the various factors interact and how they influence buyer behaviour, both separately and in their totality.

1.1.1 Cultural factors

These are the most fundamental of the influencing factors, and include culture, subculture and social class.

KEY CONCEPT

Culture comprises the values and attitudes in the life adopted by people that help them to interpret and communicate with others, as members of a society.

Culture is largely the result of a learning process. As we grow up we learn a set of values, perceptions, preferences and behaviour patterns through socialisation in the family and other institutions such as school and work.

This broad set of values is then influenced by the **subcultures** in which we develop. Sub-cultural groups can be defined in terms of religion, ethnic characteristics, racial characteristics and geographical areas, all of which further influence attitudes, tastes, taboos and lifestyle.

A third cultural influence is that of **social stratification**, or **class**. The key characteristics of social class have been highlighted as follows.

(a) People within a particular social class resemble each other more than they resemble those from other social classes.

(b) Social class is determined by a series of variables such as occupation, income, education and values, rather than by a single variable.

(c) Individuals can move from one social class to another.

1.1.2 Social factors

Within the context of culture, an individual is also influenced by a series of social factors, such as **reference groups**, family, social roles and status, all of which can have a direct effect on buying behaviour.

Reference groups are groups 'with which an individual identifies so much that he or she takes on many of the values, attitudes or behaviours of group members' (Dibb et al, 1996). Four types have been identified.

(a) **Primary membership groups**, which are generally informal and within which individuals interact frequently(family, friends, neighbours, work colleagues).

(b) **Secondary membership groups**, which tend to be more formal than primary groups and within which less interaction takes place (trade unions, religious groups and professional societies are examples).

(c) **Aspirational groups**, to which an individual would like to belong.

(d) **Dissociative groups**, whose values and behaviour the individual rejects.

WORKSHEET ACTIVITY 1

application

The CIM is, presumably, one of your own 'aspirational' groups. What other reference groups do you have? Divide them according to the following classifications.

Primary membership groups:

Secondary membership groups:

Aspirational groups:

Dissociative groups:

The family

A major social influence is the family, particularly with regard to the roles and relative influence exerted by different family members. Research has indicated three patterns of decision making within the family. The typical 'lead' in making decisions in different according to the product group.

- **Husband dominated**: life insurance, cars and television
- **Wife dominated**: washing machines, carpets, kitchenware and furniture
- **Equal**: holidays, housing and entertainment

Families now have many different forms and roles: unmarried partners, single-parent families, blended families and so on. The dominant role adopted within different product groups is therefore more complex in reality. Marketers have had to therefore adapt.

MARKETING AT WORK

application 

Tour operators looking to attract holiday makers to book through them found that as a large proportion of single parent families were discouraged from booking because free child places were subject to two adult fares. Some holiday companies changed their price structures as a result to appeal to this significant market.

1.1.3 Personal factors

Influencing factors that can be classified as personal include such things as age and life cycle, occupation, economic circumstances and lifestyle.

Individuals will buy different types of product depending on their age. This is particularly relevant to such products as clothes, furniture and recreation. However, consumption may also be shaped by the stage of the **family life cycle** within which an individual falls.

MARKETING AT WORK

application 

Think about the cars you may have throughout your life. A classic example may be as follows. A young driver passes their driving test aged seventeen and opts for a small, two door, economical car because it is affordable, easy to park and seen as being 'cool' with peers. By the time they have a family they may want something larger with four doors to easily help get children in and out. Once the children have left home and they have more disposable income and savings, a two-seater sports car becomes a prize possession.

A person's occupation will influence consumption and the task for marketers is to identify the occupational groups that have an above average interest in their products and services.

Buying patterns are also heavily influenced by an individual's economic circumstances. Kotler states that an individual's economic circumstances consist of:

- Spendable income: its level, stability and time pattern
- Savings and assets, including the percentage that is liquid
- Borrowing power
- Attitude toward spending versus saving

However, people coming from the same subculture, social class and occupation may lead completely different lifestyles.

Marketers will search for relationships between their products and lifestyle groups.

MARKETING AT WORK

Advertisers are failing to notice the growing population of over 50 year olds, according to research by Datamonitor. By 2025 there are expected to be 177 million in this age group in Western Europe.

Three groups of over 50 year old consumers have emerged:

'Woofs': well off older folk

'Youthfully spirited': less financially secure then 'woofs', but willing to experiment

'Self preservationists': older, more conservative than the other groups.

Companies are obsessed with youth, and the staff in advertising agencies are predominantly under 30.

1.1.4 Psychological factors

The process of buyer behaviour is also influenced by four major psychological factors:

- Motivation (how driven the consumer is to achieve specific goals)
- Perception (the way in which the consumer makes sense and process the meaning of the product or service)
- Learning (the way consumer behaviour changes according to their experience of the product or service)
- Beliefs and attitudes (the consumers evaluation of the product or service)

concept

You do not need to understand these psychological factors in detail for your examination. We wanted to provide you with a complete overview of consumer buying behaviour and so have included them as a means of assisting your overall knowledge.

1.2 Organisational buyer behaviour

A number of differences between organisational and consumer markets exist which mean that a modified approach needs to be taken when considering the process of buying behaviour.

Organisational markets normally comprise fewer buyers, with those buyers often being very concentrated (a few buyers are responsible for the majority of sales). Because of this smaller customer base and the importance and power of larger customers there is generally a close relationship between buyer and seller in organisational markets, with a great degree of customisation and co-operation on product specification and other requirements. Often organisational buyers are geographically concentrated.

The specific characteristics of organisational markets may vary according to the type of organisation that comprises the market.

(a) Producer markets comprise those organisations that purchase products for the purpose of making a profit by using them to produce other products or by using them in their own operations. This may include buyers of raw materials and of semi-finished and finished items used to produce other products.

(b) Reseller markets consist of intermediaries such as retailers and wholesalers who buy the finished goods in order to resell them to make a profit. Other than minor alterations, resellers do not change the physical characteristics of the products they handle.

(c) Government markets comprise those national and local governments who buy a variety of goods and services to support their internal operations and to provide the public services that are within their remit, normally making their purchases through bids or negotiated contracts.

(d) Institutional markets comprise those organisations that seek to achieve charitable, educational, community or other non-business goals.

2 Decision making processes

Decision making processes refer to the processes and stages that are used by consumers and organisations go through when making a purchase.

2.1 Consumer decision making processes

To influence consumers with regard to a specific product or service offered, it is essential the practitioner has some understanding of the process by which consumers reach decisions to buy or not buy.

Steps in the buying process:

Step 1 Need recognition

Step 2 Information search

Step 3 Evaluation of alternatives

Step 4 Purchase decision

Step 5 Post purchase evaluation

Step 1: Need recognition

The process begins when the buyer recognises a **need or problem**. This can be triggered by internal **stimuli**, such as hunger or thirst, or external stimuli, such as social esteem. If the need rises to a threshold level it will become a **drive**, and from previous experience the buyer will know how to satisfy this drive through the purchase of a particular type of product. The task for the marketer is to identify the stimuli that trigger a particular need, and use this knowledge to develop marketing strategies that trigger consumer interest.

Step 2: Information search

Once aroused, the customer will search for more information. The information search stage can be divided

into two levels.

(a) '**Heightened attention**', where the customer simply becomes more receptive to information about the particular product category.

(b) '**Active information search**'. The extent of the search will depend on the strength of the drive, the amount of information available, the ease of obtaining additional information and the satisfaction obtained from the search.

The task for the marketer is to decide which are the major information sources that the customer will use and to analyse their relative importance. Kotler (1994) suggests that **consumer information sources fall into four groups**:

- **Personal sources**: family, friends, neighbours, work colleagues
- **Commercial sources**: advertising, salespeople, packaging, displays
- **Public sources**: mass media, consumer rating organisations
- **Experiential sources**: handling, examining, using the product

A consumer will generally receive the most information exposure from commercial sources, but **the most effective information exposure comes from personal sources**. Each information source performs a somewhat different function, with consumers being informed by commercial sources and this information being legitimised (or not) by personal sources.

Through this information-gathering process the consumer will learn about competing brands and their relative pros and cons. This will enable the consumer to narrow down the range of alternatives to those brands that will best meet his or her particular needs: what has been called the **choice** or **evoked set**.

Step 3: Evaluation of alternatives prior to purchase

Trying to describe the process of evaluation of alternatives is not easy as there is no generally accepted single evaluation process. Most current models of evaluation are **cognitively** oriented: in other words they take the view that **the customer forms judgements largely on a conscious and rational basis**. Kotler (1994) states that, as the consumer is trying to satisfy some need with the buying process, he will be looking for certain benefits from the product chosen and each product will be seen as a **'bundle of attributes'** with varying capabilities of delivering the benefits sought.

Step 4: Purchase decision

Having evaluated the range of brand choices the consumer may have formed a purchase intention to buy the most preferred brand. However, some factors could intervene between the purchase intention and the purchase decision. The first factor is the **attitude of others**. If, for example, a friend or relative of the consumer expresses a strong negative opinion regarding the brand choice, this may influence the consumer to change his or her mind. Purchase intention is also influenced by **unanticipated situational factors** that may intervene between purchase intention and decision. Such factors could include a change in financial circumstances such as redundancy, or circumstances in which some other purchase becomes more urgent.

Step 5: Post purchase evaluation

Having purchased the brand the consumer will experience some level of **satisfaction or dissatisfaction**, depending on the closeness between the consumer's product expectations and the product's **perceived performance**. These feelings will influence whether the consumer buys the brand again and also whether the consumer talks favourably or unfavourably about the brand to others.

2.2 Organisational buyer behaviour

The following stages in the process of organisational buying behaviour must be considered.

Step 1 Recognise the problem

Step 2 Develop product specifications to solve the problem

Step 3 Search for products and suppliers

Step 4 Evaluate products relative to specifications

Step 5 Select and order the most appropriate product

Step 6 Evaluate the product and supplier performance

This process is, in outline terms, similar to that for consumer buying behaviour. It begins with the recognition that a problem exists, the stimulus for which may come either from within or outside the company. The second stage of the process requires those people participating in the buying decision to assess the problem or need and determine what will be required to resolve or satisfy it. Here, the DMU comes into operation.

The third stage of the process is similar to that of information search; utilising trade shows, trade publications, supplier catalogues, and soliciting proposals from known suppliers. This should result in a list of alternative products which are then evaluated to ascertain whether they meet the product specifications. Suppliers may also be evaluated according to criteria such as price, service and ability to deliver.

3 Decision making units

One of the major differences between consumer and organisational buying behaviour is the fact that organisational purchase decisions are rarely made by a single individual. Normally purchasing decisions are made by a number of people from different functional areas, possibly with different statuses within the organisation. This obviously complicates the process of marketing and selling the product and it is important that the marketer is fully aware of the **composition of the buying group** and the relative importance to the purchase decision of the individuals within it.

KEY CONCEPT

concept

The **decision making unit (DMU)** is a group of people who participate in or influence the purchase decision at any stage in the buying process.

The **decision making unit** (DMU) comprises all stakeholders in a decision. This may involve a number of roles: gatekeeper, initiator, influencer, decider, financier, buyer and user.

Although the **buyer** may appear to be the 'customer' at the point of sale, the entire decision-making unit can be identified as the target market for the marketer

The marketing organisation needs to understand the complexity of the DMU in each market and market segment in which it operates. It is clearly relevant to marketers whether, for example, the woman or man in a household is the buyer/decision maker; whether a young or older person is the user; which gender or age group consumes which promotional media. This kind of information determines the product's positioning (masculine/feminine? youthful/mature?), media choices and target audience for marketing communications. It will also direct the product specifications.

MARKETING AT WORK

application

Mobile phone designs vary according to the target market they are to appeal to. Pink 'girly' designs are developed for young females whist professional looking models are designed for working professionals. Children are also targeted with some models designed specifically to appeal to them

---

With marketing communications in mind, the communication mix should **leverage influence** on the purchase decision: reaching and persuading the **most influential role** in a given purchase with the **least expenditure** of effort and cost. The decider may be an obvious target, but for price sensitive decisions, for example, it may be important to target the financier (if a separate individual); if deciders are difficult to reach, it may be important to target gatekeepers; and for shared or complex decisions, it may be more cost effective to target influencers (co-opting them to share the work of promotion).

- Identify **gatekeepers** (who is most likely to be open to, or in charge of acquiring, product information?) and the most effective information **media** to reach them (where do they prefer to gather product information and in what format?)
- Identify **indicators/initiators** (who is most likely to notice and draw attention to product information?) and target them with messages that arouse **interest** (how is the product relevant to needs, wants or interests of the DMU?)
- Identify **influencers** (whom will the decider consult or listen to?) and target them with persuasive information to arouse or reinforce **desire** (how does the product solve a problem, meet a need? How can it be endorsed or validated?)
- Identify **deciders** (who will have the final say?) and target them with information to arouse or reinforce **intention** (what are the decisive benefits of the product for meeting needs and wants? How can the perceived risks of decision be lowered – and the benefits of acting quickly be conveyed?)
- Identify **buyers** (who actually makes the purchase?) and target them with messages which facilitate **action** (what does the buyer need to do next? How can it be made easy?)

- Identify **financiers** (who pays or authorises payment?) and target them with information to help them to **justify** expenditure (what benefits can be weighed against the costs?) and to complete the transaction (how can payment be made easy?)
- Identify **users** (who uses, consumes or benefits?) and target them with practical information to enable them to **use** the product safely and satisfyingly (what are possible areas of ignorance or difficulty? What on-going support may be required?)

The marketing organisation will also seek appropriate forms of **feedback** to fine-tune its marketing mix in satisfying the needs of each of the DMU roles. (Is product packaging effectively attracting the attention of initiators? Are promotional messages effectively persuading influencers and deciders? Is customer service effectively satisfying users?), are models effectively meting needs and wants?

3.1 Consumer decision making units

The people who make up a DMU will vary according to the context in which the purchase decision is being made and the stakeholders who will be affected by and involved in the decision. Consumers belong to a number of different groups and networks.

(a) The **family** is a primary group for most individuals: family norms and influences are particularly strong. Socio-cultural factors influence customary decision-making roles within the family structure: be aware that such norms vary from culture to culture. In a traditional Western or Latin family model, marketing messages may be targeted at the child (initiator/influencer) in the purchase of a toy; at the wife/mother (decider/buyer) in the case of household items; or at the husband/father (decider/buyer) in the case of the family car. Be aware, however, that gender roles and household structures are becoming more diverse, as discussed in Chapter 2.

(b) The **work group** can be an important influence, especially if colleagues are also part of the individual's social network. Needs to project status, professionalism and image at work also influence decisions: cars, clothes, office furniture and other products are often positioned accordingly.

(c) **Friendship groups** are an important influence on buyer behaviour: the desire to form and maintain social relationships is a basic human need. People often trust friends to advise them: marketers frequently depict product choice, in advertising, in the context of friendly sharing, advice and encouragement – and attempt to capitalise on positive word-of-mouth promotion.

(d) **Interest groups** (action groups, pressure groups, consumer groups and so on) may influence purchase behaviour. Membership of (or advocacy by) groups may lead to supporting or boycotting brands that do or do not conform to the group's values. Marketing messages may be targeted defensively or positively to address environmental, human rights or consumer concerns.

WORKSHEET ACTIVITY 2

application

Think about a recent purchase you have made:

a. consider who was part of the decision making unit.

b. How would you describe the various stages of the decision making process for your purchase scenario

3.2 Organisational decision making units

The DMU of a buying organisation is called its **buying centre**. This is not to be confused with a purchasing function or team: it is a set of buying roles exercised by different individuals and units that participate in the business decision making process. As Kotler(1996) notes, 'the buying centre concept presents a major marketing challenge. The business marketer must learn who participates in the decision, each participant's relative influence and what evaluation criteria each decision participant uses.'

The buying centre will involve those formally involved in purchase decisions, such as department managers, purchasing managers and accountants. It may also involve less obvious, informal participants who may initiate or influence the buying process.

4 Types of markets

4.1 Consumer marketing

There are two principal types of consumer marketing.

- **Fast moving consumer goods** are goods such as packaged food, beverages, toiletries, and tobacco.
- **Consumer durables** are items such as home appliances and cars.

Classical marketing theory was designed with consumer marketing in mind as we have discussed within this text so far.

4.2 Business to business

Business-to-business marketing (often abbreviated as **B2B**) is concerned with **industrial goods and services**, which are bought by manufacturers, distributors and other private and publicly owned institutions, such as schools and hospitals, to be used as part of their own activities.

In addition, of course, many of the products involved in business-to-business markets are the same as those bought within the ordinary consumer markets, for example, company cars, computers, mobile phones and so on. As we'll see in a moment, however, organisational **buying behaviour** may be quite different from that of an ordinary consumer.

B2B market categories (to recap) can be classified as follows.

(a) **Capital goods** include such items as buildings, machinery and motor vehicles.

(b) **Components and materials** include raw, partly and wholly processed materials or goods which are incorporated into the products sold by the company.

(c) **Supplies** are goods which assist production and distribution. This would include small but important items such as machine oil, computer disks and stationery, and cleaning products.

(d) **Business services** are services used by businesses, for instance employer's liability insurance.

4.2.1 Business products

When bought in a business-to-business context, products are distinct from consumer goods in several ways.

(a) **Conformity with standards**. Industrial products are often bound by legal or quality standards, and as a consequence, products within a particular group are often similar. Differentiation, which is such a key dimension of *consumer* goods, is more difficult here. At the same time, buyers lay down their own specifications to which manufacturers must adhere.

(b) **Technical sophistication**. Many products in this area require levels of complexity and sophistication which are unheard of in consumer products. Often the industry standard gradually influences the consumer equivalent as, for instance, in the case of power tools in the DIY market. After-sales and maintenance contracts have become essential in certain areas.

(c) **High order values**. As a consequence of (a) and (b), many business goods, particularly capital equipment, are very often extremely costly items. Even in the case of supplies, where the single unit value of components and materials may be comparatively low, the quantity required frequently means that orders have a very high value.

(d) **Irregularity of purchase**. Machinery used to produce consumer goods is not bought regularly. Materials used to produce the goods certainly are, but components and materials are often bought on a contract or preferred supplier basis, so that the opportunity to get new business may not arise very often.

4.3 Service organisations

Services are distinguished from products mainly because they are generally produced at the same time as they are consumed, and cannot be stored or taken away. An enhanced marketing mix needs to be deployed.

Characteristics of services which make them distinctive from the marketing of goods have been proposed. There are five major differences

- Intangibility
- Inseparability
- Heterogeneity/variability
- Perishability
- Ownership

4.3.1 Intangibility

Intangibility refers to the **lack of physical substance** which is involved with service delivery. Unlike a product there is nothing to touch, feel or smell. Clearly, this creates difficulties and can inhibit the propensity to consume a service, since customers are not sure what they have.

MARKETING AT WORK

application

The online retailer Amazon is a service provider with many intangible elements to its service. In order to provide reassurance and a more tangible dimension Amazon will focus on aspects such as the look and quality of the packaging and related paperwork they use when sending out goods to consumers. The retailer will also be able to use the physical look of their website and incorporate features such as order tracking so that the consumer gains more of an understanding of the service process. With very few exceptions, credible online retailers will include a page on their website called something along the lines of 'About Us' where often there are photographs of actual shops, warehouses and other corporate premised to reassure consumers that although they are an online company, they are real, actually do have a physical representation and are not just a cyberspace image or are operating from a dodgy lounge.

4.3.2 Ownership

Services do not result in the transfer of property. In the case of purchasing a product, there is permanent transfer of title and control over the use of an item. An item of service provision is often defined by the length of time it is available. This may very well lessen the perceived customer value of a service, and consequently make for unfavourable comparisons with tangible alternatives. Attempts have been made to overcome this problem by providing symbolic tangible items which can be taken away and kept. Car brochures, theatre programmes and the plethora of corporate giftwares such as golf umbrellas, pens and key rings are all examples of this.

Inseparability

A service often cannot be separated from the provider of the service. The **performance of a service often occurs at the same instant as its consumption.** Think of having dental treatment or going on a journey. Neither exists until actually consumed by the purchaser.

4.3.3 Perishability

Services cannot be stored. They are innately perishable. Performances at a theatre or the services of a chiropodist consist in their availability for periods of time, and if they are not occupied, the service they offer cannot be used later. This presents

specific marketing problems. Meeting customer needs in these operations depends on staff being available when they are needed. This must be balanced against the need to minimise unnecessary expenditure on staff wages. Anticipating and responding to levels of demand is, therefore, a key planning priority. There are two risks.

- Inadequate level of demand, accompanied by substantial fixed costs.
- Excess demand may result in lost custom through inadequate service.

Policies must seek to match demand with supply by price variations and promotions to stimulate off-peak demand.

4.3.4 Heterogeneity and variability

Many services face a problem of maintaining consistency in the standard of output. Variability of quality in delivery is inevitable, because of the number of factors which may influence it. This may create problems of operations management. For example, it may be difficult or impossible to attain:

(a) Precise standardisation of the service offered. The quality of the service may depend heavily on who delivers the service and when it takes place, eg. booking a holiday using standard procedures may well be quite different on a quiet winter afternoon than on a hectic spring weekend, and may well vary according to the person dealing with the client.

(b) Influence or control over perceptions of what is good or bad customer service. From the customer's perspective, it is very difficult to obtain an idea of the quality of service in advance of purchase.

WORKSHEET ACTIVITY 3

application

Think about a service that you use and consider how each of the elements below can be described

- Intangibility
- Inseparability
- Heterogeneity/variability
- Perishability
- Ownership

4.4 Not for profit

KEY CONCEPT

concept

Not-for profit organisation can be defined as: '...an organisation whose attainment of its prime goal is not assessed by economic measures. However, in pursuit of that goal it may undertake profit-making activities.' This may involve a number of different kinds of organisation with, for example, differing legal status — charities, statutory bodies offering public transport or the provision of services such as leisure, schools, health or public utilities such as water or road maintenance.

Not for profit refers to organisations such as non private education establishments and charities that do not have profit maximising objectives. Charity marketing is akin to service marketing and the extended service marketing mix is appropriate. The guiding philosophy of the charity says what it is for and how it goes about its business. Clearly, just as the components of the normal marketing mix must be in harmony with one another, so too must they be in harmony with the charity's philosophy.

4.4.1 Product

A charity's **products** include **ideas** as well as goods and services. Ideas are very important in fund-raising, pressure-group activity and communicating with the public.

(a) When a supporter provides money to a charity, the idea of what the money will be used for is a kind of product, providing satisfaction to the supporter. Often supporters give their time and skills to assist as volunteers and thereby offering a service.

(b) Pressure groups work, in part, by promoting new ideas into the public consciousness, so that bodies with power can be persuaded to take a desired course of action.

(c) Ideas can also be promoted to the public with the aim of changing their behaviour. Governments often take this approach, as, for instance, with energy conservation and road safety campaigns.

4.4.2 Price

Price is very important to larger charities since sales of goods and services provide their largest single source of income. Proper cost accounting techniques must be applied where appropriate. Since supporters are crucial to a charity's income and beneficiaries are the reason why it exists, **processes** must be as customer-friendly as possible. This is certainly an area where philosophy is important.

4.4.3 Place

Place. It is common for charities to have significant problems with the distribution of physical goods when they rely on volunteer labour. This is especially true of charities that operate internationally, unless they are well established. In particular, the type of charity fund that is set up to relieve a disaster overseas is likely to have great difficulty moving the necessary supplies to where they are needed. On the other hand, charities that merely disburse funds within one country, to the poor, for instance, or to pay for medical research, may have very short and easily managed distribution chains.

4.4.4 Promotion

The major principles of marketing communications for non-profit organisations are the same as for consumer and business-to-business marketing. There are, however, considerable differences of emphasis. Promotion is often dominated by personal **selling**, with street corner and door-to-door collections or awareness campaigns. The sum of money available for organised communication may be less. Public scrutiny of policies may be higher. Almost certainly there will be a different set of communication objectives.

- Making target customers **aware** of a product, service or social behaviour
- **Educating** consumers about the offer or changes in the offer
- **Changing beliefs** about negative and positive consequences of taking a particular action
- **Changing the relative importance** of particular consequences
- Enlisting the **support** of a variety of individuals
- Recruiting, motivating or rewarding **employees or volunteers**
- Changing **perceptions** about the sponsoring organisation
- Influencing **government bodies**
- Preventing the **discontinuity** of support
- **Proving benefits** over 'competitors'
- **Combating** injurious rumours
- **Influencing** funding agencies

MARKETING AT WORK

application

Northern England Springer Spaniel Rescue (NESSR) is a registered charity which cares for and re-homes spaniels (and often other breeds of dogs) throughout the UK.

Established over thirty years ago, NESSR has become an active charity with the increasing number of dogs arriving each year due to their owners neglecting or abandoning them, divorcing, losing their jobs, emigrating and other such 21st century related problems.

NESSR generates funds via:

- Donations made when people adopt a dog
- Donations given by supporters
- The sale of items made by volunteers
- Raffles and Tombola'
- A NESSR Weather Lottery

100% of the money raised for NESSR goes towards the direct work of rescuing and re-homing dogs. All "staff" are volunteers.. NESSR pays for food, neutering and veterinary treatment of all the dogs in NESSR's care.

NESSR uses a range of promotional tools to help fundraise, raise awareness about dogs in need of rescuing and find homes for the dogs in their care. The promotional tools used include:

- **Events** such as an annual fun day, sponsored dog walks, in-store stands in collaboration with the retailer Pets at Home
- A highly interactive **website with an active forum** to co-ordinate volunteers, offer support to dog owners and 'advertise' dogs looking for a home
- **Public relations** efforts by Cynthia Turvey (who set up NESSR) to raise awareness of NESSR amongst interested parties such as pet food companies, press and networking with other not for profit organisations.

For more information about NESSR visit www.nessr.net

4.5 Online businesses

Online business has provided an opportunity for businesses to reach customers in a more streamlined way and has enabled smaller organisations and small business start ups to compete effectively with larger players in many markets. The scope and potential of the Internet are still developing. Its uses within business already embrace the following:

(a) Dissemination of information

(b) Product/service development – through almost instantaneous test marketing

(c) Transaction processing

(d) Relationship enhancement – between various groups of stakeholders, but principally between consumers and product/service suppliers

(e) Recruitment and job search – involving organisations worldwide

(f) Entertainment – including music, humour, games and some less wholesome pursuits!

(g) Social networking – business and social networks, increasing the ability to review and rate organisations and utilise word of mouth promotion on a larger scale

Although the traditional marketing mix and laws of marketing apply to online business (Blythe, 2006), there are several features of the Internet which differentiate it from what has gone before.

4.5.1 Changing models

The Internet challenges traditional business models – because, for example, it enables product/service suppliers to interact directly with their customers, instead of using intermediaries (like retail shops, travel agents, insurance brokers, and conventional banks). Businesses are finding that they can cut out the middle man, with electronic banking, insurance, publishing and printing as primary examples.

4.5.2 Benefits for small companies

Although the Internet is global in its operation, its benefits are not confined to large (or global) organisations. Small companies can move instantly into a global market place, either on their own initiative or as part of what is known as a 'consumer portal'. For example, Ede and Ravenscroft is a small outfitting and tailoring business in Oxford: it could easily promote itself within a much larger 'portal' called OxfordHighStreet.com, embracing a comprehensive mixture of other Oxford retailers.

4.5.3 Economies of information

The Internet offers a new economics of information – because, with the Internet, information is free. Those with Internet access can view all the world's major newspapers and periodicals without charge.

4.5.4 Transaction costs

The Internet reduces transaction costs and thus stimulates economic activity. According to one US calculation, a banking transaction via the Internet costs 1 cent, 27 cents at an ATM (automated teller machine) and 52 cents over the telephone.

4.5.5 Speed

The net supplies an almost incredible level of speed – virtually instant access to organisations, plus the capacity to complete purchasing transactions within seconds. This velocity, of course, is only truly impressive if it is accompanied by equal speed so far as the delivery of tangible goods is concerned.

4.5.6 New networks of communication

Networks have sprung up between organisations and their customers (either individually or collectively), between customers themselves (through mutual support groups), and between organisations and their suppliers. Facebook, MySpace, You Tube are now key reasons why people use the internet.

4.5.7 New business partnerships

Small enterprises can gain access to customers on a scale which would have been viewed as impossible a few years ago. For example, a university can put its reading list on a website and students wishing to purchase any given book can click directly through to an online bookseller such as Amazon.com. The university gets a commission; the online bookseller gets increased business; the student gets a discount. Everyone benefits except the traditional bookshop.

4.5.8 Transparent prices

Potential customers can readily compare prices not only from suppliers within any given country, but also from suppliers across the world.

4.5.9 Personal attention

Even if personal attention is actually administered through impersonal, yet highly sophisticated IT systems and customer database manipulation.

4.5.10 Flexibility

The web can either be a separate or a complementary distribution channel.

4.5.11 Presentation

Presentation is continuously improving from single text and graphics to sophisticated multi-media sites.

4.5.12 Interactivity

The level and power of interactivity is also increasing.

4.5.13 Pricing

A new phenomenon is emerging called dynamic pricing. Companies can rapidly change their prices to reflect the current state of demand and supply. These new trends are creating **pressure** for companies. The main threat facing companies is that prices will be driven down by consumers' ability to shop around.

MARKETING AT WORK

application 

The success of the **Internet auctioneers** e-Bay has highlighted how the Internet can provide additional mechanisms for doing business. Auctions can serve various purposes. They can establish a price for items that do not have a clear market price, such as antiques. They can be used to sell products that it would be difficult to sell through more traditional channels such as last minute deals on flights. They are also a mechanism for distributing products to a number of customers.

Hill & O'Sullivan (2004) Introductory Marketing. Chapter 2 covers marketing in the real world and is a useful chapter to read. Jobber (2007) also has a highly relevant chapter on services marketing which includes not for profit- chapter 22

Blythe's (2006) chapter 19 (in part) covers buyer behaviour from the perspective of internet based sales The theme of E–marketing also runs through the entire text as a chapter feature. ■

Learning objective review

Learning objectives	Covered
1 Describe ways in which customers and consumers make buying decisions	☑ Decision making process ☑ Decision making units ☑ Differences exist between consumer and organisational customers
2 Explain how the marketing mix is used in different markets	☑ Consumer goods- FMCGs and convenience goods ☑ Services marketing ☑ Business to business ☑ Not for profit ☑ Online business

Quick quiz

1 What does the decision making process refer to?

A The people involved with making a decision

B The stages that are gone through when making a purchase decision

C The outcome of a purchase decision

2 What is a gatekeeper?

A Someone who suggests a purchase

B A person able to restrict the flow of information

C The person who pays for a product or service

3 Which is not stage in the decision making process?

A Need identification

B Evaluation of alternatives

C Idea generation

4 Which is not a reference group?

A Aspirational group

B Dissociative group

C Social class

5 Which list shows the components of culture?

A subculture and social class

B subculture and reference groups

C reference groups and media

6 Services are said to be perishable which means what ?

A They cannot be stored for later use

B They cannot be touched

C Customers play a role in service delivery

7 Consumer goods do not include

A FMCG's

B Convenience goods

C Industrial purchases

8 Which statement is true?

A Traditional marketing rules are not relevant to internet based businesses

B Online businesses are less flexible

C Traditional marketing rules still apply to online businesses

Quiz answers

1	B	The stages and considerations people go through when making purchases.
2	B	Gatekeepers can withhold information from the deciders, the marketer must get through the gatekeeper
3	C	Idea generation is part of the NPD process – covered in another chapter
4	C	Social class is not directly a reference group, the other 2 option are
5	A	The first option
6	A	B is because they are intangible, C refers specifically to the customers role
7	C	Industrial goods are relevant to business to business sales
8	C	Traditional marketing theory is still relevant online

Activity debriefs

Worksheet activity 1

This will depend on your own personal circumstances.

Worksheet activity 2

Much of your response will depend on the category of product you purchased.

For part b of the activity, two example scenarios are provided below

	Buying a snack at a train station	Buying a car
Need recognition	Feeling peckish and train due in five minutes	Car has failed an MOT test
Information search	Look for a vending machine or shop	Visit local garages View car section of local newspapers Buy and read Auto trader, Browse on Ebay
Evaluation of alternatives	Consider – sweet or savoury, decide on sweet, view alternative sweets in shop – close to the till for speed	Circle all relevant cars– make a short to view and then go and look at the cars for sale. Test drive the cars. Decide between new, used or repair of existing car
Purchase decision	Make decision based on known brands – chose Cadbury flake	Confirm criteria for selection, choose between shorted short list
Post purchase evaluation	Regret as difficult to eat on the train due to the crumbly nature of the product – decide not to buy again for a train journey	Thoughts about the car following the purchase, reliability, satisfaction with the drive, comments from friends.

Worksheet activity 3

Again, your answer will depend on the type of service you have chosen.

References

Blythe, J. (2006) Principles and Practice of Marketing, Thompson, London.

Dibb, S. et al (1996) Marketing Concepts and Strategies, Houghton Miffin, London.

Hill, L. And O'Sullivan, T. (2004) Foundation Marketing 3rd Edition, Prentice Hall, London.

Jobber, D. (2007) Principles and Practice of Marketing. 5th Edition, McGraw Hill education, Maidenhead, Berks.

Kotler, P. (1994) Marketing Management: Analysis, Planning, Implementation and Control, Eighth Edition, Prentice Hall, New Jersey.

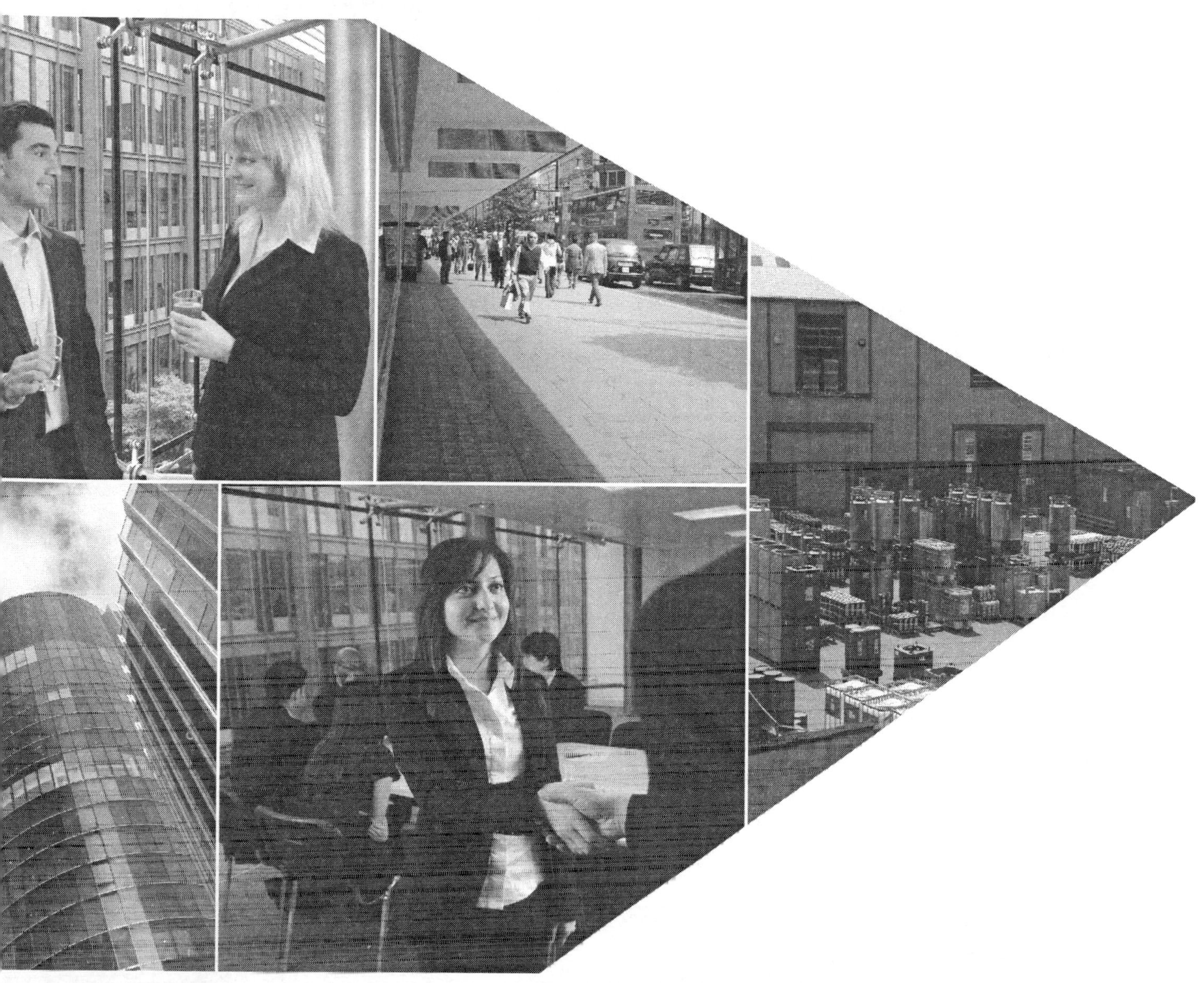

Chapter 5
Understanding Customers

Topic list

1 Customers and users
2 The use of information to understand customers
3 Customer databases

Introduction

This is the first chapter which covers Unit 2 (Understanding Customer Relationships) of the qualification. As a result we now focus specifically on customers and how organisations should be aware of their needs and how to build better relationships.

The features within the text will also change to reflect your needs in preparing for the assignment based unit. In chapters 1-4 we featured worksheet activities and related debriefs to help with your learning. We also used quick quizzes at the end of the chapters so that you could test yourself as you would in the exam. Within the next few chapters however we replace these activities with Work based Project Tips as below. We will use these as activities for you to complete in order to build a portfolio and gather evidence about your own organisation as you work progress through the workbook. The purpose of this is so that you will have a range of material to assist you in your assessment once it is released to you.

WORK BASED PROJECT TIP

application

You will have a range of different activities to conduct. Any tables etc will also be reproduced within our online materials to make it easy for you to adapt them according to your needs.

As these are based on your own organisation, it is pointless us providing debriefs because we obviously have no idea about your own organisation.

The content of this chapter looks specifically at the nature of customers and how they differ from users. We then move on to consider how information may help organisations better understand customers before moving on to discuss the use of customer databases.

Syllabus linked learning objectives

By the end of the chapter you will be able to:

Learning objectives	Syllabus link
1 Discuss need for organisations to understand the distinction between customers and users and their differing needs and wants	1.1
2 Consider the importance of information used to understand customer needs and behaviour	1.2, 1.4
3 Explain how information is collected to develop a database	1.3

1 Customers and users

In chapter 4 we looked at buyer behaviour and the different groups of customers that exist. We shall briefly elaborate and put this into the context of Unit 2 but please refer back to previous chapters too where necessary.

KEY CONCEPT

concept

A **customer** is the purchaser of goods and services: a **user or consumer** is the recipient or end-user of the goods and services

---

Not all organisations would find this distinction between the 'customer' (the person who pays) and the 'user' (the person who consumes) relevant. However, not-for-profit organisations, such as local authorities, charities, libraries and schools, for example, often have a diversity of people and groups interested in the products and services they supply. These may be

variously described as 'clients', 'users' or 'customers', even though the products/services are paid for by other parties: taxpayers, government, donors and so on, who may or may not be recipients of the products or services themselves.

It is important that you should be able to distinguish, where appropriate, between the customer and the user from a marketing point of view. Users may or may not be the same people who have bought the product, and may or may not have had a direct say in the purchase decision – but they are the ones who experience the product or service, and their needs and wants may influence the purchase decision made by the customer.

Customer satisfaction with the experience of purchase – including product availability, cost, the convenience of the transaction and the quality of in-store service – will be an important factor in maintaining loyalty, repeat business and word-of-mouth promotion of the product/service and/or of the intermediary through which it is sold. However, user satisfaction is also important, as it is likely to motivate customers who have bought a product/service on their behalf to make repeat or related purchases – or not.

WORK BASED PROJECT TIP

application

1 List your organisations customers and users.

Customers	Users

MARKETING AT WORK

application

The sweet manufacturer Haribo has a clear distinction between their customers and users (consumers). Parents and adults tend to purchase the sweets while both adults and children eat (or consume) them. Haribo will need to meet the needs of both groups in order to be successful. Adults may look for natural ingredients to prevent childhood hyperactivity and children will want sweets that taste best and are seen as 'cool' amongst their peers.

WORK BASED PROJECT TIP

application

Are the requirements of your organisations customers and users similar or different?

Level of similarity	Due to...

In chapter 1 we looked at a definition of marketing.

KEY CONCEPT

concept

The CIM's definition of marketing is;

"Marketing is the management process responsible for identifying, anticipating and satisfying customer requirements profitably"

In order to identify, anticipate and then work towards satisfying customer requirements, information must first be gathered.

2 The use of information to understand customers

Information is a **marketing asset**. It impacts on performance in several ways.

- It helps to increase **responsiveness** to customer demands.
- It helps to identify **new customer opportunities** and new product/service demands.
- It helps to anticipate competitive attacks and threats.

Overall, marketers need information to help them to make decisions. These decisions should ultimately be to better meet the needs of customers by understanding.

- differing customer needs and wants
- why customers purchase eg what makes them choose certain products over others
- the factors that influence customer decision making

This information can then be used to develop appropriate and effective marketing mix activities to meet those needs.

MARKETING AT WORK

application

Heinz learnt that many consumers heated baked beans in a microwave and that often the portion was prepared for just one person. The manufacturer launched a new product in the form of multipack beans in a yoghurt style individual container that could be put in the microwave and heated.

2.1 The organisation's marketing information requirements

Here is a list of questions that marketers might need answered.

(a) **Markets**. Who are our customers? What are they like? How are buying decisions made?

(b) **Share of the market**. What are total sales of our product? How do our sales compare with competitors' sales?

(c) **Products**. What do customers think of our product? What do they do with it? Are our products in a 'growth' or 'decline' stage of their life cycle? Should we extend our range?

(d) **Price**. How do our prices compare with others: higher, average, lower? Is the market sensitive to price?

(e) **Distribution**. Should we distribute directly, indirectly or both? What discounts are required?

(f) **Sales force**. Do we have enough/too many salespeople? Are their territories equal to their potential? Are they contacting the right people? Should we pay commission?

(g) **Advertising**. Do we use the right media? Do we communicate the right message? Is it effective?

(h) **Customer attitudes**. What do they think of our product/firm/service/delivery?

(i) **Competitors' activities**. Who are our competitors? Are they more or less successful businesses? Why are they more or less successful?

(j) **Environmental factors**. What factors impact on marketing planning (SLEPT factors)?

2.2 Types of information

The following diagram shows just some of the information which is available to marketers to assist in decision making. Generally it is grouped into formal primary marketing research projects, external secondary sources and internal secondary sources.

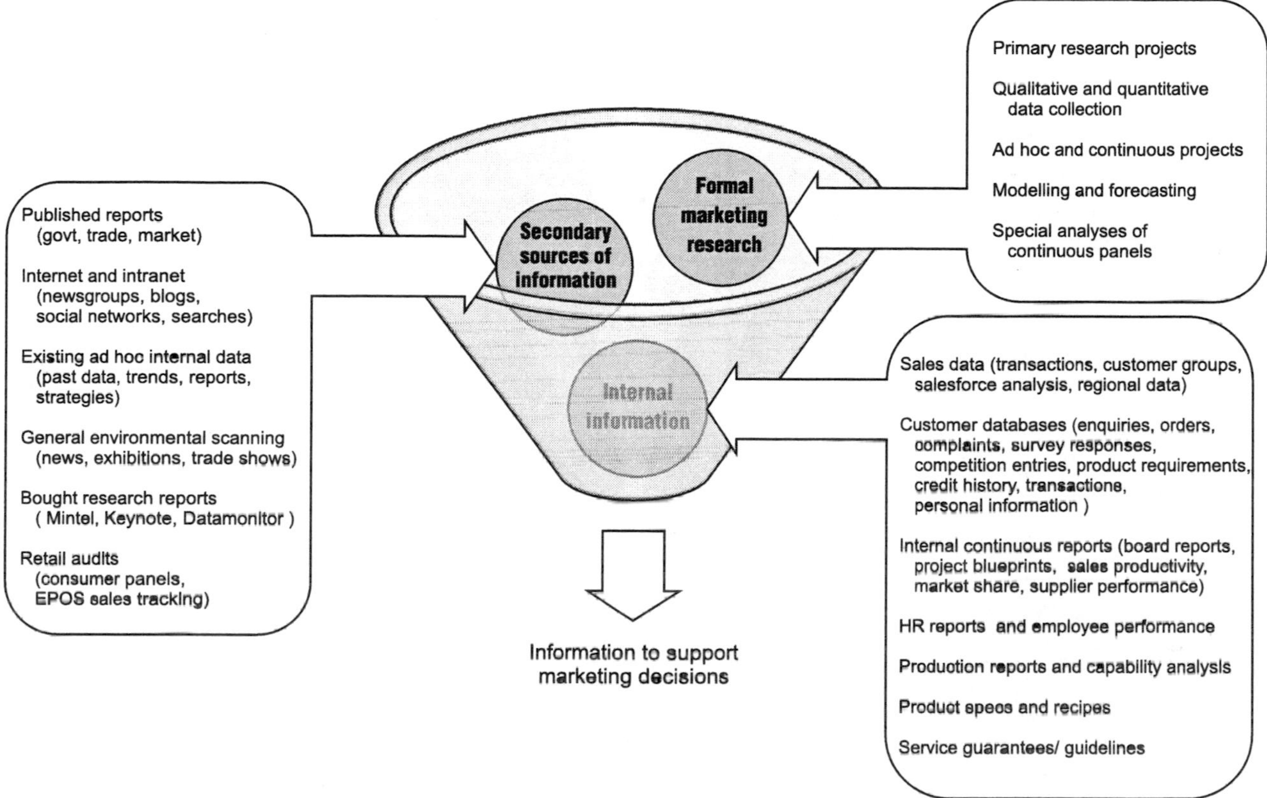

WORK BASED PROJECT TIP

application

Try to find out what sources of internal information sources exist within your own organisation.

2.3 Secondary information

KEY CONCEPT

concept

Secondary data is data that already exists in some form. Collection of secondary data is known as 'desk research'. Originally this was to distinguish it from research that involves getting out and about in the world, talking to people and watching them. In fact a great deal of research can now be **done from your desk** in a literal sense, using your desktop computer and the Internet.

Secondary data is data (including internal data) not created specifically for the purpose at hand but used and analysed to provide marketing information where primary data is not (yet) available or not sufficient.

Desk research is the term used to describe a proactive search for existing data, usually as an initial, exploratory research task.

It may seem odd that we deal with 'secondary' data **before we look at primary data**, but it would very silly to embark on substantial amounts of **primary** research without seeing what secondary data already exists. **Checking what is known already** is also likely to give insights into how and what to investigate further.

2.4 The use of secondary data

Secondary information is now **available** in every form and on a **huge scale**. The problem is how to decide what information is required. The use of secondary data will generally come **early** in the process of **marketing research**. In some cases, secondary data may be sufficient in itself, but not always.

Secondary data:

- Can provide a backdrop to primary research
- Can act as a substitute for field research
- Can be used as a technique in itself

2.4.1 Backdrop to primary research

In **unfamiliar territory**, it is natural that the marketer will carry out some **basic research** in the area, using journals, existing market reports, the press and any contacts with relevant knowledge. Such investigations will aid the marketer by providing guidance on a number of areas.

- Possible data sources
- Methods of data collection (relevant populations, sampling methods)
- The general state of the market (demand, competition and the like)

2.4.2 Substitute for primary research

The often substantial **cost** of primary research **might be avoided** if existing secondary data is sufficient. This data might not be perfect for the needs of the business, though and to judge whether it *is* enough, or whether primary research ought to be undertaken, a cost-benefit analysis should be implemented weighing up the advantages of each method.

There are some situations in which secondary data is bound to be **insufficient**. For instance if your brand new version of an existing product is hugely superior to your competitors' versions because of your unique use of new technology, you have changed the entire market. Primary research will be a necessity to find out the impact of your product.

2.4.3 A technique in itself

Some types of information **can only be acquired** by examining secondary data, in particular **trends over time**. Historical data cannot realistically be replaced by a one-off study and an organisation's internal data would only give a limited picture (Dillon, 1994).

There are many varied secondary sources and it can be quite complex to classify them in specific ways. The diagram that follows shows a basic overview.

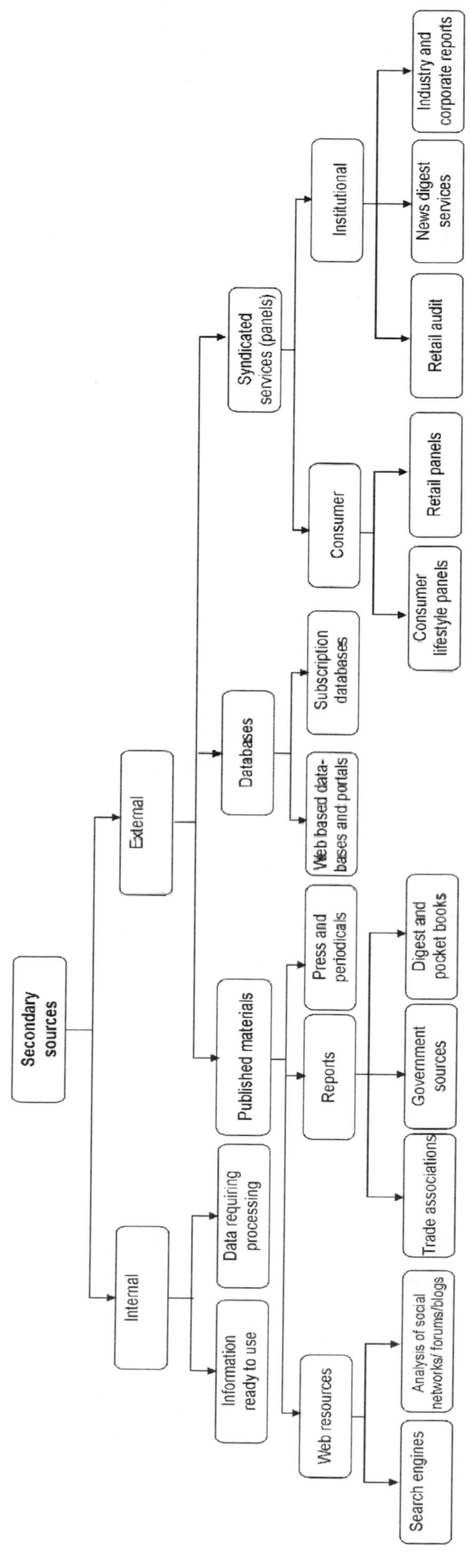

Secondary sources
Internal
External
Information ready to use
Data requiring processing
Published materials
Databases
Syndicated services (panels)
Web resources
Reports
Press and periodicals
Web based data-bases and portals
Subscription databases
Consumer
Institutional
Search engines
Analysis of social networks/ forums/blogs
Trade associations
Government sources
Digest and pocket books
Consumer lifestyle panels
Retail panels
Retail audit
News digest services
Industry and corporate reports

2.5 Primary data

KEY CONCEPT

concept

Primary data is information **collected specifically** to address a question posed by the marketer.

Primary data may be qualitative (figures and statistics) or quantitative (attitudes and feelings) in nature.

A range of methods to collect primary data exist. The following table shows just a few as an example.

Qualitative data collection methods	Quantitative data collection methods
In-depth interview	Survey
Focus groups	Observation eg scanned bar code data
Analysis of online discussion forums	Online voting buttons

2.6 Some of the limitations of data collected

All data collected should be evaluated using the following criteria.

(a) Is the data relevant to the purpose for which it was collected?

(b) Is it up-to-date?

(c) Is it reliable and accurate?

(d) Is the source of the data credible and objective, or unbiased? Look for the following.

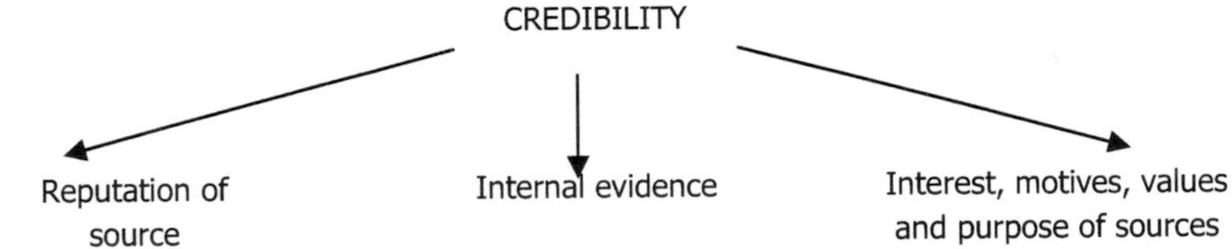

(e) Is the data subject to confirmation, or comparison with data from other sources? Are you prepared to risk basing decisions on uncorroborated data? The term triangulation refers to the ability to produce similar findings from multiple sources. If once source verifies another, the findings are viewed as more credible.

(f) Is the data based on a large and representative statistical sample of the relevant population (the group or issue under investigation)?

(g) Has the data been gathered in a way that makes it meaningful and reliable? Has the same question been put to all respondents? Were all terms consistently defined? Did researchers lead or suggest 'right' answers? Were the respondents influenced by the researcher, or each other, or the desire to be nice?

(h) Has the data collection and analysis been worthwhile? Has it fulfilled its purposes at a reasonable cost in money, time and effort?

3 Customer databases

A marketing database can provide an organisation with much information about its customers and target groups. **Every purchase a customer makes has two functions**.

- Provision of **sales revenue**
- Provision of **information** as to future market opportunities

3.1 Typical data held

A typical customer database might include the following.

Element	Examples
Customer or company details	Account numbers, names, addresses and contact (telephone, fax, e-mail) details; basic 'mailing list' data, relationship to other customers. For business customers these fields might include sales contact, technical contact, parent company or subsidiaries, number of employees
Professional details	Company; job title; responsibilities – especially for business-to-business marketing; industry type
Personal details	Sex, age, number of people at the same address, spouse's name, children, interests, and any other relevant data known, such as newspapers read, journals subscribed to
Transaction history	What products/services are ordered, date, how often, how much is spent (turnover), payment methods
Call/contact history	Sales or after sales service calls made, complaints/queries received, meetings at shows/exhibitions, mailings sent, etc
Credit/payment history	Credit rating, amounts outstanding, aged debts
Credit transaction details	Items currently on order, dates, prices, delivery arrangements
Special account details	Membership number, loyalty or incentive points earned, discount awarded,(where customer loyalty or incentive schemes are used)

3.1.1 Sources of information and applications of the database

The **sources** of information in a customer database and the **uses** to which it can be put are outlined in the diagram below.

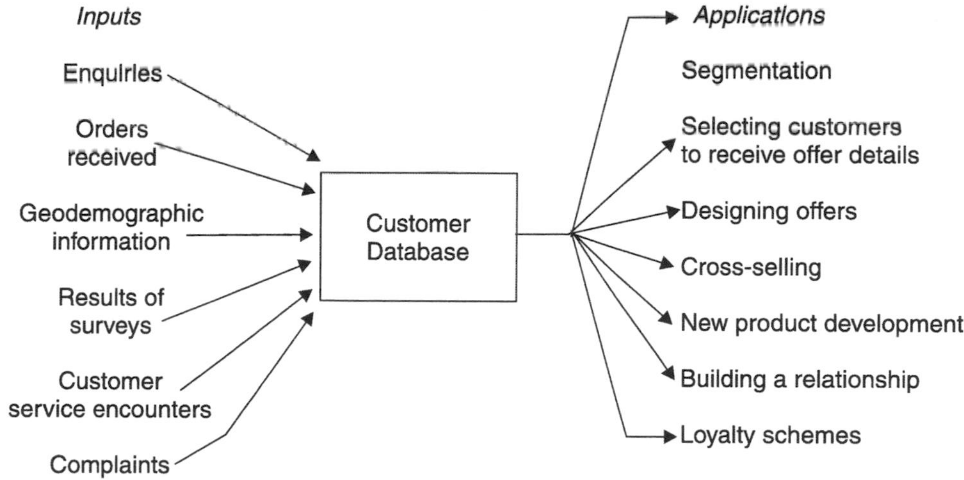

MARKETING AT WORK

application

Let us take the example of a theatre which is in a tourist city and which wants to build a **database**. The types of data it may wish to include are as follows.

(a) Analysis of theatregoers by specific **characteristics**: age, sex, home address
(b) How many **performances** each theatre customer sees in the year

(c) How many days visitors stay in the city and how they choose a day or night at the theatre
(d) **Types of production** customers like to watch
(e) **Factors** important to their decision to visit the theatre, such as price, location, play, cast, facilities
(f) Where they obtained **information** on the theatre and its productions: press, hotel, leaflets, mailings and so on
(g) **Other purchases** customers make when visiting the theatre
(h) **Other entertainment** that theatregoers choose to spend their money on

This data could then be used by the theatre management to build relationships with customers and to exploit sales and promotional opportunities.

3.2 Setting up a database

A database need not be computerised. A paper address book that you keep in your briefcase is a form of database and so is a card index. However most modern business databases will be created and maintained **centrally on a computer**. This is obviously the most efficient method where **large amounts of data** are involved and for several important additional reasons.

(a) **Common data** for all users to share

(b) Avoidance of **data duplication** in files kept by different users

(c) **Consistency** in the organisation's use of data, and in the accuracy and up-to-dateness of data accessed by different users, because all records are centrally maintained and updated

(d) **Flexibility** in the way in which shared data can be queried, analysed and formatted by individual users for specific purposes, without altering the store of data itself

(e) **Speed** of data retrieval

WORK BASED PROJECT TIP

application

Find out what type(s) of database your organisation (or college) uses, and for what applications. If possible, get access to the database and browse through the index, directory or switchboard to see what databases/catalogues contain what database files or tables, queries, reports and forms, with what fields.

3.2.1 Database formats

There are two basic kinds of **computerised** database.

(a) A **flat file system** lumps all the data into single file. A single worksheet in a spreadsheet is an example.

(b) A **relational database system** allows greater flexibility and storage efficiency by splitting the data up into a number of tables, which are linked and can be integrated as necessary. For example, one table may contain customer names and another customers' payment histories. A linking field such as a customer ID number would allow the user to interrogate both tables and generate an integrated report on a particular customer's purchases and payments, or a list of customers who had made multiple purchases, or a list of those with a poor payment record.

Flat systems are easy to build and maintain, and are quite adequate for applications such as mailing lists, or membership databases. **Relational systems** integrate a wider range of business functions, for invoicing, accounting, inventory and marketing analysis: they are, however, complicated to develop and use properly. If your organisation already operates a relational system, learn how to use it. If you are required to set up or build a relational system, get help: use a 'wizard' or template (in the database package) or ask an expert, at least the first time.

All databases have some kind of structure, otherwise you would never be able to retrieve information from them. For instance a telephone directory stores entries in alphabetical order. Computer database packages store data as follows.

(a) **Fields** are the labels given to types of data. A simple customer database, for example, might include fields such as: Title, First name, Last name, Address fields, and other contact details. The fields are the **columns** in a tabular database.

(b) **Records** are the collection of fields relevant to one entry. So all the above data fields for a particular customer make up one customer record. The records are the **rows** in a tabular database.

ID	Title	First name	Last name	Address 1	Address 2	Address 3	City	County	Postcode	Country	Telephone	Fax	Email
1	Mr	Kieran	Davies	25 Dill Street	Merton		London		SW17 4QF	UK	020 7884 1122		kieran.davis@virgin.net
2	Mrs	Shagura	Jumal	37 Nelson Road	Trafford		Manchester		M41 2BD	UK	01584 452291		sjumal@freeserve.com

(c) **Tables** are collections of records that describe similar data. All the customer records for a particular region or product may be stored in one table.

(d) **Databases** are collections of all the tables relating to a particular set of information. So your customer database may include tables for various regions, products and customer contacts.

3.2.2 Data cleansing

KEY CONCEPT

concept

A key issue in setting up a database is **data cleansing**: ensuring that the information is correct, up-to-date and not duplicated. Much can be done at the data entry stage, but where data is imported from other systems a good deal of preparatory work may be needed to ensure that it is in the correct format.

Data cleansing is the process of amending or removing data in a database that is incorrect, out of date, incomplete, improperly formatted, or duplicated.

3.2.3 Control access to the database to stored information across the organisation

Enabling open access to all within the organisation may not be required or indeed sensible in many instances. The organisation must take steps to protect their customers data from external hackers and only share internally where there is a legitimate need in order to maintain customer privacy.

WORK BASED PROJECT TIP

application

Within your organisation, find out:

- Who has access to different databases
- How the data is sourced
- How the data is cleansed.

How effective do you think your database is?

Blyhe (2006) a chapter on marketing research (chapter 19) and a section within chapter 19 on databases

Jobber (2007) covers research and information in chapter with useful case study on iPod

Both these texts go into much more detail than you require so don't worry too much about the finer details for your own work. The chapters however will provide more examples for you to consider.

Learning objective review

Learning objectives	Covered
1 Discuss need for organisations to understand the distinction between customers and users and their differing needs and wants	☑ Definitions of customers v's users ☑ Differing needs of customers and users ☑ Reminder of the benefits of a marketing approach
2 Consider the importance of information used to understand customer needs and behaviour	☑ Uses and benefits of information ☑ Sources of primary and secondary information ☑ Limitations of information
3 Explain how information is collected to develop a database	☑ Sources of information within a database ☑ Organising and managing the database

References

Blythe, J. (2006) Principles and Practice of Marketing, Thompson, London, .

Hill, L. And O'Sullivan, T. (2004) Foundation Marketing 3rd Edition, Prentice Hall, London.

Jobber, D. (2007) Principles and Practice of Marketing 5th edition, McGraw Hill, London.

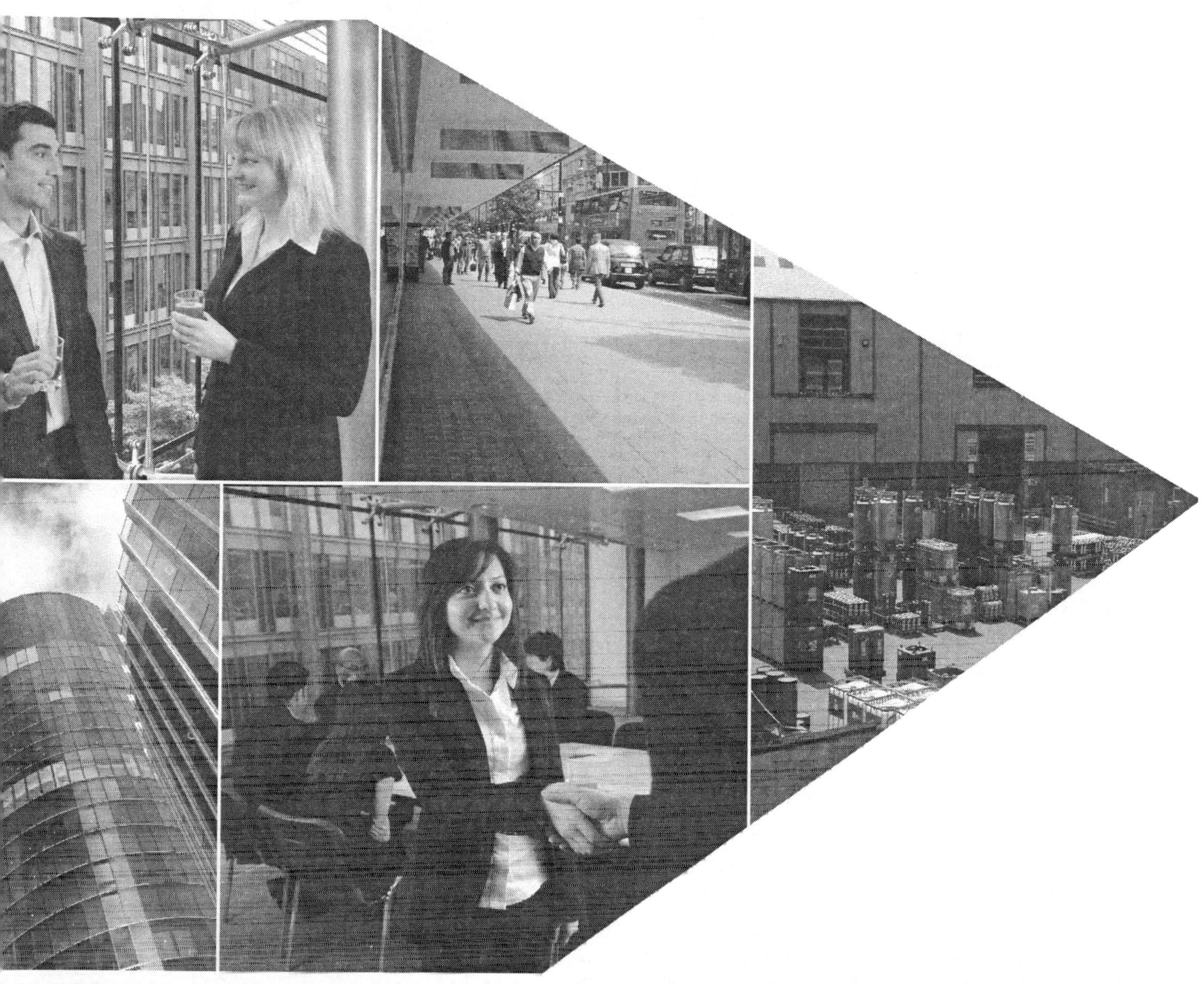

Chapter 6
Effective relationships

Topic list

Introduction

Building effective long terms relationships with *stakeholders* is considered essential for success within the world today. Organisations do not exist in their own right but are a collection of *people*. To get along in business, these people form interpersonal relationships. Who we want to work with or purchase goods and services form is often based on how well we get along. The strength of the relationships formed is therefore often a key criteria in our decision making and can change our behaviour.

Stakeholders are, broadly, individuals or groups who have a legitimate 'stake' or 'interest' in an organisation and its activities: they may depend on the organisation to fulfil their own goals and needs, or they may contribute in some way to the fulfilment of the purposes and goals of the organisation.

Within this chapter we begin by considering the nature and scope of stakeholders. We then address a modern marketing theory- relationship marketing. Section three looks specifically at the organisations supply chain and the relationships that are formed with suppliers and distributors in order to better meet the needs of the organisations customers. We conclude with a thorough assessment of the relationships that are formed within the organisation and specifically between departments. These relationships are important because they help the organisation to unite and work together to provide high levels of quality in their outputs for customers.

Syllabus linked learning objectives

By the end of the chapter you will be able to:

Learning objectives	Syllabus link
1 Explain the characteristics of different organisational stakeholders	2.1
2 Explain relationship marketing	2.2
3 Discuss how relationships are developed and sustained with suppliers and distributors	2.4
4 Explore inter-organisational relationships	2.5, 2.6, 2.7, 2.8, 2.9

1 Stakeholder relationships

For any given organisation, there will be a number of individuals and groups who have some kind of a relationship with it, or have invested in it in some way, or are affected by its activities – and who therefore have a legitimate interest or 'stake' in it. These parties are called **stakeholders**.

KEY CONCEPT

concept

'Stakeholders are those individuals or groups who depend on the organisation to fulfil their own goals and on whom, in turn, the organisation depends.' (Johnson & Scholes, 2005, p 179)

'Stakeholders are individuals and/or groups who are affected by or affect the performance of the organisation in which they have an interest. Typically they would include employees, managers, creditors, suppliers, shareholders (if appropriate) and society at large.' (Worthington & Britton, 2006, p 220)

'A stakeholder of a company is an individual or group that either is harmed by, or benefits from, the company *or* whose rights can be violated, or have to be respected, by the company. Other groups, besides shareholders, who typically would be considered stakeholders are communities associated with the company, employees, customers of the company's products, and suppliers.' (Jobber, 2007, p 201)

1.1 Categories of stakeholders

There are three broad categories of stakeholder in an organisation.

- **Internal** stakeholders, who are members of the organisation. Key examples include the directors, managers and employees of a company – or the members of a club or association, or the volunteer workers in a charity. They may also include other functions of the organisation (eg marketing, production or finance) which have a stake in marketing activity, and/or separate units of the organisation (eg regional or product divisions) which have a stake in its plans.
- **Connected** stakeholders (or primary stakeholders), who have an economic or contractual relationship with the organisation. Key examples include the shareholders in a business; the customers of a business or beneficiaries of a charity; distributors and intermediaries; suppliers of goods and services; and financiers/funders of the organisation.
- **External** stakeholders (or secondary stakeholders), who are not directly connected to the organisation, but who have an interest in its activities, or are impacted by them in some way. Examples include the government, pressure and interest groups (including professional bodies and trade unions), the news media, the local community and wider society.

The following diagram shows a quick visual snapshot of the total stakeholder environment:

Stakeholders in the marketing organisation

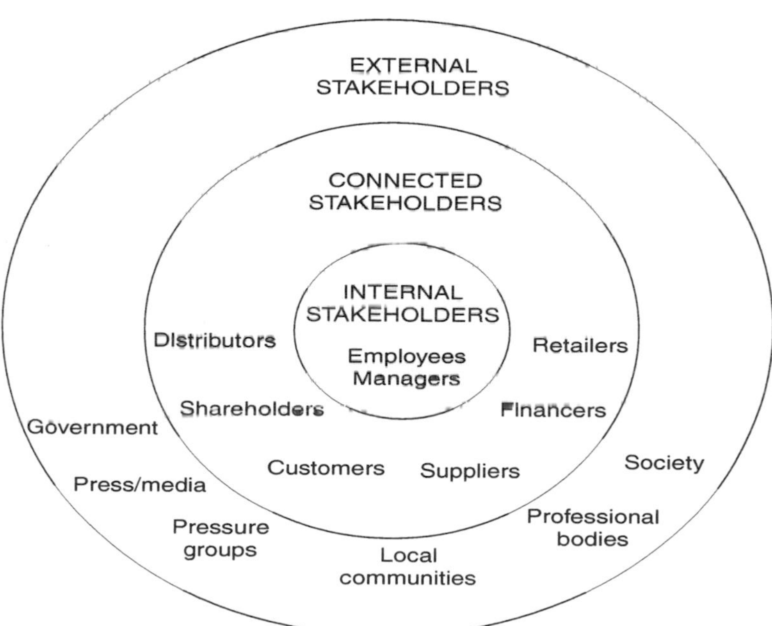

While it is useful to categorise stakeholders in this way, it would be a mistake to think of them as entirely separate groups. Customers are also members of the wider community, and may be shareholders in the company and/or members of a consumer or environmental protection group, for example. Employees of the organisation may also be customers, shareholders and perhaps members of a trade union which can bring influence to bear on their behalf with the management of the organisation. So there are always areas in which membership and interests intertwine.

The key point of stakeholder theory is that an organisation affects its environment and is affected by its environment. The boundaries of the organisation are highly permeable: influence flows from internal stakeholders outwards (eg through marketing) and from external stakeholders inwards (eg if a major customer pressures sales staff to represent its interests within the organisation, or more generally if a marketing-oriented organisation seeks to listen to its customers and meet their needs).

MARKETING AT WORK

application

Cadbury Schweppes is an international confectionery and beverages company, selling chocolate, sweets, gum and beverages around the world. It uses different ways to communicate with different stakeholder groups.

Shareowners – Cadbury Schweppes has over 60,000 registered shareowners. These include private individuals as well as large institutional investors, such as pension funds and banks. All shareowners are also entitled to attend the Annual General Meeting, at which they have the opportunity to ask questions, discuss the company's performance and vote on certain issues.

Consumers – Consumers can contact the company by various means and Cadbury Schweppes deals with consumer enquiries on a daily basis. It performs market research to track changing consumer trends. Many parts of the business also use survey and market research panels to find out what consumers think of products.

Customers – The company has ongoing discussions with its customers. Wholesalers and retailers (intermediaries) provide the vital link to consumers and it is they who make Cadbury Schweppes' brands widely available.

Employees – Managers hold regular individual and team meetings to inform colleagues about the business and hear their views. The company also conducts surveys to check how its employees feel about working at Cadbury Schweppes. Internal newsletters, a group website and many local websites help employees keep up to date with what is going on.

Society – The company enters into regular dialogue with organisations such as national governments and international bodies such as the World Health Organisation (WHO), to discuss issues that affect the company. These issues can be anything from agricultural policy to education and skills.

1.2 Stakeholders in marketing

Each function, unit or even sub-project of an organisation may be said to have stakeholders, whose needs and influence may need to be taken into account. For any given marketing activity or decision, it should be possible to identify relevant stakeholder groups.

- The **owners or sponsor** of the project or activity, who puts authority behind it, initiates it and sets its objectives (for example, the marketing manager or director).
- **Customers**, **users or beneficiaries** of the activity or its outputs: for example, internal departments who receive marketing advice or input, and external customers at whom products/services are targeted.
- The various **target audiences** of marketing messages: the customer base, consumer or industrial markets, the press, the recruitment and financial markets and so on.
- **Other functions** of the organisation, who may share marketing's overall aims (profitable and competitive business) – but may have differing goals, priorities, technology, culture and timescales.
- **Suppliers** of goods and services used by marketing (eg advertising agencies and media, research consultants, intermediaries) – and suppliers of goods and services to the organisation in general, since they also contribute to the products and services it offers to its customers.
- External **collaborators**, **partners or allies** eg in joint promotions, sponsorship or knowledge-sharing networks.
- **Secondary stakeholders** impacted by marketing: for example, communities affected by the environmental and economic impacts of marketing plans (eg waste packaging or price changes) or interest groups concerned with the environment, trading practices, consumer rights, advertising standards and so on.

WORK BASED PROJECT TIP

For your own employing organisation, or an organisation which you know well:

- Identify its major stakeholders
- Categorise them as internal, connected or external stakeholders
- Identify the major internal stakeholders of the marketing function(even if you do not have a dedicated marketing team, there will be somebody who is responsible for marketing activities).

Where possible, and where they are sufficiently significant, identify particular, named stakeholders (eg individual managers, major customers/suppliers, organisational functions or departments).

1.3 Stakeholders and the marketing oriented firm

A marketing oriented firm is one which operates according to the belief that 'achieving organisational goals depends on determining the needs and wants of target markets and delivering the desired satisfactions more effectively and efficiently than competitors' (Kotler, 2002).

Note that Kotler's definition does not just focus on the needs and wants of 'customers', but of '**target markets**'. It is possible to see a range of stakeholder groups as targets for marketing activities and as audiences for marketing messages, as we will see in later chapters.

The important point is that the marketing oriented firm recognises that its reason for existence and activity lies outside itself, in the market. It cannot simply do or produce whatever it likes and then push the results on people, or do or produce whatever it is good at and assume that people will respond positively. It has to analyse the complex needs and drivers of the **people who keep it in business**, and attempt to satisfy them, profitably and competitively – and those people include not just customers, but other stakeholder groups as well. It also needs the input of **internal and external contributors** in order to deliver customer satisfaction – and these contributors are also stakeholder groups.

WORK BASED PROJECT TIP

application

What influence do stakeholders have in your own organisation?

Building strong relationships with stakeholders is then a key priority for marketers.

2 Relationship marketing

2.1 What is a relationship?

If you shop regularly at the same supermarket, does this mean you have a 'relationship' with that supermarket? If you regularly buy a particular brand, does this form a 'relationship' with the brand or the organisation that created it? And what if you have given your details as part of a sales promotion, and the marketer starts e-mailing you regularly with special offers: is this a 'relationship'? How can a person have a meaningful relationship with an organisation?

2.2 The nature of organisational relationships

Relationships require at least two parties who are in contact with each other. If we focus on only two parties (for example, a supplier and its customer), the relationship will be a **'one to one' or 'dyad'** (two-party) relationship.

However, basic supplier-customer exchanges usually happen within the wider context of a supply process: a producer of raw materials supplies a processing plant or producer of components, which supplies a manufacturing organisation, which supplies a distributor or retail outlet, which supplies the consumer. This configuration is often called a **chain or channel**.

However, even this picture is simplified. The fact is that each organisation in the supply chain has multiple other relationships with customers, suppliers, industry partners and so on.

2.2.1 One to one (dyadic) relationships

The relationship between a supplier and a customer is the classic two-sided relationship (dyad) of marketing (Gummesson, 2002). Marketing and supply management often focus on this dyad: focusing on how the firm could secure and exploit the contribution of its immediate suppliers – and what it could offer to its immediate customers.

Classic dyadic (one-to-one) relationships

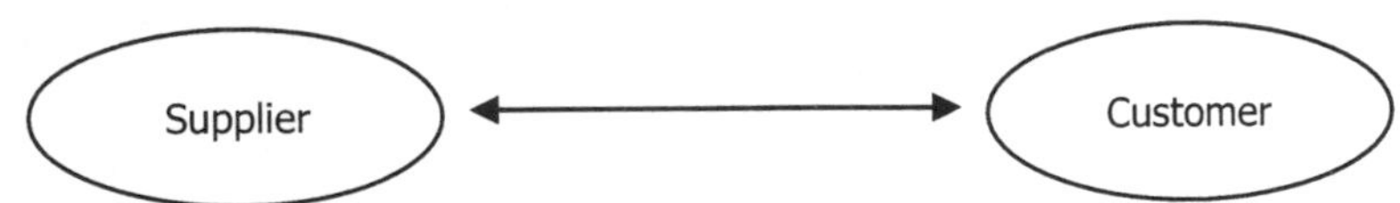

(based on Gummesson, 2002)

In many instances, relationships are much more complex and are more akin to a **network** of inter-related parties. Each of these relationships will take significant time and resource to build and so it is much cheaper (as a result of being less resource hungry) to try to effectively strengthen them as opposed to building new ones.

KEY CONCEPT

concept

The Pareto theory is also known as the 80/20 rule. This relates specifically to the nature of customer relationships in terms of how much profit is generated from customer sales. The rule states that 80% of an organisations profit is generated from 20% of their customers.

Identifying which customers fall within the 20% category and focussing on building strong relationships with them is sensible to remain profitable. Understanding why they are the 'best' customers may also help you to develop a marketing mix to meet their needs.

Customers are often described in relationship marketing terminology as markets.

2.2.2 The six markets model

The six markets model offers a helpful overview of the key categories of relationships for any given firm (sometimes called the 'core' or 'focal' firm, because we are looking at relationships from its point of view). It presents six role-related market domains or 'markets', each involving relationships with a number of parties – organisations or individuals – who can potentially contribute, directly or indirectly, to an organisation's marketplace effectiveness (Peck *et al*, 1999, p 5).

The model has developed since its formulation in 1991, to take account of changing views and priorities in marketing, but the most commonly used version of the framework is as follows (Peck, et al 1999).

Domain	Comments
Customer markets	The concept of relationship marketing is based on the belief that firms must invest in building relationships with customers, in order to enhance profitability through customer retention and loyalty. The importance of customer relationships has long been recognised in professional and financial services, business-to-business marketing, and the market for regularly replaced consumer durables (such as cars). More recently it was applied in FMCG (fast moving consumer goods) markets. • For consumer goods or services, the customer market domain represents **end customers**, users and consumers. • For business-to-business marketing, it also embraces channel **intermediaries**, including agents, retailers and distributors who are effectively 'customers' of the organisation, but operate between them and the end users.
Referral markets	Referrals, recommendations and endorsements by existing customers are an important source of new business: either directing potential new customers to the supplier (eg business-to-business sales 'leads' and professional referrals) or guiding consumer choice (eg through word-of-mouth recommendations or endorsements by trusted third parties). Potential sources of referrals must be cultivated and motivated. 'Given that satisfied customers will happily endorse the products or services of the supplier if prompted, relationships with existing customers are an unrecognised or underutilised facility for many organisations'. (Peck *et al*, 1999) Companies can create formal or informal cross-referral agreements between themselves and suppliers of complementary products (eg a weight loss consultancy and a local gym). Such referrals may also add value for customers, as part of a total service.
Internal markets	The internal market comprises all employees, and other functions, divisions and strategic business units (SBUs) of the firm. The concept of 'internal marketing', argues that employees and units throughout an organisation can contribute to the effectiveness of marketing to customers: most notably, through value-adding customer service and communications. It has been shown that employee satisfaction and retention (the aims of internal marketing) correlate directly with customer satisfaction and retention (the aims of customer relationship marketing) in service businesses (Schlesinger & Heskett, 1991).

Domain	Comments
Recruitment markets	The recruitment market comprises: • The **external labour pool**, and more specifically, those with the attributes and competencies needed by the firm: that is, quality potential employees. • **Third parties**, such as colleges, universities, recruitment agencies and other employers, who can give the firm access to those quality potential employees. Relationships with these markets must be cultivated in order for the firm to be able to compete with other employers to attract the best people, particularly in times, regions and disciplines in which there are acute skill shortages.
Influence markets	• Customers' buying decisions are often made with input from a group of key influencers, referred to as a **'decision making unit' (DMU)**. • A range of **external third parties** also exercise influence over consumers – and over the marketing organisation itself. These influencers include governments and government agencies, the press/media, investors and pressure groups. Relationships with these markets can be exploited to generate positive PR (and/or minimise negative PR); influence public opinion in the organisation's favour; gain access to markets (eg through cause-related marketing); and enhance or replace other marketing activities (as in The Body Shop's exploitation of referral, media and pressure group relationships, in place of advertising). *'While relationships with these parties may not directly add value to a product or service, they can directly influence the likelihood of purchase or prevent an offer from even reaching the market'* (Peck *et al*, 1999).
Supplier & Alliance markets	The supplier market refers to the relationships that the firm must cultivate with its supply chain or network, in order to enable reliable, flexible, value-adding, cost-effective flows of supplies into and through the firm to the end customer. The concept of supply chain management recognises the need for long-term, collaborative relationship development with a small number of suppliers, particularly for strategic or critical items – rather than hard-bargaining, adversarial, one-off transactions (which may still be used for routine items, where price is the main criterion). The alliance market recognises a wide range of opportunities to add value through collaborative relationships between the core firm and partners (other than its immediate suppliers) in joint promotions, strategic alliances, joint ventures, knowledge-sharing networks, 'virtual' collaborations, and so on.

" For a full outline-level explanation of the six markets model (by its originators), together with a helpful short survey of other relational models, you might like to get hold of Peck, Payne, Christopher and Clark: Relationship Marketing: Strategy & Implementation (1999: Elsevier Butterworth Heinemann). See Chapter 1: Relationship Marketing: the six markets framework." pg 2

MARKETING AT WORK

Coutts Bank: It's not just about clients

Coutts considers at the way it services five distinct markets, in addition to its traditional client market, to make sure it maintains consistent, high quality relationships with them.

- **Internal markets**: Coutts communicates with all staff – client account managers, product managers and support staff – about its relationship management priorities. The aim is to ensure there is no weak link in the chain that makes up the Coutts service offering.
- **Referral markets**: Lawyers, consultants and financial advisers are a significant source of new business for the bank: they meet prospective clients every day and advise them on how best to invest their wealth. Coutts contacts these sources regularly and delivers regular, tailored information to them so that the bank is in their minds when they are advising their clients.
- **Supplier markets**: Although the bank is a service provider, it needs to ensure that its tangible offerings –brochures, events, premises or staff lapel badges – match its service quality image. It works closely with a few suppliers who, over time, get to know its ways and standards.
- **Recruitment markets**: In banking, new client account managers can often bring a portfolio of business with them, so Coutts works hard to sustain its quality image among its peers, and to be an organisation that people want to work for, in order to attract the best recruits.
- **Influence markets**: One of Coutts' key influence markets is the governments and financial authorities in the countries in which it operates. They may actively seek the bank's views on legislative changes and new product opportunities that might attract investment to their countries.

(Adapted from Christopher *et al*, p 81)

WORK BASED PROJECT TIP

application

Look back at your list of stakeholders you prepared earlier for your organisation. Try to re-classify them within the six markets model frame.

2.3 The relationship marketing ladder of loyalty

The ladder of loyalty (Kotler, 1997; Peck *et al*, 1999) is designed to illustrate how relationship marketing seeks to increase the loyalty of customer groups (including buyers, intermediaries and consumers), in order to reap the benefits of their retention, support and engagement. It can be applied in many relational settings: for example, charities and pressure groups use it to gauge the loyalty of donors, volunteers and members.

Ladder of loyalty

PARTNERS	Those who have become an active part of the value-creating process, closely linked in a long-term relationship of trust and collaboration (most common in B2B buyer-supplier relationships).
ADVOCATES	Those who actively support your marketing through word-of-mouth endorsement, recommendations and referrals
SUPPORTERS	Those who like you, but only support you passively by responding to your marketing
CLIENTS	Those who do business with you repeatedly, but may nevertheless be neutral (or even negative) towards the organisation.
CUSTOMERS (or Purchasers)	Those who have done business with you once: a first-time or one-off purchaser of your product/service.
PROSPECTS	Potential customers: people who might be persuaded to do business with you. (Better quality if profiled, qualified, referred to you – or active enquirers.)

Finding **prospects** and converting them into **customers** (ie securing purchase) is the preoccupation of traditional or transactional marketing. Relationship marketing emphasises the conversion of new or one-off customers into repeat customers – followed by progressive conversion to each higher rung of the ladder, which represents a strengthening of the relationship over time.

Getting customers to **advocate** level is a particularly helpful source of leverage, as recommendations and referrals by existing customers are an easy and cost-effective way of both getting new prospects and converting them into customers and clients.

Few consumer relationships go beyond the advocate level to **partnership** (which is mainly a feature of B2B buyer-supplier relationships). However, some ladder models include an intermediate stage called '**membership**', which implies genuine affiliation of some sort. This has long been a feature of voluntary sector relationships: membership of political parties and charities, for example, requires commitment and cost/effort, and offers corresponding opportunities for active involvement in fund-raising and policy development. In the consumer sector, some organisations have introduced tactics to create or simulate membership-type relationships.

"Travel organisations are perhaps the furthest advanced and many (particularly airlines) have developed clubs where members are seen to enjoy privileges that ordinary consumers do not enjoy. Some organisations, for example British Airways, have taken this a step further by openly differentiating between levels of membership dependent on the customer's commitment (determined by expenditure) to the airline. Executive Club Members (who can be blue, silver or gold card holders) receive different levels of privileges dependent on their status." Egan (2004)pg 68

3 Supplier and distributor relationships

We mentioned earlier that dyadic relationships are somewhat simplistic and that in reality groups of networks surround relationships.

3.1 Networks and alliances

Organisations tend to form a number of relationships and depend on a range of **network alliances** to provide access to:

- **markets** (eg through joint ventures with overseas partners)
- **technology** and intellectual property (eg through licensing)
- **resources** and competences (eg through strategic alliances or outsourcing)
- **wider distribution**
- brand profile or reputational **credibility** (eg through co-branding, joint promotion, sponsorship, endorsements and affiliations).

Such partnerships are often based on shared interests and objectives (eg associations between commercial organisations and pressure groups to promote causes or raise funds, while enhancing the ethical or environmental credentials of the business).

3.2 Co-operation and collaboration

One of the key principles of relationship management is that relationships can be co-operative rather than adversarial or competitive: buyers and suppliers, and even industry competitors, can work together to add value, to mutual benefit. It is widely acknowledged that in order to compete successfully in the global marketplace, firms cannot 'go it alone'.

- They depend on the contribution of their total **supply chains** to enable them to deliver value to the customer better and more profitably than competitors, through: better quality materials or access to scarce materials; reliable and flexible delivery; cost savings on materials and logistics; streamlined processes enabling late customisation of products (eg Dell Computers, the specifications for which are put together by the individual buyer, from a menu of components); and the quality of service given by intermediaries to the end consumer.

Collaboration is increasingly also embracing **customers and consumers**, who were previously regarded as passive recipients of marketing activity and offerings. For example:

- **Customer self-service.** Customers are being empowered to 'self-serve' products, services and marketing information. Examples include: self pick-up and home assembly furniture (eg from Ikea); on-line information and customer support via database searches and FAQs; self-administered purchase-and-payment transactions via e-commerce; on-line travel and entertainment bookings; and so on.
- **User-generated product and marketing content**. Examples include: magazine readers being allowed to nominate feature content; TV viewers contributing news and current affairs content, via on-line and SMS services; web-based blogs and wikis (eg Wikipedia) written by users; 'viral' marketing via word-of-mouth, content-sharing (eg on You Tube) and so on. Virgin Mobile in Australia recently invited consumers to define the brief for an advertising campaign. "What we love about the campaign is that it's flipping advertising on its head. By asking people to be part of it, we're guaranteeing that they'll want to watch it." (*Ad News,* Australia, 21 April 2006).

3.3 Negotiation

Within a given supply chain there is often an imbalance of power. In order to ensure that the needs of all parties are met fairly, careful and in a constructive manner, careful negotiation is required. Negotiation involves discussing issues and coming to an agreement.

Two starting points (or states of mind) exit for negotiation:

- **Distributive negotiation** – characterised by a desire to 'beat the opposition'
- **Integrative negotiation** – a friendly form with both parties looking to reach a mutually beneficial agreement

4 Inter-organisational relationships

We have mentioned previously the need to ensure that the organisation works together to meet customer needs. To do this effectively, it isn't enough to work on a within a shared mission, strong working relationships have to exist.

4.1 Building relationships across the organisation

KEY CONCEPT

concept

How might you describe a 'good working relationship'? A precise definition would include different things for different for different people, but there are two main components.

(a) **Good working**

A good working relationship allows or facilitates work transactions, the completion of tasks and the fulfilment of objectives.

(b) **Good relationships**

A good working relationship allows or facilitates ongoing and mutually satisfying interpersonal relations.

Elements in (a) might include prompt and willing service, co-operation and co-ordination, communication, expertise, teamworking skills and mutual reward or benefit.

Elements in (b) might include politeness, friendliness, trust, openness, respect and the ability to resolve conflict.

'In principle, business functions should mesh harmoniously to achieve the overall objectives of the firm. In practice, departmental interfaces are often characterised by deep rivalries and misunderstandings... Some inter-departmental conflict stems from differences of opinion about what lies in the best interests of the firm; some from real trade-offs between departmental well-being and company well-being; and some from unfortunate departmental stereotypes and prejudices'. (Kotler, 2002).

The **marketing concept** is designed to foster a deeper appreciation by all departments of the value and benefits of a **customer orientation**, but how much influence should marketing have over other departments to bring about co-ordinated effort in customer service, say, or product development? Other departments naturally stress their own special contribution to company goals, and view problems and opportunities in the light of their own expertise and culture.

Kotler (2002) summarises the potential for conflict as follows.

Other Departments	Their Emphasis	Marketing Emphasis
R & D	Basic research Intrinsic quality Functional features	Applied research Perceivable quality Sales features
Purchasing	Narrow product line Standard parts Price of material Economical lot sizes Purchasing at infrequent intervals	Broad product line Non-standard parts Quality of material Large lot sizes to avoid stockouts Immediate purchasing for customer needs
Manufacturing	Long production lead time Long runs with few models No model changes Standard orders Ease of fabrication Average quality control	Short production lead time Short runs with many models Frequent model changes Custom orders Aesthetic appearance Tight quality control
Finance	Strict rationales for spending Hard and fast budgets Pricing to cover costs	Intuitive arguments for spending Flexible budgets to meet changing needs Pricing to further market development
Accounting	Standard transactions Few reports	Special terms and discounts Many reports
Credit	Full financial disclosures by customers Low credit risks Tough credit terms Tough collection procedures	Minimum credit examination of customers Medium credit risks Easy credit terms Easy collection procedures

So what can you do as a member of the marketing department to overcome such obstacles to co-operative working? You may not be able to influence orientation or policy but you will be involved in **communication** and **co-ordination**. Organisations generally try to foster support for the marketing department

4.2 Internal co-operation and support for marketing

Gaining support for marketing activities will include encouraging other departments to take an interest in the plans. Clearly communicating the rationale behind plans will help to foster support. Listening to the needs of other departments and lookin for ways to work together on mutually beneficial projects will

Interpersonal skills include:

- The ability to build **rapport**, or a sense of relationship, with another person
- The ability to **persuade** or **influence** another person
- The ability to gain the **trust**, **confidence** and **co-operation** of another person
- The ability to **resolve conflict or disagreements**

Obviously, these are not things you can really learn in a book. You need to develop your communication skills, and to practise applying and adjusting them in every interaction that you encounter, until you consistently get the results you want.

4.3 Dealing with internal conflict

Interdepartmental **conflict** stems from genuine clashes of emphasis as well as prejudice and politics, and the marketing department needs to exercise internal promotion and employee relations in order to integrate its activities with those of other departments.

WORK BASED PROJECT TIP

Think about sources of potential conflict within your own organisation. Try to outline where these instances of conflict may have arisen from.

There are a number of formal methods available to deal with internal conflict;

- Internal **Arbitration** involves involving a third party within the organisation (possibly from a different function or a manager)to help resolve differences in an unbiased manner
- **Conciliation** involves an external third party but they are trained in conciliation and are there to establish a legally binding agreement between the parties.

ACAS are a government funded body who formally provide arbitration advice and conciliation services to organisation. Their website provided lots of useful information on dealing with conflict www.acas.org.uk

Three alternative outcomes exist when looking to resolve conflict.

Outcome	Likelihood	What it means in reality
Win-lose	This is quite common.	**One party gets what (s)he wants at the expense of the other party**: for example, Department A gets the new photocopier, while Department B keeps the old one (since there were insufficient resources to buy two new ones). However well-justified such a solution is (Department A needed the facilities on the new photocopier more than Department B), there is often lingering resentment on the part of the 'losing' party, which may begin to damage work relations.
Lose-lose	This sounds like a senseless outcome, but actually **compromise** comes into this category. It is thus very common.	**Neither party gets what (s)he really wanted**: for example, since Department A and B cannot both have a new photocopier, it is decided that neither department should have one. However 'logical' such a solution is, there is often resentment and dissatisfaction on both sides. (Personal arguments where neither party gives ground and both end up storming off or not talking are also lose-lose: the parties may not have lost the argument, but they lose the relationship ...) Even positive compromises only result in half-satisfied needs.
Win-win	This may not be common, but working towards it often brings out the best solution.	**Both parties get as close as possible to what they really want**. How can this be achieved?

Learning objective review

Learning objectives	Covered
1 Explain the characteristics of different organisational stakeholders	☑ Types and characteristics of range of people who are stakeholders ☑ Internal and external, connected and other stakeholders
2 Explain relationship marketing	☑ links between the marketing orientation and customer focus ☑ customer acquisition and retention- Pareto law ☑ benefits of building long term relationships ☑ ladder of loyalty
3 Discuss how relationships are developed and sustained with suppliers and distributors	☑ networking ☑ collaboration and cooperation ☑ negotiation
4 Explore inter-organisational relationships	☑ building relationships across the organisation ☑ internal co-operation and support for marketing ☑ overcoming conflict through co-operation , arbitration and conciliation

References

Blythe, J. (2006) Principles and Practice of Marketing, Thompson, London, .

Egan, J (2004) Relationship Marketing: Exploring Relational Strategies in Marketing (2nd edition). Pearson Education, Harlow, Essex.

Gummesson, E (2002) Total Relationship Marketing (2002) Elsevier Butterworth-Heinemann, Oxford.

Jobber, D. (2007) Principles and Practice of Marketing 5th edition, McGraw Hill, London.

Johnson G, Scholes K & Whittington R (2005) Exploring Corporate Strategy: Text and Cases (7th edition). Pearson Education, Harlow, Essex.

Kotler, P (2002) Marketing Management (11th edition). US Imports and PHIPES.

Peck HL, Payne A, Christopher M & Clark M (1999) Relationship Marketing: Strategy and Implementation. Elsevier Butterworth-Heinemann, Oxford.

Schlesinger, LA & Heskett, JL (1991). Breaking the cycle of failure in services. Sloan Management Review, Spring, pp 17-28.

Worthington I & Britton C (2006) The Business Environment. 5th edition. Pearson Education, Harlow, Essex.

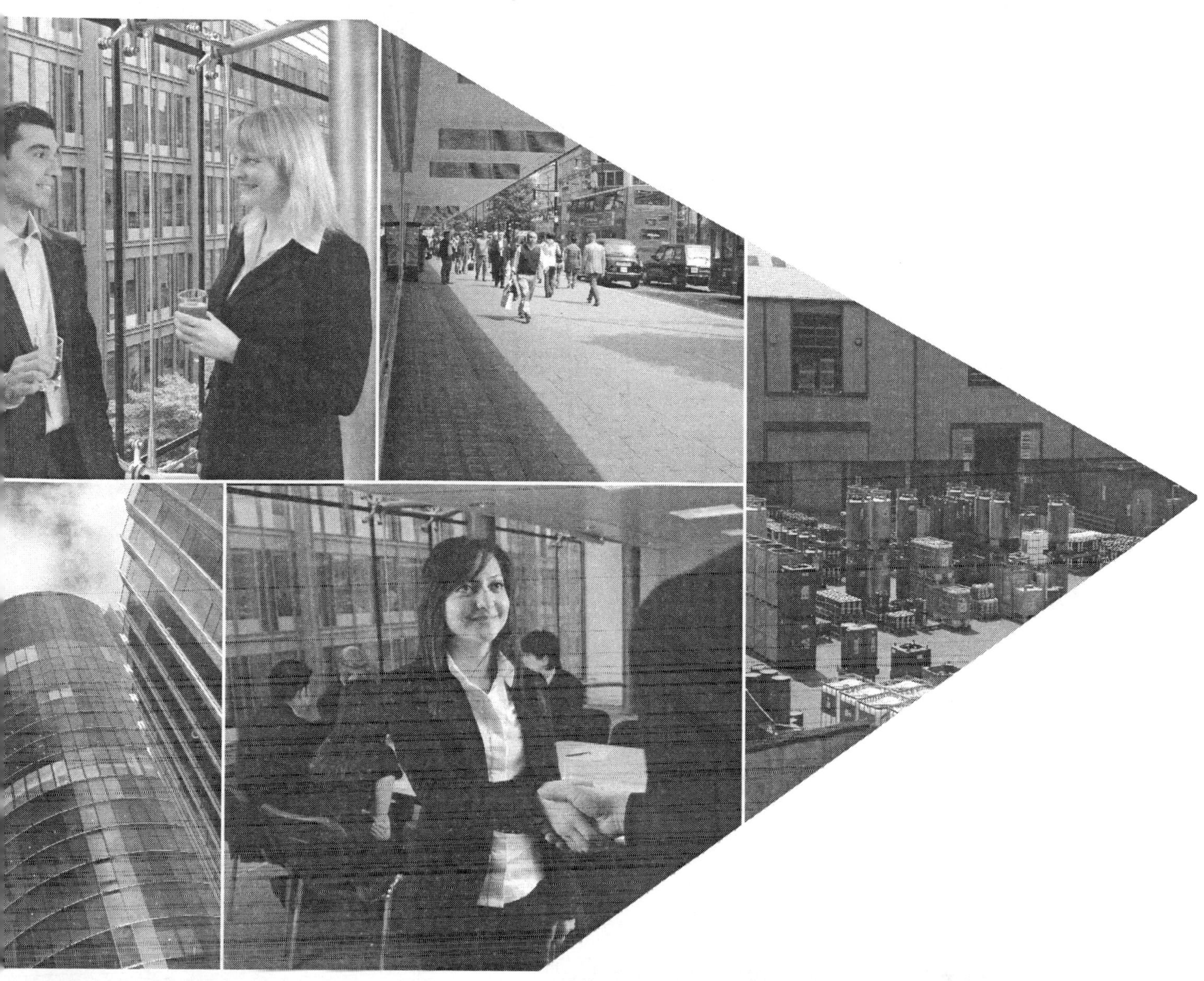

Chapter 7

Marketing communications and promotion

Topic list

1 The nature and theory of communications
2 Communication skills, medium and tools
3 Promotional communication tactics
4 Managing and monitoring marketing communications

Introduction

Within this chapter we look at marketing communications. For effective relationships with stakeholders, communications play a central role. There are many models of communication; we will address a couple of basic ones. We then consider specific communication tools and skills required by marketers. Written, verbal and non-verbal communications are discussed. Specific marketing communications promotional tools are then covered. A range of promotional communication tools are reviewed building on from the coverage in chapter 3. Finally, how to manage and monitor a specific communications tactic brings the chapter to a close.

Syllabus linked learning objectives

By the end of the chapter you will be able to:

Learning objectives	Syllabus link
1 Explain the importance, nature and scope of communication	3.1, 3.2
2 Explain the tools of written, verbal and non-verbal communication	3.3, 3.4
3 Evaluate a range of promotional marketing communication activities	3.5, 3.6, 3.7
4 Explain how to manage and monitor marketing communications	3.8, 3.9

1 The nature and theory of communication

The **key functions of communication** are: initiating action; exchanging information and ideas; and to establishing, maintaining and developing relationships with others. These can be applied to any given *marketing* function, such as: creating brand awareness, motivating or facilitating purchase, or managing customer/network/working relationships.

1.1 The purpose of communications

Communications are used in marketing for a range of specific purposes:

- **Creating brand awareness**: reaching consumers with brand messages widely and consistently enough to enable recognition and association with the right kind of images (for example, through advertising, public relations, brand identity). Like celebrities, brands need to be 'seen in all the right places' and to project their 'personality' in order to be instantly recognisable by the public.
- **Motivating purchase**: highlighting product benefits that are relevant to the needs of the target audience (for example, through advertising); offering incentives to purchase (for example, through sales promotion).
- **Facilitating purchase**: direct marketing (for example, through mail order advertising or Internet marketing); informing consumers how and where to purchase ('available at...' messages, web addresses); offering sales service.
- **Forming and maintaining customer relationships**: customer contacts (for example, through personalised mailings, loyalty programmes); personal client contacts (in business markets); after-sales service (for example, through care lines and customer service).
- **Forming and maintaining network relationships**: networking with suppliers, distributors and marketing service agencies; supplying information to support transaction and decision making.
- **Forming and maintaining working relationships**: supplying management and staff in the marketing and other departments with the information they need to integrate their marketing (especially customer-facing activities); fostering a customer-focused organisation culture through 'selling' quality values to staff.

1.1.1 The AIDA model

The AIDA model is a simple framework, which usefully suggests the desirable qualities of an effective promotional message. It also serves to outline the purpose of a marketing communications, that is: to draw attention, create interest, create desire and initiate action.

AIDA	
Attention	An effective message will get the attention of the target audience: it must have sufficient sensory (visual, audible) impact to get noticed.
Interest	An effective message will hold the interest of the target audience: it must be sufficiently relevant or intriguing to create engagement
Desire	An effective message will arouse desire in the target audience: it must offer to satisfy a need or want or solve a problem
Action	An effective message will obtain response from the target audience: it must describe next steps and helpful contacts to facilitate action

WORK BASED PROJECT TIP

application

Review some communications messages sent within your organisation. How can you see AIDA applied?

1.2 The communication process

KEY CONCEPT

concept

Effective communication is a two-way process, perhaps best expressed as a cycle. Signals or messages are sent by the communicator and received by the other party, who sends back some form of confirmation that the message has been received and understood ('feedback').

If you ask somebody the time and get a response, or send an invoice and receive payment, this corresponds to a single cycle of communication.

A more detailed model of the communication cycle (known as the **'radio signal' model**: Schramm, 1961) can be depicted as follows.

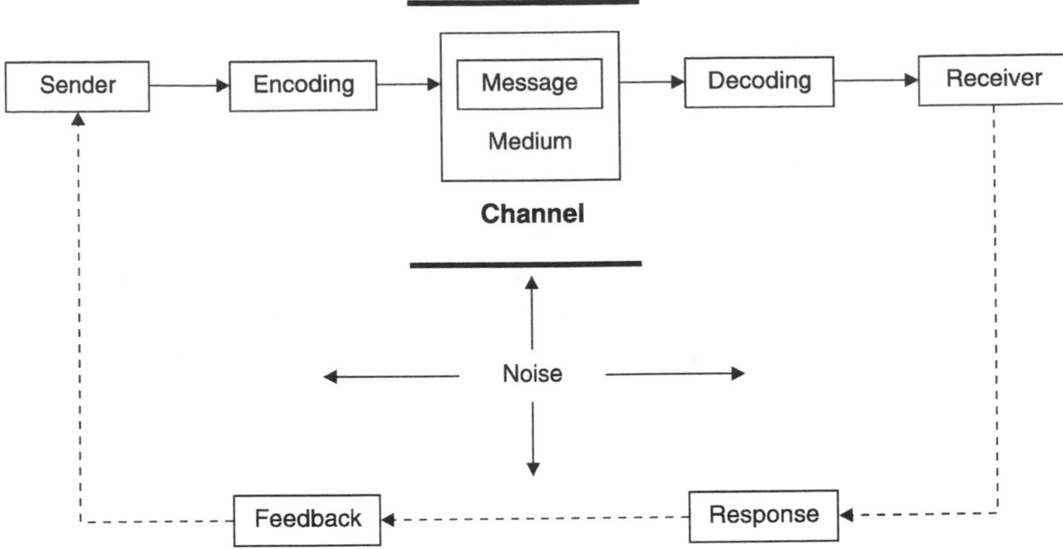

The 'radio signal' model of communication

1.2.1 Planning the message

The **sender** decides to communicate and plans what and how to communicate. In written communications (drafting an advertisement or report, say) you have 'off-line' decision and planning time in which to work out how best to present your ideas to get the desired response from your target audience. In face-to-face and oral communication (answering a telephone or customer query, say) you may have to plan and formulate messages 'live': this is why oral and face-to-face communication skills are so important.

1.2.2 The code analogy

Encoding is an analogy for how the sender puts his or her intentions into a form which can be transmitted: a form which the sender and receiver must *both* understand, if the sender's message is to be correctly interpreted at the other end by the receiver. This is like a code, because the words, numbers, pictures and gestures we use are only symbols representing our ideas: in communicating we must translate our ideas into a code which we think the receiver will be able to 'decipher' or translate back into the idea.

It is important to bear in mind that a symbol that we use and understand may be ambiguous (have more than one possible meaning) or mean something different to a person of different age, nationality, experience or beliefs. Just because we understand what we mean, it does not necessarily follow that someone else will: another reason to consider the needs and capacities of the target audience. Never mind what you think you'll say: what do you think *they'll hear*?

1.2.3 Media and the channels

Once the idea has been encoded as a message, the sender needs to choose how to **transmit** or get it across to the receiver/target audience.

(a) The particular route or path via which the message is sent, connecting the sender and receiver, is called the **channel** of communication: examples include a notice board, postal/telecommunications system and the Internet.

(b) The tool or instrument which is used is the **medium** (plural 'media'). The selected medium will usually come under one of the broad headings of:

- **Visual** (non-verbal) communication: a gesture, chart, graphic poster or Web page
- **Written** (verbal) communication: a letter, memo, report, press-release, e-mail or text advertisement
- **Oral** (verbal) communication ('by mouth'), which includes both face-to-face media (meetings, presentations) and remote media (telephone, television)

The choice of medium is an important communication skill: we will discuss it further later in the chapter.

If everything has gone well so far, the **receiver** receives the message – and must then **decode** its meaning, using his or her own knowledge, skills and perceptions to interpret its meaning.

KEY CONCEPT

concept 

Feedback is a response of the receiver which indicates to the sender that the message has (or has not) been successfully received, understood and interpreted.

1.2.4 Feedback

Seeking and giving **feedback** (especially in oral and face-to-face communication) is a key communication skill. Communication is prone to a wide range of factors which interfere with the effective transmission of the message from sender to receiver: these factors are often known by the collective term '**noise**'.They include technical interference (such as a bad phone line or poorly printed advertisement) and sources of misunderstanding (such as emotion, prejudice and differences in perception) and so on. Only by seeking feedback can the sender trust that the message has been both received and understood.

Examples of **positive feedback** include: a staff member accurately reading back your instructions; a presentation audience nodding agreement; a customer sending back the reply form as requested; your target audience buying the advertised product – or, as an example of more systematically gathered feedback, a market research focus group confirming that their response to a brand is as you expected.(You can probably work out what the negative equivalents would be.)

WORK BASED PROJECT TIP

application 

Think of a recent piece of communications within your organisation and break down it's components using the radio-signal model of communication.

2 Communication skills, medium and tools

In this section we consider the tools and media used to communicate. There are many everyday business formats used for communication.

ASSIGNMENT TIP

format 

We cover the range of written formats that you may be asked to complete for your assignment as well as the specific tools specified within the syllabus.

2.1 Written communication

A range of formats are specified within the syllabus, they include: letters; memo, emails and informal reports.

2.1.1 Letters

KEY CONCEPT

The **letter** is a 'high profile' medium of communication. It is in many cases the first or only contact between organisations and the outside world.

A **letter** is a written (or printed) communication addressed *to* a person or organisation *by* a person or organisation and usually sent through the post.

- As you can see, this definition allows a great deal of scope for variations: the letter is an extremely versatile medium and format, which can be adapted to almost any purpose. At the same time, its direct person-to-person nature makes it particularly well suited to private, confidential or 'sensitive' communications.
- A letter is the main method of written business-to-business communication, although e-mail is swiftly replacing it.

Format

A business letter contains various **standard elements**. You can see these elements laid out on the following page, with an example following the 'template' version.

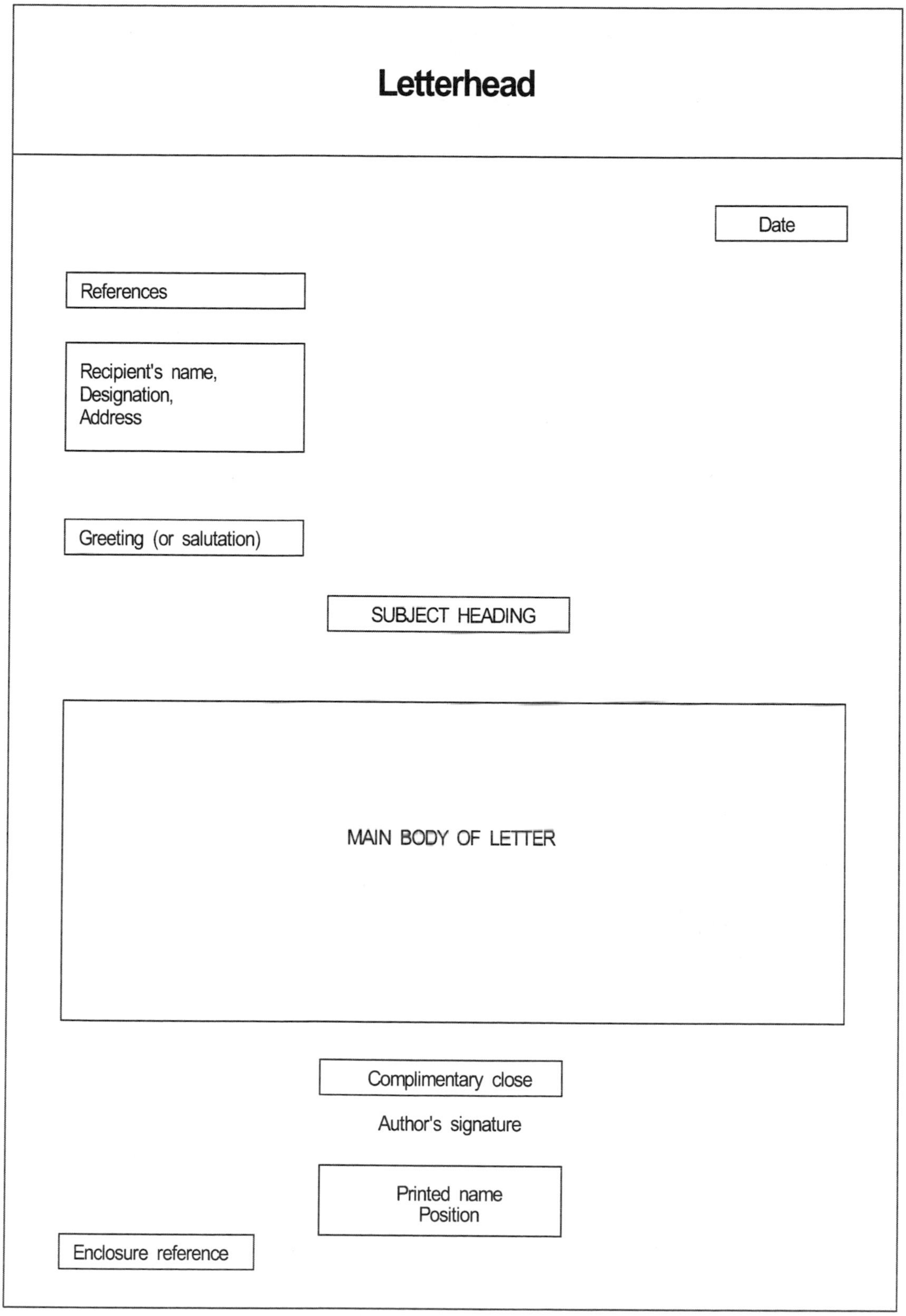

Letterhead

Date

References

Recipient's name,
Designation,
Address

Greeting (or salutation)

SUBJECT HEADING

MAIN BODY OF LETTER

Complimentary close

Author's signature

Printed name
Position

Enclosure reference

Hi-Tech Office Equipment Ltd

Micro House, High St, Newtown, Middlesex NT3 0PN

Telephone: Newtown (01789) 1234 Fax: (01789) 5678

Directors:
I. Teck (Managing)
M. Ployer
D. Rechtor
N. Other

Registered Office:
Micro House, High St, Newtown
Middx NT3 0PN
Registered No 123 4 56 789
Registered in England

7th June 200X

Your Ref: JB/nn
Our Ref: IW/cw

J M Bloggs Esq
Communications manager
Toubai Forze Timber Yard
Wood Lane Industrial Estate
SUSSEX SX1 4PW

Dear Mr Bloggs

DESK TOP PUBLISHING (DTP) SOFTWARE AND EQUIPMENT

Thank you for your letter of 3rd June, 200X, in which you request further details of Hi-Tech's of PCs and high performance printers with DTP software. I am delighted to hear that our discussions were of help to you.

Please find enclosed our list of hardware and software with current prices. I have also included leaflet entitled 'Desktop', which outlines some of the options for DTP: I trust this answers questions and gives you an idea of the exciting possibilities.

I would also take this opportunity to remind you that two of your old photocopiers are under maintenance contract with us, and that both of them become due for routine servicing the next month. Perhaps you would contact my secretary to arrange a convenient date for engineer to call at your offices.

I look forward to hearing from you, when you have thought about your DTP plans. If you have queries or need further information on DTP printers or accessories do not hesitate to let me know.

Yours sincerely

I M Wright

I M Wright
SALES MANAGER

Enc

Structure

A letter should have a **beginning**, a **middle** and an **end**. The reader will have a very general idea of the letter's contents already, from the letterhead, subject heading and the signature, name and designation at the foot of the letter. However,

you can 'lose' your reader very quickly if you do not at each stage make it clear why you are writing, what it is that you are trying to say, and what you think he can do for you and, more importantly, what *you* can do for *him*.

The reader will not be as familiar with the **context of the message** as you are. Describe it briefly: it may be a response to a previous communication from the reader, or you may be making initial contact (if you are introducing yourself or advertising goods). You would usually put the following in your opening.

- A straightforward (brief) explanation of why you are writing. ('Thank you for your letter of 3rd March, in which you requested information about conference bookings'.)
- An acknowledgement of any relevant correspondence received, noting its date and nature. ('As requested [or agreed] in our telephone conversation [or meeting] of 4 September, I am sending you ...'.)
- Important details of the circumstances leading to the letter. ('I have been asked by my colleague, George Brown, to contact you in regard to... .')

The *middle paragraph(s)* should then be used to set out the letter's message, which will elaborate on or move forward from the introductory paragraph. This section will contain the substance of your response to a previous message, details of the matter in hand, or the information you wish to communicate. If you are making several points, start a new paragraph with each, so that the reader can digest each part of your message in turn.

Your letter will not be effective unless it has the desired result of creating understanding or initiating action. It is a good idea to *summarise* your points briefly or make clear exactly what *response* is required. Here are some examples.

- I look forward to meeting you to discuss the matter in more detail.
- Thank you again for your order. I trust our service will be to your satisfaction.
- If you require any further information, please [do not hesitate to] call me.
- I will be contacting you in the next few days to arrange a meeting.

2.1.2 E-mails

KEY CONCEPT

format

E-mails can take the role of letters, memos, notes and messages. They are deceptively secure and informal: care must be taken to ensure sensitivity to the recipient's needs, confidentiality and effective tone.

Many organisations now conduct both internal and external communications via e-mail systems. E-mail can be used for a wide variety of communication purposes, in place of letters, circulars, internal memos, notes and other brief messages. Lengthier messages (such as briefs and reports) and graphic messages (such as diagrams and maps) can be attached as file attachments.

Most organisations have **guidelines for the use of e-mail**.

(a) E-mail messages have a **legal effect**. Firms can be sued for libellous, offensive or misleading remarks made in e-mail, and e-mail messages can be cited as evidence in court.

(b) E-mail can be **used excessively**, to the exclusion of other forms of communication which might be more appropriate. Excessive personal use (or abuse) is also an issue for many organisations (as it has been with the telephone).

(c) E-mail is **not private**, and remains on the server. There are thus dangers in using it to send confidential messages.

E-mail format

The most common e-mail software is Microsoft Outlook. In Outlook, depending on which version you use, a new (empty) mail message looks something like this :

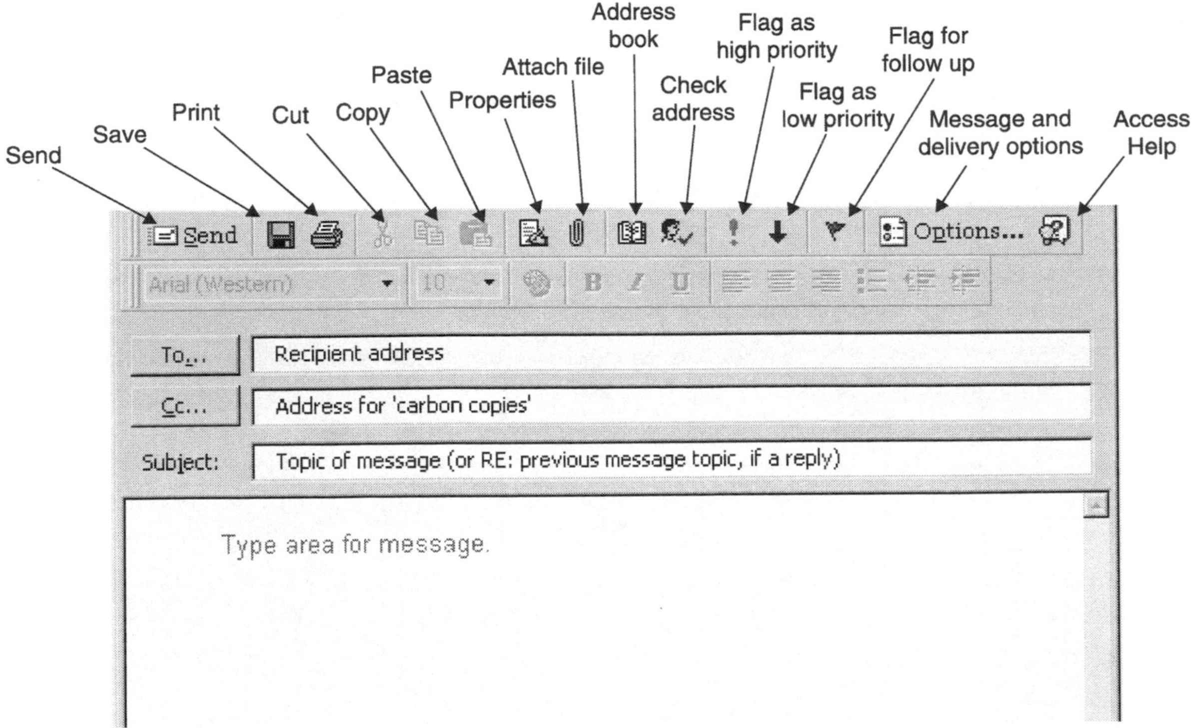

E-mail 'page'.

Most organisations also require employees to add a signature to the end of a message, This is usually set up similarly to a business card with job title and contact details. Increasingly common are branded templates which look similar to corporate letter head paper.

2.1.3 Guidelines for drafting e-mail messages

The following are general hints on composing e-mail messages.

Composing emails
Do not commit to e-mail any message that is private or confidential. As mentioned above, it is not a secure medium in general: a co-worker may cover someone's e-mail while (s)he is absent, the system administrator may access messages and companies may monitor e-mail.
Do not send illegal or offensive messages. (This should not be on your agenda anyway – especially for marketing purposes – but abusive, discriminatory and harassing messages do get sent.) E-mails can be traced to their source, and systems administrators can be liable for the misdeeds of users.
Beware of informality. Writers of e-mails may dash off a friendly note, but the recipients may (quite rightly) regard it as a written (and legally valid) response which may imply contract terms.
Beware of 'tone of voice'. Sarcasm and irony do not come across well in brief, typed, computer-mediated messages. If you wish to be humorous (in an informal context), there are conventions: adding 'emoticons' such as 'smiley faces' (☺) or the typed equivalent :).
Use mixed case letters. All uppercase (ie capitals) IS INTERPRETED AS SHOUTING!
Keep the line-length reasonably short, to ensure that it displays effectively on most recipient terminals.
Ensure that you give the **recipient's address** correctly and that you state a **subject**. The first will avoid getting the message returned to you (remember that computers are very literal) and the second will avoid getting the message deleted by the recipient as possible junk or virus mail.
Remember that sending e-mail is instant and that you **cannot usually recall a message**. Check your message carefully before you click on 'send'.

Because e-mail messages can be easily personalised and sent to mass mailing lists (as well as instantly, cheaply and conveniently sent to individual recipients), they have particular advantages for marketing communications. The use of e-mail for **transaction processing** and **relationship marketing** can be extremely effective: e-mailed newsletters, product information and order confirmation from known senders is likely to be welcomed – or at least not filtered out by bulk mail avoidance tools.

2.2 Memoranda

KEY CONCEPT

format

A **memorandum** is the internal equivalent of a letter: it can be used for a variety of purposes. Memoranda have highly structured introductory elements, including sender, recipient, subject, date and reference: thereafter there are no formal elements required.

The memorandum or 'memo' is a very flexible form used within an organisation for communication at all levels and for many different reasons.

(a) It performs *internally* the same function as a letter does in *external* communication by an organisation, but can in effect be used for reports, briefings or instructions, brief messages or 'notes' and any kind of internal communication that is more easily or clearly conveyed in writing (rather than face-to-face or on the telephone).

(b) A memorandum may be sent upwards, downwards or sideways in the organisation. It may be sent from one individual to another, from one department to another or from one individual to a department or larger body of staff, via the internal mail system of the organisation.

(c) Nowadays, internal e-mail (using networked computers) often substitutes for hard-copy memoranda.

Format

A memorandum may be typed onto blank sheets but many companies which generate a large volume of memoranda streamline the system and have 'memo pads' with appropriate headings already printed or memo styles set up in word processing or e-mail software.

Memorandum format will vary slightly according to the degree of formality required and the organisation's policy on matters like filing and authorisation of memoranda. Follow the conventions of **'house style'** in your own organisation. A typical format, including all the required elements, is illustrated below. (You may note the similarity to e-mail message windows.)

Organisation's name (optional) 'MEMORANDUM' heading	
To: (recipient's name or designation) From: (author's name or designation) Subject: (main theme of message)	Ref: (for filing) Date: (in full)
The message of the memorandum is set out like that of a letter: good English in spaced paragraphs. Note, however, that *no* inside address, salutation or complimentary close are required.	
Copies to: (recipient(s) of copies)	Signed: (optional) author signs/initials
Enc.: to indicate accompanying material	

Forrest Fire Extinguishers Ltd

MEMORANDUM

To: All Staff — Ref: ID/mp

From: I. Drant, Managing Director — Date: 13 October 20XX

Subject: Overtime arrangements for October/November

I would like to remind you that thanks to Guy Fawkes celebrations on and around the 5th November, we can expect the usual increased demand for small extinguishers. I am afraid this will involve substantial overtime hours for everyone.

In order to make this as easy as possible, the works canteen will be open all evening for snacks and hot drinks. The works van will also be available in case of transport difficulties late at night.

I realise that this period puts pressure on production and administrative staff alike, but I would appreciate your co-operation in working as many hours of overtime as you feel able.

Copies to: All staff — Signed: I. Drant

Structure and style

The structure and style of the message will vary according to its nature, the number of people it is addressed to, who those people are and what position they occupy. The flexibility of the medium means that some memos can be less formal than others. The same guidelines apply as with a letter.

The audience of a memo will be people within your organisation or business network.

- You may be writing to a fellow-specialist, and so be able to use technical language and complex ideas. Think first, however: a memo to all staff might cover a vast range of fields and abilities, from tea lady to accountant to engineer.
- If you are reporting to, or making a suggestion to, someone higher in the hierarchy than yourself, your tone will have to be appropriately formal, businesslike and tactful.
- If you are dashing off a handwritten note on a memo pad to a colleague with whom you enjoy an informal working relationship, you can be as direct, familiar and friendly as you like.
- If you are instructing or disciplining junior personnel, you will have to retain a certain formality for the sake of authority; a more persuasive and less formal tone might be appropriate if you are congratulating, motivating or making a request.

Here is an example of a memorandum used to make an **informal report**.

MEMORANDUM

To: M. Ployer, Office Manager — Date: 17 September 20XX

From: M. Ployee, Supervisor — Ref: MP/XX/913

Subject: ABUSE OF TELEPHONE PROCEDURES

As you requested, in view of the rising costs of maintaining current telephone equipment and procedures, I have investigated the possible causes of the rise in costs over the last quarter. I have identified three main causes.

(a) There are more telephones in the office than are necessary for efficient communication.

(b) Staff have become accustomed to making personal calls on office apparatus.

(c) Many calls are made at expensive charge rates and unnecessary length.

I outline below a number of courses of action which could be taken to prevent further increases.

(a) *Remove superfluous equipment.* Several extensions are unallocated or little used for business purposes, and are therefore not only unnecessary but open to abuse. These could be disconnected immediately.

(b) *Circularise all staff and Department Heads.* This might discourage personal and unnecessarily lengthy calls on office apparatus, and encourage staff to be more conscious of economy.

(c) *Monitor the length and cost of calls.* A variety of devices are currently available at a reasonable cost, capable of displaying the value of units used on calls and logging long-distance calls.

(d) *Route all calls through the central switchboard.* This would provide control over use of the apparatus, each call having to be verified. The risk of congestion at the switchboard and the inconvenience to the operator, however, make this an unacceptable long-term option.

(e) *Provide alternative telephone facilities to staff.* The installation of pay telephones at generally accessible locations within the building would allow staff to continue to make personal calls, thereby preserving good working relations in the office.

If you wish to discuss these suggestions, I would be more than happy to supply further details, at your convenience.

2.2.1 Reports

'Report' is a general term and one that may suggest a wide range of formats. If you give someone a verbal account, or write them a message in a letter, memo or e-mail informing them of facts, events, actions you have taken, suggestions you wish to make as a result of an investigation and so on, you are reporting. In this sense the word means simply 'telling' or 'relating': we have seen reports of this kind in memorandum form, in the visual presentation of statistics, and in the minutes of meetings.

There will be variety in the format and style of a report, according to the context.

- **Formal or informal**. You may think of reports as huge documents with sections, subsections, paragraphs, subparagraphs, indexes, appendixes and so on. There *are* extensive, complex reports like this, but a single-sheet ordinary memorandum may be sufficient in many contexts.
- **Special reports** may be commissioned for one-off planning and decision-making, such as a market research report, or reports on a proposed project or particular issue.

- **Routine reports** are produced at regular intervals. Examples of routine reports are budgetary control reports, sales reports or progress reports. **Occasional** reports include an accident report or a disciplinary report.

Report-writing style

KEY CONCEPT

format

Report writing involves particular requirements for objectivity, impersonality, ease of reading, precision and appropriate formality.

There are certain stylistic requirements in the writing of reports, formal or informal.

(a) **Objectivity and impersonality**. Even in a report designed to persuade as well as inform, subjective value judgements and emotions should be kept out of the content and style as far as possible: the bias, if recognised, can undermine the credibility of the report and its recommendations.

(b) **Ease of understanding**.

   (i) Avoid technical language and complex sentence structures for non-technical users.

   (ii) The material will have to be logically organised, especially if it is leading up to a conclusion or recommendation.

   (iii) Relevant themes should be signalled by appropriate headings, or highlighted for easy scanning.

   (iv) The layout of the report should display data clearly and attractively. Figures and diagrams should be used with discretion, and it might be helpful to highlight key figures which appear within large tables of numbers.

   (v) Background or supporting information may be removed to 'appendices' at the end of the report, in order to keep its main body concise and relevant at the appropriate level of detail.

(c) **Precision**

   (i) Do not use vague language. 'This option is likely to exceed expenditure budgets' is far superior to 'it would cost an awful lot of money'.

   (ii) Recommendations should be specific and firm. 'I feel more could be done...' is too vague to be helpful. Say precisely what should be done: 'customers should receive a verbal explanation in layman's terms...'.

Formal report structure

KEY CONCEPT

format

Reports are highly structured (especially formal reports), with sections covering: context-setting, description of methodology and findings, and conclusion/recommendation (as required).

A formal report is laid out according to certain basic guidelines. It will be split into logical sections, each referenced and headed appropriately.

TITLE		*Ask yourself....*
I	TERMS OF REFERENCE (or INTRODUCTION or BACKGROUND)	*What was I asked to do?*
II	PROCEDURE (or METHOD)	*How did I go about it?* [if relevant]
III	FINDINGS (or ANALYSIS or appropriate topic headings)	*What did I discover?*
1	Section heading	
2	Section heading	
	(a) sub heading	
	(i) sub point	
IV	CONCLUSIONS	*What is the general 'thrust' of the result?*
V	RECOMMENDATIONS	*What particular recommendations do I wish to make?* [if requested to do so]

2.2.2 Example: a short formal report

REPORT ON COMPACT DISC STORAGE SAFETY AND SECURITY

To: Mr M Ployer, Personnel Department Manager

From: M Ployee, Supervisor

Date: 3 October 20XX

I INTRODUCTION

This report details the findings of an investigation into methods of CD storage currently employed at the Head Office of the bank. The report includes recommendations for the improvement of current procedure.

II METHOD

In order to evaluate the present procedures and to identify specific shortcomings, the following investigatory procedures were adopted:

1 Interview of all staff using CD to back up data

2 Storage and indexing system inspected

3 Computer accessory firm consulted by telephone and catalogues obtained (see Appendix I)

III FINDINGS

1 *Current system*

(a) CDs are 'backed up' or duplicated irregularly and infrequently.

(b) Back-up discs if they exist are stored in plastic containers in the personnel office, the same room as the discs currently in use.

(c) Discs are frequently left on desk tops during the day and even overnight.

2 *Safety and security risks*

(a) There is no systematic provision for making copies, in the event of loss or damage of discs in use.

(b) There is no provision for separate storage of copies in the event of fire in the personnel office, and no adequate security against fire or damage in the containers used.

(c) There appears to be no awareness of the confidential nature of information on disc, nor of the ease with which discs may be damaged by handling, the spilling of beverages, dust etc.

IV CONCLUSIONS

The principal conclusions drawn from the investigation were that there was insufficient awareness of safety and security among non-specialist staff, that there was insufficient formal provision for safety and security procedure, and that there was serious cause for concern.

V RECOMMENDATIONS

In order to rectify the unsatisfactory situation summarised above, the author of the report recommends that consideration be given as a matter of urgency to the following measures.

1 Immediate backing up of all existing discs.

2 Drafting of procedures for backing up discs at the end of each day.

3 Acquisition of a fire-proof safe to be kept in separate office accommodation.

4 Communication to all staff of the serious risk of loss, theft and damage arising from careless handling of computer discs.

2.2.2 Informal reports

An **informal report** is used for less complex and lower-level information. Its structure is less developed: it will not require elaborate referencing and layout. There will be three main sections, each of which may be headed in any way appropriate to the context in which the report is written:

- Introduction/background/situation
- Findings/analysis/information
- Summary/conclusion/recommendations

In informal reporting situations within an organisation, the 'short informal report' may well be presented in memorandum or e-mail format, which incorporates title headings and can thereafter be laid out at the writer's discretion.

2.3 Verbal and non verbal communication

2.3.1 Oral communication

Oral communication means, simply, communication by speech, or 'word of mouth'. Face-to-face oral media include conversations, meetings, interviews, negotiations and public addresses, presentations or briefings. Interactive oral communication can also take place when the sender and receiver are not physically face-to-face, through telephone calls, video conferencing or Webcasting.

The advantages and disadvantages of such communication may be summarised as follows.

Advantages	Disadvantages
Speed/directness: little or no time lapse between sending and receiving	**Less planning time** to formulate and check message and responses
Interactivity: real-time exchange of ideas, opinions, questions. Ability to respond directly to questions, make decisions	**Ephemeral** (passes with time): does not allow for reception at audience's own pace, repeated reference etc (as writing does)
Feedback: immediate and versatile (non-verbal messages). Ability to clarify, check, reinforce messages.	**Ambiguity**: people's perceptions and memory of what was said may differ. (May need written checking, confirmation.)
Influence: interactivity (plus use of non-verbal messages) supports ability to persuade, motivate	**Influence**: strong personalities/voices can prevent others being heard
Sensitivity: interactivity and personal nature (voice, non-verbals) allows for sensitive handling of difficult messages	**Technical noise**: potential for interference (for example, from noise, bad phone lines)

2.3.2 Face-to-face communication

Face-to-face communication is particularly effective in:

- Allowing **non-verbal cues**, both **audible** (for example, tone of voice) and **visual** (body language), to be used to enhance understanding and persuasion
- Allowing immediate **exchange and feedback**
- Humanising the **context** of communication by opening the parties to each other's direct scrutiny and to personal factors

The advantages and their applications can be summarised as follows.

Advantages	Examples of application
Encourages **ideas generation**: participants encouraging and prompting each other	Brainstorming meeting for promotion planning or customer care improvement
Encourages **problem solving** and **conflict resolution**: allows exchange and supportive communication, sensitivity to personal factors	Customer complaint handling, or employee counselling
Improves **decision-making**: adds different viewpoints and information in real time	Team meetings to decide strategies or allocate roles
Facilitates **persuasion**: use of personal charisma, logic, adjustment to feedback	Sales negotiations, pitching ideas to internal/external clients
Encourages **co-operation**: information sharing, participation	Team meetings
Shows the **human face** of an organisation, and encourages identification with it	Personal customer service

2.3.3 Non-verbal communication

KEY CONCEPT

concept

Non-verbal communication is basically anything that conveys a message without using words or symbols. There are three forms of non-verbal communication;

- Kinetics eg body language such as facial expressions, gestures, movement
- Meta-communications eg the importance of silences, pauses in conversation for effect, slamming a door
- Paralanguage eg tone of voice

What is non-verbal communication?

Non-verbal communication may be linked to words (for example, a tone of voice), or it may be independent of any verbal message. Information is perceived by all the senses: tastes and smells and movements convey messages. Think what you can convey through, for example, frowning or smiling, nodding, scratching your head, putting your head in your hands, slamming a door, turning your back, screaming, being silent, keeping your office door open or closed, slouching or sitting up straight, dressing casually or turning up late to a formal meeting.

All these examples have aspects in common.

(a) They **convey a message** from or about the person 'doing' them.

(b) They are the kind of things done by everybody all the time: *every* action (or non-action) and every communication (or non-communication) conveys or adds a non-verbal message. (Remember: you cannot NOT communicate.)

(c) The message conveyed is **not consistent from culture to culture**, person to person, or in one person over time. A nod, for example may mean agreement, non-agreement (as in India, where a shake of the head means agreement), a friendly greeting, an *unfriendly* greeting (if you expected a handshake or hug, say), an instruction to sit or move in the direction indicated, the easing of a stiff neck, and so on. We depend on context, expectation, perception and attitude to interpret the message – and frequently get it wrong! (If someone has her arms folded across her chest, this is not necessarily defensiveness: she may just be cold!)

(d) They may or may not be **conscious or intentional**. In general, we are much more aware of *other* people's gestures and tone of voice, and sensitive to possible meanings in them (even if we misinterpret them), than we are of the things we are doing ourselves, and the signals they convey.

(e) They may **reinforce or contradict** a verbal message. The words 'I'd love to stay for dinner', for example, would be reinforced by a smile, warm tone of voice, or arm around the shoulders: they would be undermined by a worried look, glance at the watch, or getting up and heading for the door.

2.4 Taking control of non-verbal communication

Non-verbal communication can be controlled (by the sender) and interpreted (by the receiver) to add depth and accuracy to the communication process.

You can see what a complex and involved process non-verbal communication is, and the extent of misunderstanding or misinterpretation that can occur. What can be done about this? Non-verbal communication can be **controlled** and used fruitfully to:

Effect of controlling NVC
Provide appropriate 'physical' **feedback** to the sender of a message (a yawn, applause, clenched fists, fidgeting)
Create a desired **impression** (smart dress, a smile, punctuality, a firm handshake)
Establish a desired **atmosphere** or conditions (a friendly smile, informal dress, attentive posture, a respectful distance)
Reinforce our spoken messages with appropriate indications of how our interest, seriousness and feelings are engaged (an emphatic gesture, sparkling eyes, a disapproving frown)

If we can learn to **recognise** non-verbal messages given by others, we can also:

Additional value of NVC
Receive non-verbal **feedback** from a listener and modify the message accordingly
Recognise people's **real feelings** when their words are constrained by formal courtesies (an excited look, a nervous tic, close affectionate proximity)
Recognise existing or potential **personal problems** (the angry silence, the indifferent shrug, absenteeism or lateness at work, refusal to look someone in the eye)
'Read' situations in order to modify our own communication and response strategy. Is the potential customer convinced? (Go ahead.) Is the complaining customer on the point of hysteria? (Be soothing.)

Body language

KEY CONCEPT

concept

Non-verbal cues (body language) include: facial expression, eye contact, gestures, posture and personal appearance..

Let's look briefly at some of the 'signals' we give and receive, and how they may be interpreted.

Facial expression

The eyebrows, nose, lips and mouth, jaw, musculature, skin colour and movement all contribute to the expression on someone's face. Some of these things can be controlled, making facial expression in isolation an unreliable guide to true feelings – especially since different races and cultures have different facial characteristics which make unfamiliar expressions hard to 'read'.

Eye contact

Eye contact – the meeting of the other person's gaze – signals interest in the West. *Intermittent* eye contact is usual in interpersonal communication: *less* might indicate disinterest or avoidance, while *more* implies a desire for intimacy (which may or may not be desirable to both parties and is particularly intrusive in Eastern cultures). People also tend to look away if they are thinking, or planning their message: they make contact when communicating directly, or seeking feedback. Excessive eye movement is often interpreted as avoidance, distraction or nervousness.

Gestures

People make gestures unconsciously: jabbing a finger in the air for emphasis, or tapping the fingers when impatient. They also make *conscious* gestures (and not only impolite ones): finger against the lips for silence, jerk of the head to indicate a direction, shrug to indicate indifference. Like any other form of non-verbal communication, there is a wide variety of possible interpretations of any given gesture. Some gestures take on an 'agreed' common meaning within a culture, but you should bear in mind that these meanings can be lost or changed – like words – and that other cultures may not share them. Indeed, some cultures use gestures more or less than others: a level of gesticulation that would seem natural to an Italian, for example, might suggest impending nervous breakdown to a native American.

Posture

Posture is positioning. It includes conscious or unconscious decisions about whether you sit, stand, walk or lie down, and *how:* lounging, hunching and sitting up straight, for example, may convey relaxation, negativity or alertness respectively.

WORK BASED PROJECT TIP

application

Make a list of the common uses of non-verbal communications used frequently within your own organisation. Think about the positive and negative aspects of the behaviour demonstrated. Consider how colleagues could be trained to improve their use of non-verbal communication.

2.5 Presentations

KEY CONCEPT

concept

Presentations are used in a wide variety of internal and external contexts, to convey information persuasively to a group of people.

ASSIGNMENT TIP

format

We have included presentations because you are likely to have to prepare slides and speaker notes as part of your assignment.

You may associate **presentations** with a particular context – possibly not one relevant to you personally. However, consider the following situations.

(a) Consultants and advertising agencies make presentations to senior management, to sell their conclusions and recommendations.

(b) Sales people make 'pitches' to clients or potential clients, discussing and demonstrating the benefits of a product, service or brand.

(c) Specialists make technical presentations to management or staff, briefing them on findings or facts relevant to their work. A market researcher might brief the sales force on findings with regard to buyer motivation, for example.

(d) A member of staff who has researched and written a report may be asked to present it orally to a group of interested parties who may not have time to read its contents, or who may require the opportunity to challenge its findings, ask questions, or be persuaded further.

As you can see, presentations may vary widely in a number of aspects.

- The size of the audience
- The composition, knowledge, interests and motivations of the audience
- The purpose and approach of the presentation (information/briefing, persuasion/pitch, demonstration/explanation, entertainment/welcome and so on).
- The length and complexity of the content
- The formality of the situation

Preparing presentations

Points to consider when preparing a presentation	
Prioritise	Select the **key points** of the subject, and a **storyline** or theme that gives your argument a unified sense of 'direction'. The **fewer** points you make (with the most emphasis) and the clearer the **direction** in which your thoughts are heading, the easier it will be for the audience to grasp and retain your message.
Structure	Make notes for your presentation which **illustrate** simply the **logical order** or **pattern** of the key points of your speech.
Outline	Following your structured notes, **flesh out** your message. • **Introduction** • **Supporting evidence, examples and illustrations** • **Notes** where **visual aids** will be used • **Conclusion**
Practise	Rehearsals should indicate difficult logical leaps, dull patches, unexplained terms and other problems: adjust your outline or style. They will also help you gauge and adjust the **length** of your presentation.
Cue	Your outline may be too detailed to act as a cue or **aide-memoire** for the talk itself. **Small cards**, which fit into the palm of the hand may be used to give you: • **Key words** for each topic, and the logical links between them • Reminders for when to use **visual aids** • The **full text** of any detailed information you need to quote

An effective presentation requires two key structural elements.

(a) An **introduction** which:

- Establishes your credibility
- Establishes rapport with the audience
- Gains the audience's attention and interest (sets up the problem to be solved, uses curiosity or surprise)
- Gives the audience an overview of the **shape** of your presentation, to guide them through it: a bit like the scanning process in reading.

(b) A **conclusion** which:

- **Clarifies and draws together** the points you have made into one main idea (using an example, anecdote, review, summary)
- **States or implies what you want/expect your audience to do** following your presentation

- Reinforces the audience's **recall** (using repetition, a joke, quotation or surprising statistic to make your main message **memorable**).

Clarity

Your structured notes and outline should contain cues which clarify the **logical order**, shape or progression of your information or argument. This will help the audience to **follow you** at each stage of your argument, so that they arrive with you at the conclusion. You can signal these logical links to the audience as follows.

(a) **Linking words or phrases**

Therefore ... [conclusion, result or effect, arising from previous point]
As a result ...

However ... [contradiction or alternative to previous point]
On the other hand ...

Similarly ... [confirmation or additional example of previous point]
Again ...

Moreover ... [building on the previous point]

(b) **Framework**: setting up the structure

'Of course, this isn't a perfect solution: There are advantages and disadvantages to it. It has the advantages of ... . But there are also disadvantages, in that ... '

(c) You can use more elaborate devices which summarise or repeat the previous point and lead the audience to the next. These also have the advantage of giving you, and the listener, a 'breather' in which to gather your thoughts.

Other ways in which content can be used to clarify the message include the following.

(a) **Examples and illustrations** – showing how an idea works in practice.

(b) **Anecdotes** – inviting the audience to relate an idea to a real-life situation.

(c) **Questions** – rhetorical, or requiring the audience to answer, raising particular points that may need clarification.

(d) **Explanation** – showing how or why something has happened or is so, to help the audience understand the principles behind your point.

(e) **Description** – helping the audience to visualise the person, object or setting you are describing.

(f) **Definition** – explaining the precise meaning of terms that may not be shared or understood by the audience.

(g) The use of **facts, quotations or statistics** – to 'prove' your point.

Your **vocabulary and style** in general should contribute to the clarity of the message. Remember to use short, simple sentences and non-technical words (unless the audience is sure to know them): avoid jargon, clichés, unexplained acronyms, colloquialisms, double meanings and vague expressions (like 'rather', 'good'). Remember, too, that this is **oral** communication, not written: use words and grammatical forms that you would **normally use in speaking** to someone – bearing in mind the audience's ability to understand you, and the formality of the occasion.

Visual aids will also be an important aspect of content used to signal the structure and clarify the meaning of your message. We discuss them specifically below.

Visual aids

KEY CONCEPT

concept

Visual aids include slides (acetates and PowerPoint), videos, flipcharts, handouts and props and demonstrations.

The term **visual aids** covers a wide variety of forms which share two characteristics.

(a) They use a visual image.

(b) They act as an aid to communication. This may seem obvious, but it is important to remember that visual aids are not supposed to be impressive or clever for their own sake, but to support the message and speaker in achieving their purpose.

A number of media and devices are available for using visual aids. They may be summarised as follows.

Equipment/medium	Advantages	Disadvantages
Slides: photographs, text or diagrams projected onto a screen or other surface	• Allow colour photos: good for mood, impact and realism • Pre-prepared: no speaker 'down time' during talk • Controllable sequence/ timing: pace content/audience needs	• Require a darkened room: may hinder note-taking • Malfunction and/or incompetent use: frustration and distraction
Film/video shown on a screen or TV monitor	• Moving images: realism, impact: can enhance credibility (eye witness effect)	• Less flexible in allowing interruption, pause or speeding up to pace audience needs
Overheads: films or acetates (hand drawn or printed) projected by light box onto a screen behind/above the presenter	• Versatility of content and presentation • Low cost (for example, if hand written) • Clear sheets: can be used to build up images as points added	• Require physical handling: can be distracting • Risk of technical breakdown: not readily adaptable to other means of projection
Presentation software: for example, Microsoft PowerPoint. PC-generated slide show (with animation, sound) projected from PC to screen via data projector	• Versatility of multi-media: impact, interest • Professional design and functioning (smooth transitions) • Use of animation to build, link and emphasise as points added	• Requires PC, data projector: expensive, may not be available • Risk of technical breakdown: not readily adaptable to other means of projection • Temptation to over-complexity and over-use: distraction
Flip charts: large paper pad mounted on frame – sheets are 'flipped' to the back when finished with	• Low cost, low-risk • Allows use during session (for example, to 'map' audience views, ideas) • Can be pre-prepared (for example, advertising 'story boards') • Easy to refer back	• Smaller, still, paper-based image: less impact • Hand-prepared: may lack perceived quality (compared to more sophisticated methods)
Handouts: supporting notes handed out for reference during or after the session	• Pre-prepared • Audience doesn't need to take as many notes: reminder provided	• Audience doesn't need to take as many notes: may encourage passive listening.
Props and demonstrations: objects or processes referred to are themselves shown to the audience	• Enhances credibility (eye witness effect) • Enhances impact (sensory solidity)	• May not be available • Risk of self-defeating 'hitches'

The following illustrations show two of the media discussed above, demonstrating some of their key features – and showing how a picture can be a helpful 'break' from reading or hearing lots of verbal content!

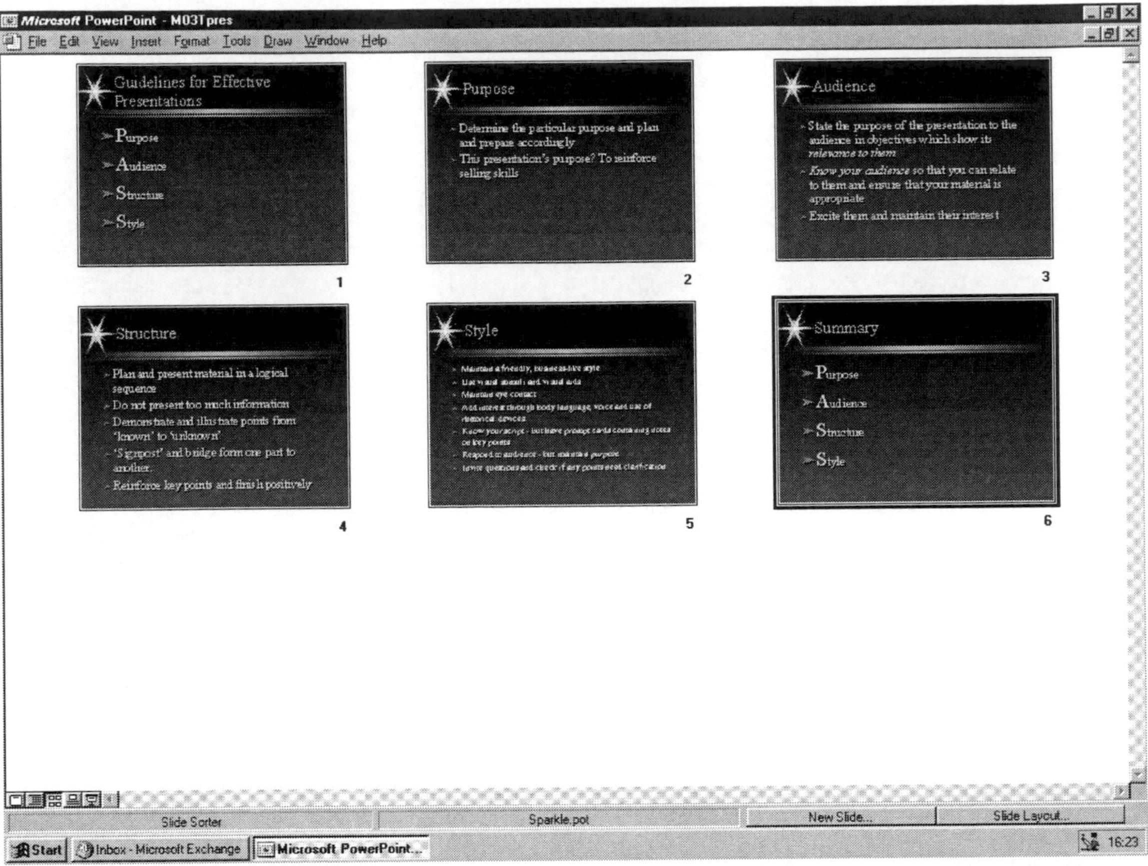

Whatever medium or device you are using, visual aids are **versatile** with regard to **content**: maps, diagrams, flowcharts, verbal notes, drawings and photographs.

When planning and using visual aids, consider the following points.

(a) Visual aids are **simplified and concrete**: they are easier to grasp than the spoken word, allowing the audience to absorb complex relationships and information.

(b) Visual aids are **stimulating** to the imagination and emotions, and therefore useful in gaining attention and recall.

(c) Visual aids can also be **distracting** for the audience – and for the presenter, who has to draw/write/organise/operate them. They can add complexity and ambiguity to the presentation if not carefully designed for relevance and clarity.

(d) Visual aids impose **practical requirements**.

   (i) The medium you choose must be **suitable** for the needs of your **audience**. Demonstrations, or handing round a small number of samples, is not going to work for a large audience. A flipchart will not be visible at the back of a large room; a slide projector can be overwhelming in a small room. A darkened room, to show video or slides, will not allow the audience to take notes.

   (ii) **Skill, time and resources** must be available for any pre-preparation of aids that may be required in advance of the presentation.

   (iii) **The equipment, materials and facilities** you require must be available in the venue, and you must **know** how to **use** them. (No good turning up with a slide projector if there is no power source, or film when there is no overhead projector, or without proper pens for a particular type of board.)

WORK BASED PROJECT TIP

Think about how you will select and create visuals which have the maximum effect within your own organisation.

3 Promotional communication tactics

In chapter 3 (section 5) we covered promotion as part of the marketing mix. In this chapter, we do not intent to repeat content by describing the tactics again but instead we will look at how they are selected and consider their use in different contexts. Any communication tactics can be used with both internal and external stakeholders in order to help forge stronger relationships.

3.1 Planning promotional tactics

When putting together a communications plan, it is best to begin with the organisational mission.

KEY CONCEPT

concept

Mission statements are broadly defined enduring statements of purpose that distinguishes a business from others of its type (Ackoff, 1987).

Mission statements essentially address two fundamental questions, 'What business are we in?' and What business do we want to be in?' (Jobber, 2007). The purpose of a mission is to provide a focus for the organisation to rally members to work together towards achieving common goals. Mission statements can be called different names including amongst others vision statements or value statements. No matter what its name, the important point is that employees and other stakeholders *believe* the statement and it should be in line with their values and expectations. Unrealistic mission statements are viewed sceptically and will be dismissed by stakeholders and so the value of writing it will be lost. They should also be more than just words written on a piece of paper, displayed on a board in a reception area or placed on mouse mats and should aim to be a living, breathing document that provides information and inspiration for members.

The communications plan will flow from the mission statement through a series of objectives set at different levels of the organisation, the following model describes this process.

ASSIGNMENT TIP

concept 

You are not expected at the Introductory Certificate level to discuss in detail the process of objective setting. We have included it here however in order to add a little context to your appreciation of planning marketing communications.

3.2 Promotional tools

If we recap the promotional mix for a moment, we can say that it is the total marketing communications programme of the organisation, consisting of a specific combination or blend of promotional tools used to reach the target audience for a given marketing task. The full range of tools that can be used to secure favourable responses from, and build sustainable relationships with, stakeholder audiences is shown in the next model.

Marketing communications tools

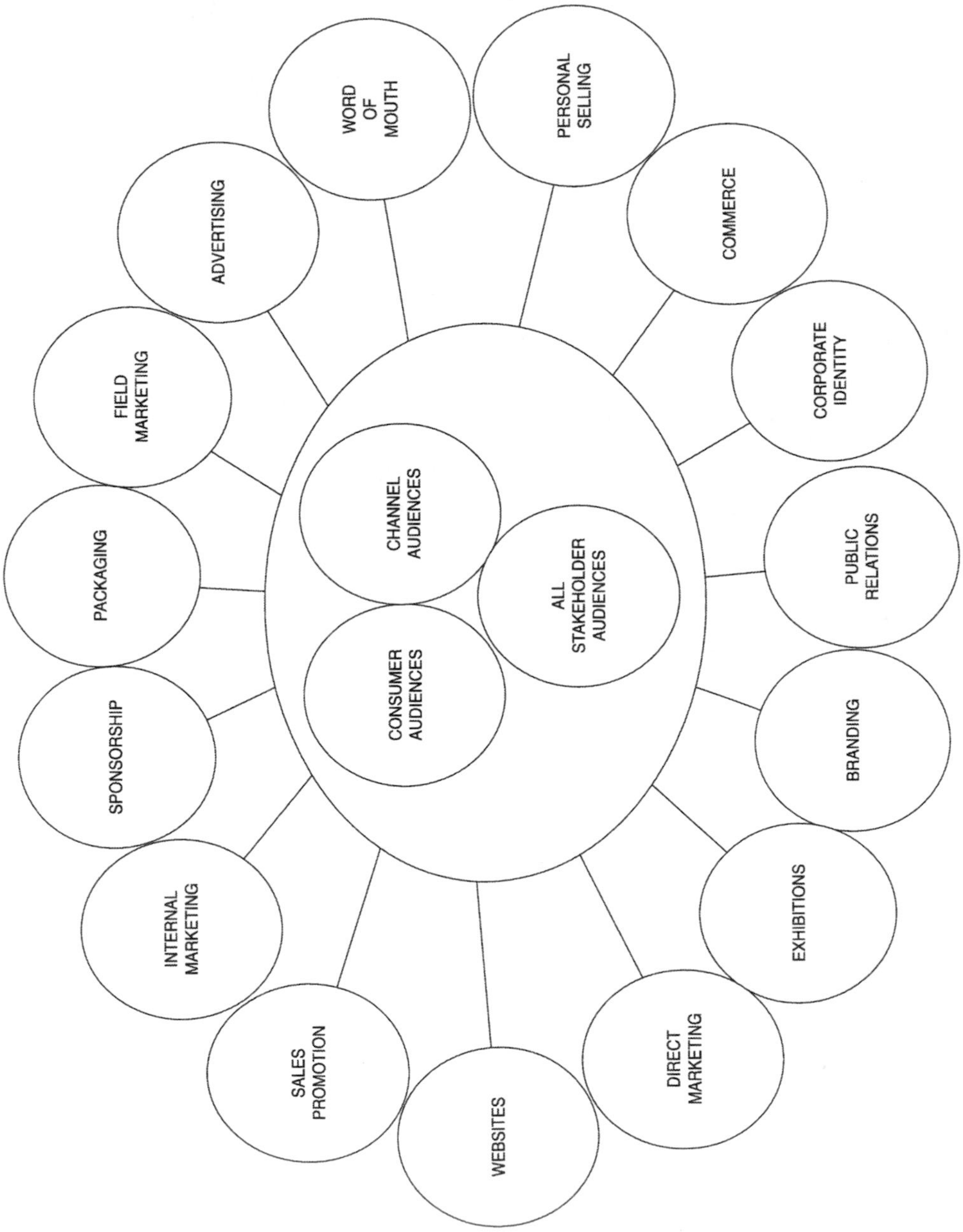

CHANNEL AUDIENCES
CONSUMER AUDIENCES
ALL STAKEHOLDER AUDIENCES

WORD OF MOUTH
PERSONAL SELLING
COMMERCE
CORPORATE IDENTITY
PUBLIC RELATIONS
BRANDING
EXHIBITIONS
DIRECT MARKETING
WEBSITES
SALES PROMOTION
INTERNAL MARKETING
SPONSORSHIP
PACKAGING
FIELD MARKETING
ADVERTISING

If the sheer range of tools available seems a bit intimidating, we have bad news – and good news.

- **The range of promotional tools and media continues to grow.** The variety of media has increased (or been fragmented) in many ways. There are more print media (publications aimed at more and more highly defined niche segments) and more broadcast media (with developments in satellite, cable and digital TV, DVD, Webcasting and Podcasting and so on). Marketing messages are being put on more and more surfaces, from buildings to tabletops to Post-It Notes – and even people! Technological developments have created new one-to-one marketing tools such as the Internet, mobile phone text messaging and database marketing.
- **There is no 'one best mix' for any given message in any given market.** While some communication tools may be identified as more or less effective in different contexts, selecting and combining promotional tools is still very much an art – *not* a science!

WORK BASED PROJECT TIP

application

Which of the tools in Figure 8.1 does your work organisation, or other organisation that you are studying, use? What audience(s) is each tool designed to address?

Which tools are particularly used to address shareholder, supplier, intermediary, pressure group and wider community audiences?

We can now add a little more detail to each of the promotional areas the CIM specify within the syllabus.

3.2.1 Sales Promotion

KEY CONCEPT

Concept

Sales promotion is 'a range of tactical marketing techniques... to add value to a product or service, in order to achieve a specific sales and marketing objective'. (Institute of Sales Promotion)

Sales promotion activity is aimed at the customer (intermediary or consumer) market, typically in order to **increase short-term sales volume**, by encouraging first time, repeat or multiple purchase within a stated time frame ('offer closes on such-and-such a date'). It seeks to do this by **adding value** to the product or service: customers are offered something extra – or the chance to obtain something extra – if they purchase, purchase more or purchase again.

The objectives of sales promotion, stated in broad terms, may be:

- To increase **awareness and interest** among target audiences: the incentive or added value element may increase engagement, and competition-style promotions may require customers to research the product to provide answers, say
- To **motivate** customers to try a product or switch from competing brands
- To **smooth seasonal fluctuations** in demand, via incentives to purchase in off-peak periods, say
- To **foster customer retention**, by encouraging repeat or multiple purchase; offering opportunities to try related products (supporting cross-selling); and capturing customer data (supporting relationship marketing)

Techniques of sales promotion

Consumer sales promotion techniques include:

- **Price promotions:** eg discounted selling price or additional product on *current* purchase, or coupons (on packs or advertisements) offering discounts on *next* purchase
- **'Gift with purchase'** or **'premium' promotions**: the consumer receives a bonus, gift or refund on purchase or repeat purchase, or on sending in tokens or proofs of multiple purchases
- **Competitions and prizes**: eg entry in prize draws or 'lucky purchase' prizes, often used both to stimulate purchase (more chances to win) and to capture customer data
- **Frequent user (loyalty) incentives**: eg air miles programmes or points-for-prizes reward cards

MARKETING AT WORK

application 

- **Coca-Cola** made glamour the theme of its 2002 sales promotion for its Diet Coke brand. The on-pack promotion, 'silver spending spree', featured an instant-win top prize of £100,000 and smaller cash prizes and trials with Cannons Health Clubs. All Diet Coke bottles were silver during the campaign. Large outdoor teaser ads supported the promotion, with strap lines such as: 'Money is the root of all evil? I'll take my chances.' These were followed by huge outdoor posters and press ads highlighting the prizes, placed in fashion and style magazines such as *Vogue* and *Glamour*, targeting consumer aspirations.
- As an example of how promotional offerings can be tailored for synergy with the brand, consider cereal maker **Kelloggs**. Its Special K brand, aimed mainly at 18-35 year old women who care about health and fitness, did a promotion offering a free hour with a personal trainer, and a pedometer. Sugar Puffs, on the other hand, are marketed to children, so the offer was a free swim voucher.
- At the other end of the scale, the most notorious cautionary tale in sales promotion is provided by the experience of **Hoover**. In 1992, Hoover and Your Leisure offered two free flights (to Europe and the US) to any customer who spent a minimum of £100 on Hoover products. Spot the mistake! Leonard Hadley, Chairman of Hoover's US parent company, Maytag, had to admit that the offer was like 'a bad accident... You can't determine what was in the driver's mind.' The promotion attracted more than double the anticipated applications, leading to the dismissal of three senior managers and a £19 million provision to cover the costs. The promotion had not been insured against unforeseen demand. The bargain was just too good. And the second-hand vacuum cleaner market would take a long time to recover from the over-supply!

Trade promotions are directed at trade customers (intermediaries), to encourage them to stock or sell more of a product or service (sometimes called a 'push' marketing strategy). Techniques include:

- **Monetary incentives** such as increased trade discounts, extended credit or 'baker's dozen' packs (13 items/packs for the price of 12)
- **Collaborative advertising and promotion**: sharing costs with the dealer or retailer to promote both the brand and the stockist
- **Point-of-sale support**: supplying display materials, information and merchandising
- **Competitions and awards** for the most successful dealers or sales people
- **Business gifts**: linked to sales or purely relational (eg diaries, calendars and other Christmas gifts – although these may be subject to ethical guidelines)
- **Consumer promotions** demonstrating an aggressive 'pull' strategy which offers the intermediary good sales

MARKETING AT WORK

'When French and other European companies want to promote their brand or services, they are increasingly doing so with computer accessories, especially mice and mouse pads, seen as an effective and long-lasting way of delivering a message and thanking a client.

When companies offer promotional gifts at holiday times and for corporate events, they still prefer 'classics', like bags, pens, lights, watches, T-shirts and other clothing, and lightweight luggage (imprinted with company logos), in that order. Objects for the office rank seventh.

However, bucking the trend, companies specialising in computer accessories have seen enormous increases in turnover. From the point of view of the end user, the target of a promotional campaign, mice and mouse pads are practical and fit neatly into office spaces crowded with other corporate gifts like mugs and promotional gadgets. Indeed, if high enough in quality and design, mice and mats become like fashion statements, ogled by colleagues and other business associates, thus extending the reach of the message.

For the company promoting its brand or services, mice and particularly mouse pads contain plenty of space to insert logos, attention-grabbing graphics or images, along with name cards, contact details and other corporation, product or service information.'

International Market News, 2004

Evaluation of sales promotion

Sales promotion is limited in its scope, aims and target audiences (intermediary and consumer customers). For these uses, its advantages and disadvantages can be summarised as follows.

Advantages	Disadvantages
Short-term measurable boost in sales	May pose fulfilment challenges (if over-subscribed)
Push tactic to gain distributor and POS support	May suggest incentive required for purchase to be worthwhile
Flexible for collaborative promotions and creative synergy	Does not necessarily create brand loyalty (if consumers switch from promotion to promotion)
Potential source of customer data (eg through competition entry)	Product given away or discounted: impact on bottom line profit

ASSESSMENT TIP

concept

It is worth being aware of the potential for confusion between the terms '**promotion**' (used as another way of saying 'marketing communications' in general) and '**sales promotion**' (which is a specialist term reserved for the techniques described here). If the word promotion comes up in an assignment brief, remember to check the context carefully – and to answer the requirement set.

MARKETING AT WORK

Expedia, the online travel company, is bolstering its database and third-party partnership ties by launching its biggest online voucher drive to date.

For one month, Expedia customers will have access to exclusive promotions from JohnLewis.com, Marksandspencer.com, Travelex, Boots.com, Fitness First, Airport Express, Body Shop, Addison Lee hire cars, Lonelyplanet.com, Kodak's Ofoto.com, Rohan and Holiday Extras.

The promotion will develop Expedia's marketing database, while its partner brands will also collect details from purchasers of their products. All vouchers will be redeemable either online or in-store.

The campaign... will be supported with direct mail. The move follows Expedia's largest integrated campaign to date, aiming to treble its database and lift flagging sales. SMS and DRTV campaigns are not being ruled out as a way to drive traffic to www.expedia.co.uk, and the company is working to improve its e-marketing.

An Expedia spokesman says: 'We wanted to create a campaign that rewarded our customers, incentivised sales and attracted new purchases. The promotion achieves this, while developing strategic relationships with major on- and offline brands.'

Mad.co.uk, 2004

3.2.2 Public relations

The scope of PR is very broad, but some frequently used techniques are as follows.

Consumer marketing support	• Publicity: generating editorial coverage in the press • Consumer and trade press releases (to secure coverage) • Sending product samples for media (or consumer) trial and review • Product placement (in TV, movies) • Product/service literature (including brochures, video and CD-ROM) • Special events (eg celebrity store openings, product launch events, in-store competitions) • Consumer exhibitions and shows • Customer magazines, e-zines, newsletters, blogs • Sport, arts and community sponsorship • Publicity 'stunts' (attention-grabbing events to gain media coverage)
B2B communication	• Corporate identity (logos, liveries, house style of communications) • Corporate literature, website, videos • Trade exhibitions and conferences • Trade and general press relations • Corporate hospitality and gifts
Internal/employee communication	• In-house magazines, employee newsletters and corporate intranet (internal-access website) • Recruitment exhibitions and conferences • Direct employee communications: briefings, consultation meetings, works councils and so on

Corporate, external and public affairs	• Corporate literature and website • Corporate social responsibility and community involvement programmes: liaison with pressure groups, community representatives, local chamber of commerce • Sponsorship of arts, sporting and community organisations and events (often as part of a CSR profile) • Media relations: networking and image management through trade, local, national (and possibly international) press • Offering spokespeople and 'experts' for media interviews, consultation or authorship of articles • Local/central government and industry/trade lobbying, to protect or promote corporate/industry interests • Crisis and issues management: minimising the negative impacts of problems and bad publicity by managing media and public relations
Financial public relations	• Financial media relations • Design of annual and interim financial reports for shareholders • Facility visits for analysts, brokers, fund managers etc • Shareholder meetings and communications

The advantages and disadvantages of PR as a promotional tool can be summarised as follows.

Advantages	Disadvantages
Raises awareness of wider audiences	The organisation can't control editorial content or guarantee coverage when desired (unlike advertising)
Builds corporate identity, supporting relationship with stakeholders (internal and external)	Media have their own agenda (circulation/ratings, public information) which may not always support positive publicity for the organisation
Relatively low cost (no media costs)	Difficult to measure effectiveness/impact
Can add legitimacy (implication of endorsement or recommendation), word-of-mouth promotion and goodwill (support in times of difficulty)	There is a risk of poor publicity and negative associations – as well as positive ones. (Yes, there is such a thing as bad publicity!)
Supports advertising, sales promotion and personal selling	

3.2.3 Personal selling

Kotler *et al* (1999) identify a number of activities that the sales force might perform.

Prospecting	Gathering leads and referrals for other potential customers
Communicating	Communicating information to existing and potential customers about the company's products and services
Selling	Establishing rapport with the customer, defining the need/problem, persuasively presenting product benefits, dealing with resistance and objections, negotiating terms (if required) and closing the sale
Servicing	Providing services to the customer, such as giving technical assistance, monitoring and replenishing stock, arranging finance or expediting delivery
Information gathering	Acting as a key source of marketing and competitor intelligence and feedback to the company, as the main direct link to the customer

If the organisation relies on consumer advertising to draw customers into stores to ask for its brands, the role of the sales force may primarily be **servicing**: ensuring that retailers carry sufficient stock, negotiating adequate shelf space and so on. In high-value consumer goods/services markets (such as car or insurance sales), where personal information and persuasion may be required to close the sale, the **selling** role may be paramount. In B2B markets, the relationship between client and sales representative (or account handler) is more complex, important and on-going.

Personal selling within the promotional mix

Personal selling is part of the co-ordinated promotional mix. It will need to be supported by a range of other marketing communication activities:

- **Product advertising, public relations and sales promotion**, drawing consumer attention and interest to the product and its sources *and* motivating retailers to stock and sell the product
- **'Leads'** (interested prospective customers) generated by contacts and enquiries made through exhibitions, promotional competitions, enquiry coupons and other methods
- **Informational tools** such as brochures and presentation kits. These can add interest and variety to sales presentations, and leave customers with helpful reminders and information.
- **Sales support information**: customer/segment profiling; competitor intelligence; access to customer contact/transaction histories and product data and so on. (This is an important aspect of Customer Relationship Management, enabling field sales teams to facilitate immediate response and transactions – without time-lags to obtain the information required.)

Evaluation of personal selling

Personal selling is an effective tool for relationship development, since it fosters deepens personal contacts between individual sellers and buyers. It is highly **interactive and flexible**, enabling the salesperson to customise the message to the audience's immediate and individual interests, needs and concerns. The two-way nature of the process allows dialogue, question-and-answer and feedback. Personal selling enables more of a **collaborative approach** to defining and creating customer value, and is therefore most appropriate for high-value consumer purchases, and for business-to-business (B2B) relationships.

The main disadvantage is that this is labour intensive, and therefore **costly**. A salesperson can only interact with one customer at a time. The organisation will have to make a value judgement between the effectiveness of relationship development and persuasion – and the relative expense.

Personal selling is often appropriate in **B2B markets**, where there are fewer, higher-value customers who are looking for a more complex total offering tailored to a more specific set of requirements. Personal selling allows a partnership relationship to be established which:

- Adds value by allowing customer needs to be met more flexibly
- Allows sales force effort to be targeted at high-return relationships; and
- Reinforces the 'inertia' of industrial markets, making it hard for buyers to switch suppliers, and creating loyalty and inter-dependency over time.

It should also be noted that although 'selling' will not be relevant to all stakeholder relationships, there may be elements of **negotiation** and/or **persuasion** involved in forming relationships and exercising influence in relation to non-customer stakeholder groups. A **one-to-one discussion approach**, similar to personal selling, may be used for:

- **Clarification and discussion of issues** eg with representatives of pressure groups
- **Supplier relationships**: eg negotiation of requirements and terms, contract and relationship management, or dispute resolution. (This is really personal selling seen from the customer's side.)
- **Internal marketing**: eg one-to-one interviews with employees or their representatives, for motivation, consultation, briefings, change management, conflict resolution and so on.

3.2.4 Web based and digital technology

Internet technology can also be used strategically to enable communication with particular audiences.

- The **Internet** itself enables public access to an organisation's website.
- An **intranet** refers to a private internal network which is normally used to enable communication with employees.
- **Extranets** allow particular external audiences such as distributors, suppliers and certain customers access to an organisation's facilities.

The Internet offers two main marketing opportunities, namely **distribution and communication**. The ability to reach customers directly and so avoid many channel intermediaries reduces transaction costs and is a prime goal for most organisations.

The use of the Internet as a communications medium is equally attractive. It is more than a medium as it **facilitates interactivity and a two-way dialogue** that no other method of communication can support. Unlike other forms of communication, dialogue is induced by the customer, the speed and duration of the communication is **customer controlled** and the intensity of the relationship (with the online brand), is again customer managed. All the traditional tools of the promotional mix can be deployed over the Internet, with varying degrees of success. E-mail campaigns and e-newsletters are cost effective means of communicating with stakeholders who have expressed an interest in receiving these communications.

- **Interactive catalogues and newsletters** can be emailed, downloaded or viewed on-line, to convey information to target audiences on topics of interest to them (new products, industry developments, exhibitions, sales promotions, training opportunities for employees and so on) with links to related website pages if stakeholders want to follow up on particular items. These approaches allow complex data to be made available to stakeholders, with the element of choice reinforcing their interest and motivation at the follow-up stage.
- **SMS text messaging** is a huge advertising growth area, and the integration of digital mobile phone networks with the Internet has also facilitated a range of m-commerce (mobile commerce) applications. SMS is low-cost, easy-to-use and highly personal and compelling (especially in the always-connected youth market). It is used for relational marketing by brands including Cadbury, Smirnoff, Avon, British Airways, Nestlé, Pepsi, Haagen-Daaz and even Liverpool FC.
- **Web advertising**. The Internet is a major advertising medium, through dedicated corporate and brand websites; pop-up and banner/button advertising (giving a click-through link to a website); and ranking on Internet search engines (to increase site exposure). The forecast global penetration of the Internet over the next few years would give it a significantly larger (international, 24/7) audience than any of the TV networks, print media outlets or other advertising vehicles. Studies have shown that brand awareness increases some five percent after using banner advertising. The other plus point for web advertising is the ability to monitor traffic, gathering information on users' interests and browsing habits, and placing 'cookies' on their computers to enable customisation of future contacts.

3.2.5 Direct Marketing

Direct marketing encompasses a wide range of media and distribution opportunities.

- Television
- Radio
- Direct mail
- Direct response advertising
- Telemarketing
- Statement stuffers
- Inserts
- Take-ones
- Electronic media
- Door to door
- Mail order
- Computerised home shopping
- Home shopping networks

In developing a comprehensive direct marketing strategy, organisations will often utilise a range of different yet complementary techniques.

Direct mail tends to be the main medium of direct response advertising. It has become the synonym for it. The reasons for this is that other major media, newspapers and magazines, are familiar to people in advertising in other contexts. Newspaper ads can include coupons to fill out and return, and radio and TV can give a phone number to ring (DRTV is now very common). However, direct mail has a number of strengths as a direct response medium.

- The advertiser can target down to **individual level**.
- The communication can **be personalised**. Known data about the individual can be used, while modern printing techniques mean that parts of a letter can be altered to accommodate this.
- The medium is good **for reinforcing interest stimulated by other media** such as TV. It can supply the response mechanism (a coupon) that is not yet available in that medium.
- The opportunity to use **different creative formats** is almost unlimited.
- **Testing potential is sophisticated**: a limited number of items can be sent out to a 'test' cell and the results can be evaluated. As success is achieved, so the mailing campaign can be rolled out.

The cornerstone upon which the direct mailing is based, however, is **the mailing list**. It is far and away the most important element in the list of variables, which also include the offer, timing and creative content.

A comprehensive customer database is an essential element to direct marketing because it is an efficient means of maintaining a mailing list with the most up to date information about specific customers. A **database** is a collection of available information on past and current customers together with future prospects, structured to allow for the implementation of effective marketing strategies. Database marketing is a customer-oriented approach to marketing, and its special power lies in the techniques it uses to harness the capabilities of computer and telecommunications technology. Building accurate and up-to-date profiles of existing customers enables the company to:

- Extend help to a company's target audience
- Stimulate further demand
- Stay close to them: recording and keeping an electronic database memory of customers and prospects and of all communications and commercial contacts helps to improve all future contacts

MARKETING AT WORK

application

Database applications

Computers now have the capacity to operate in three new ways that will enable businesses to operate in a totally different dimension.

'Customers can be tracked individually. Thousands of pieces of information about each of millions of customers can be stored and accessed economically.

Companies and customers can interact through, for example, phones, mail, e-mail and interactive kiosks. ... for the first time since the invention of mass marketing, 'companies will be hearing from individual customers in a cost-efficient manner'.

Computers allow companies to match their production processes to what they learn from their individual customers – a process known as 'mass customisation' which can be seen as 'the cost-efficient mass production of products and services in lot sizes of one'.

There are many examples of companies which are already employing or experimenting with these ideas. In the US Levi Strauss, the jeans company, is taking measurements and preferences from female customers to produce exact-fitting garments. The approach 'offers the company tremendous opportunities for building learning relationships'.

The Ritz-Carlton hotel chain has trained staff throughout the organisation to jot down customer details at every opportunity on a 'guest preference pad'.

The result could be the following: 'You stay at the Ritz-Carlton in Cancun, Mexico, call room service for dinner, and request an ice cube in your glass of white wine. Months later, when you stay at the Ritz-Carlton in Naples, Florida, and order a glass of white wine from room service, you will almost certainly be asked if you would like an ice cube in it.'

4 Managing and monitoring marketing communications

In terms of managing an overall communications plan, the following model outlines the additional stages.

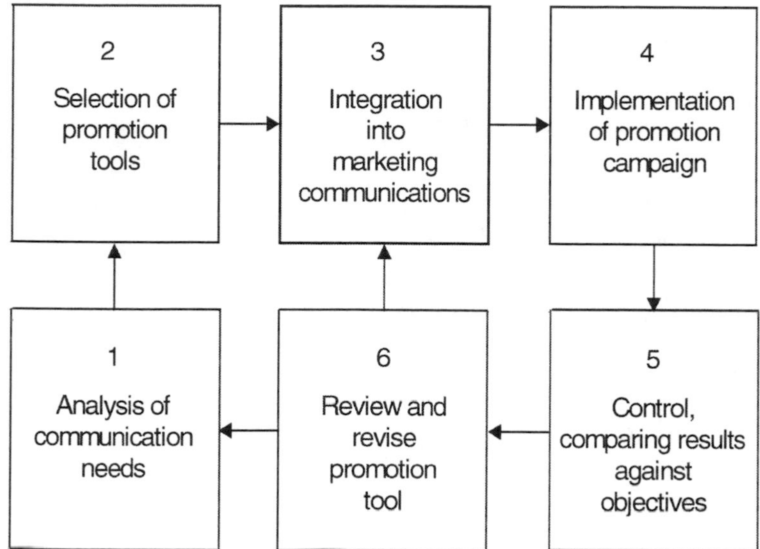

Stage 1 – **Analysing communication needs**- this will involve a consideration of the target audience, and the promotional/communication objectives.

Stage 2 – **Selection of the promotional tools**- one or several promotional tools may be applicable within different contexts. the cost, ability to effectively reach the target audience and relevance to the message will determine those chosen.

Stage 3 – **Integration into marketing communications**- there may already exist a communications campaign which the message may need to be integrated within. In these circumstances, the messages should complement the existing campaign. If it is a new campaign the messages chosen should take into account the business and promotional objectives which will include a consideration of the effect on the organisations reputation, corporate image and stakeholder expectations.

Stage 4 – **Implementation of promotional campaign** – this will involve co-ordinating and working with any external agencies to help originate and place the message. During the implementation stage it is important to carefully manage the budget of the campaign and ensure that costs are allocated correctly. Many marketers will use Excel spreadsheet type packages to keep abreast of costs and spending. We will discuss this further in section 4.

Stages 5 & 6 – **Control, comparing results against objectives/ Review and revise**- it is essential to measure the success of a campaign so that it can be revised where relevant and that future campaigns are improved. We will discuss this further in section 4.

KEY CONCEPT

concept

To **control** is to measure results against targets and take any action necessary to adjust performance.

The marketing control process can be broken down into four stages.

- Development of objectives and strategies eg 'We want to increase our market share'
- Establishment of standards eg 'We want to increase market share to 15% by the end of 20XX'
- Evaluation of performance eg 'Have we increased our market share to 15%?'
- Corrective action eg 'No, we have not. Maybe we need to reduce our prices.'

Overall marketing effectiveness can be difficult to measure. Audits, financial measures, targets and information gathering (such as customer feedback) can help. Where possible, performance should be measured in quantitative terms because these are less subjective and less liable to bias. The following are some possible techniques that relate to promotional measurement.

Personal selling – Sales increases

Public relations – Editorial coverage

Direct marketing – Enquiries generated

Advertising – Brand awareness

Sales promotion – Coupons redeemed

Exhibitions – Contacts made

4.1 Methods for measuring success

MARKETING AT WORK

application

Examples of marketing measures

Feedback information	Standards	Control actions
Sales figures	Against budget	Simulate or dampen down demand
Complaints	Number, frequency, seriousness	Improving 'customer focus'
Competitors	Relative to us	Attack/defence strategies
Costs/profitability	Ratios	Cost cutting exercises
Corporate image	Attitude measures, satisfaction surveys	Internal/external communications

4.2 Budget management

KEY CONCEPTS

concept

A **budget** is a consolidated statement of the resources required to achieve desired objectives, or to implement planned activities. It is a planning and control tool relevant to all aspects of management activities.

A **forecast** is an estimate of what might happen in the future.

In terms of measuring marketing effectiveness, **budgeted** results often comprise:

(a) Targets for the overall **financial objectives** and other strategy objectives such as productivity targets
(b) Subsidiary **financial** targets, including the sales budget and marketing expenditure budget
(c) Product-market strategy targets
(d) Targets for each element of the **marketing mix**

Budgets perform a dual role.

(a) They **incorporate forecasting** and planning information
(b) They **incorporate control measures**, because they plan how resources are to be used to achieve the targets

Marketing costs analysis can be a highly detailed process and it may be difficult to allocate costs to specific marketing activities (especially staff costs, when staff may be working on several different areas at the same time). It is however important that for the purposes of avoiding escalating marketing spend a careful check of actual spend against forecast is kept. Generally, marketers use simple Excel spreadsheets for such purposes with the budget split into specific marketing activities. The expense budgets related to promotional activities include those listed in the following table.

(a) *Selling expenses budget*

- Salaries and commission
- Materials, literature, samples
- Travelling (car cost, petrol, insurance) and entertaining
- Staff recruitment and selection and training
- Telephones and telegrams, postage
- After-sales service
- Royalties/patents
- Office rent and rates, lighting, heating
- Office equipment
- Credit costs, bad debts

(b) *Advertising budget*

- Trade journal – space
- Prestige media – space
- PR space (costs of releases, entertainment
- Blocks and artwork
- Advertising agents commission
- Staff salaries, office costs
- Posters
- Cinema
- TV
- Signs

(c) *Sales promotion budget*

- Exhibitions: space, equipment, staff, transport, hotels, bar
- Literature: leaflets, catalogues
- Samples/working models
- Point of sale display, window or showroom displays
- Special offers
- Direct mail shots – enclose, postage, design costs

There are several methods of setting the **communications budget** that have been identified.

Competitive parity	Fixing promotional expenditure in relation to the expenditure incurred by competitors. (This is unsatisfactory because it presupposes that the competitor's decision must be a good one.)
The task method (or objective and task method)	The marketing task for the organisation is set and a promotional budget is prepared which will help to ensure that this objective is achieved. A problem occurs if the objective is achieved only by paying out more on promotion than the extra profits obtained would justify.
Communication stage models	These are based on the idea that the link between promotion and sales cannot be measured directly, but can be measured by means of intermediate stages (for example, increase in awareness, comprehension, and then intention to buy).
All you can afford	Crude and unscientific, but commonly used. The firm simply takes a view on what it thinks it can afford to spend on promotion, given that it would like to spend as much as it can.
Investment	The advertising and promotions budget can be designed around the amount felt necessary to maintain a certain brand value.
Rule-of-thumb, non-scientific methods	These include setting expenditure at a certain percentage of sales or profits.

WORK BASED PROJECT TIP

application

Find out what monitoring and control activities are in operation within your own organisation. Evaluate whether or not these are appropriate. How would you make improvements?

Learning objective review

Learning objectives	Covered
1 Explain the importance, nature and scope of communication	☑ Importance of communication ☑ Models of communication, AIDA, Schramm ☑ Noise and distortion ☑ Encoding messages for a target audience
2 Explain the tools of written, verbal and non-verbal communication	☑ Business formats: letters; memos; email; meetings; reports ☑ Non verbal communication- kinetics, meta and paralanguage
3 Evaluate a range of promotional marketing communication activities and the processes involved in undertaking the campaign	☑ Planning communications ☑ Recap tools - Sales promotion, PR, Personal selling ☑ Web based – Internet, Intranet & extranet e newsletters, email, SMS mesaging ☑ Databases to assist direct marketing
4 Explain how to manage and monitor marketing communications	☑ Managing a communications budget for a specific task ☑ Monitoring and measuring tactical communications campaigns

References

Ackoff, R.I. (1987) '*Mission Statements*' Planning Review, vol 15 (4) pp 30-32.

Blythe, J. (2006) Principles and Practice of Marketing, Thompson, London, .

Jobber, D. (2007) Principles and Practice of Marketing 5th edition, McGraw Hill, London.

Kotler P, Armstrong G, Meggs D, Bradbury E and Grech J (1999) Marketing: An Introduction. Prentice Hall Australia, Sydney.

Schramm, W.(1961)"*How Communication Works*," The Process and Effects of Mass Communication, editor, Wilbur Schramm pp. 5-6, The University of Illinois Press, Urbana.

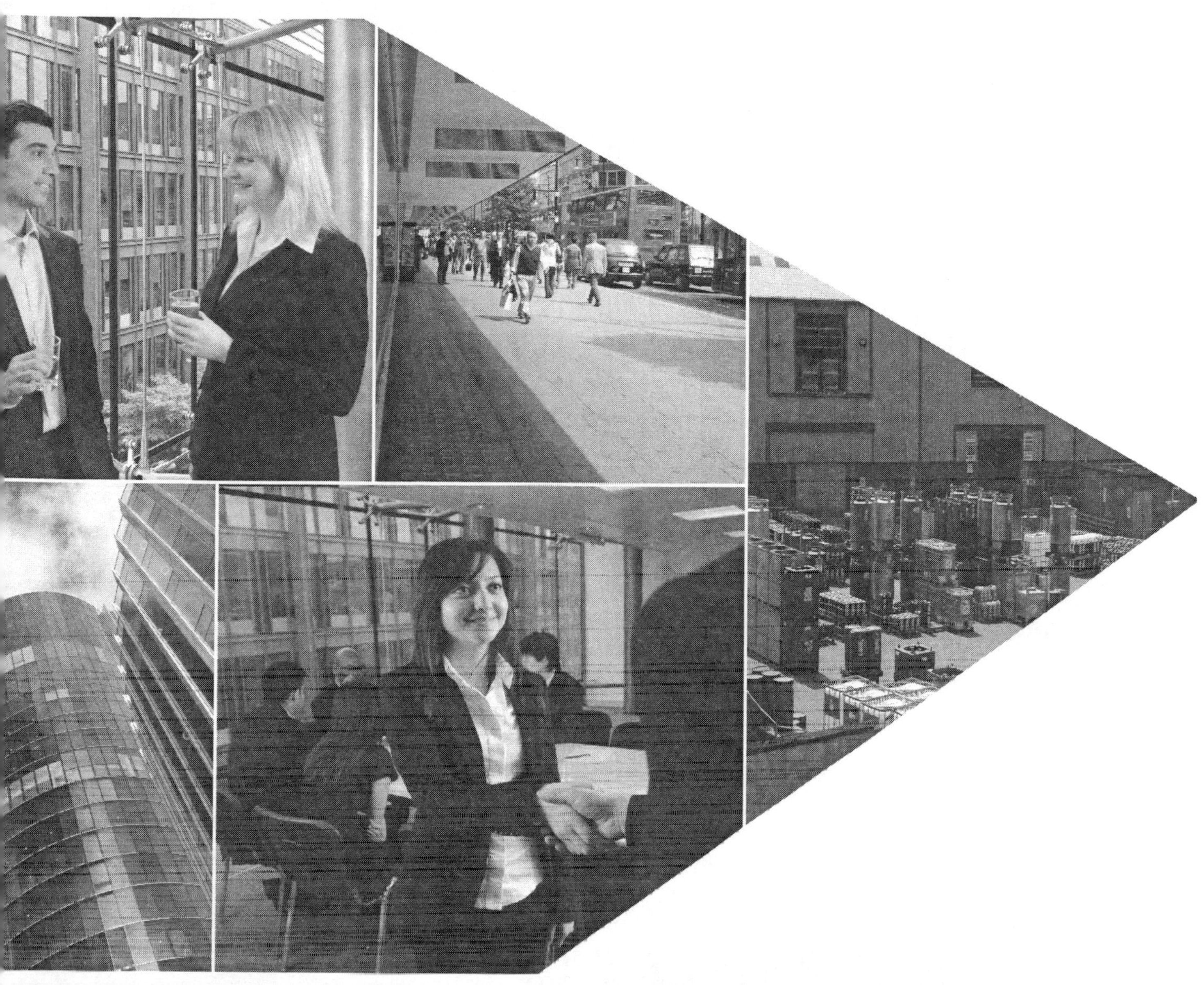

Chapter 8
Effective customer service

Topic list

1 The importance of customer care
2 Customer service
3 Seeking customer feedback
4 Setting up a customer care programme
5 Databases to assist customer service

Introduction

In this final chapter of the study workbook, we build on several areas covered within the study workbook so far in order to highlight the concept of customer service. An awareness of customer service is vital for the marketer and we have already discussed:

- The increasing **importance of the customer** for organisational survival and competitive advantage
- The nature and importance of **customer focus**: seeing marketing processes and practices from the customer's point of view, in order to meet their needs more appropriately
- The need to retain customers and win their **loyalty**: the key focus of **relationship marketing**.

We also outlined how customer retention and loyalty can be achieved: by creating customer **satisfaction** and by maintaining on-going, consistent customer **contacts**. These elements are integral to the concept of **customer care**, which embraces both customer service and customer communications.

In this chapter, we begin by looking at the nature and importance of customer care, and then focus on approaches to achieving it, through quality management and customer service. We will suggest a systematic approach to implementing a Customer Care programme in an organisation. We conclude the chapter by looking specifically at how customer care and customer service can be facilitated by the use of technology such as databases.

By the end of the chapter you will be able to:

Learning objectives	Syllabus link
1 Describe the concept of customer care and customer service in terms of how this helps to build relationships	4.1, 4.2
2 Describe how to set up a customer care programme	4.3
3 Explain the importance of collecting information and the measure used to monitor customer service	4.4, 4.5
4 Explain how IT and databases are essential to customer care and customer service	4.6

1 The importance of customer care

Customer care aims to close the gap between customers' expectations and their experience in every aspect of the customer/supplier relationship. It is an important source of product/service differentiation, competitive advantage and customer retention and loyalty.

KEY CONCEPT

concept

Customer care is 'a fundamental approach to the standards of service quality' which 'covers every aspect of a company's operations from the design of a product or service to how it is packaged, delivered and serviced'. (Clutterbuck, 2001).

The term '**customer care**' is often used interchangeably with '**customer service**'. The latter term, however, originally had a much narrower focus on order-cycle related activities: it is only comparatively recently, with the recognition of customer focus at the strategic level, that it has been extended to cover activities throughout the organisation at pre-, during- and post-transaction stages. In this chapter, we refer to customer care in this wider sense, and to customer service in the context of direct transaction-based contacts between organisational staff and customers.

1.1 Key phases for service delivery

Effective customer care requires the integration of corporate vision and values, internal human resource systems and external customer communication systems, with a view to commercial success.

The following diagram highlights the key elements required for service delivery.

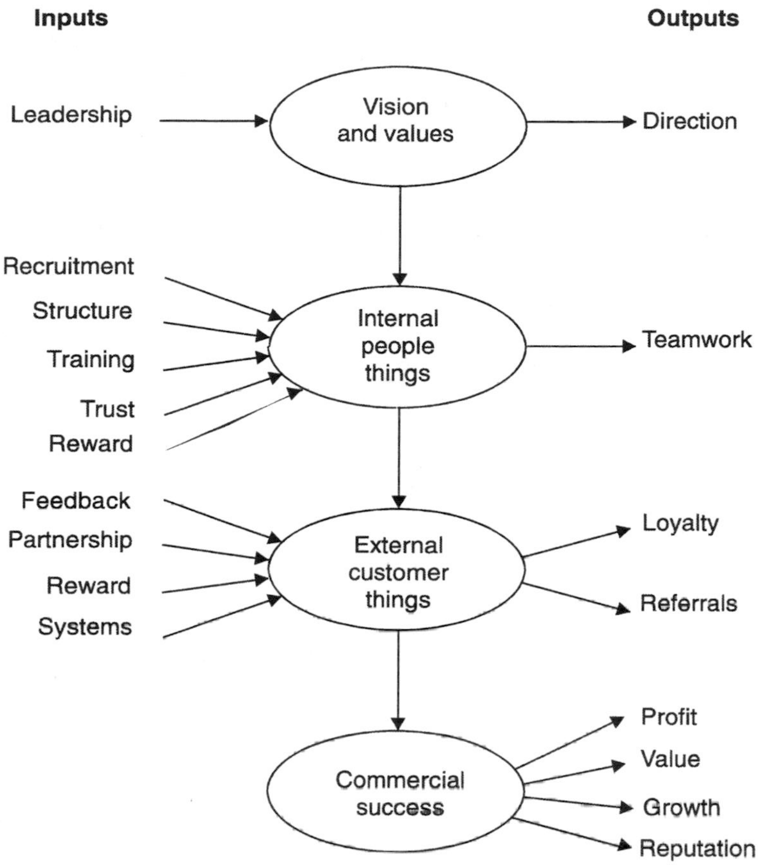

1.1.1 Vision and values

A 'fundamental approach' integrating all aspects of an organisation's activities requires a clear vision, leadership that models customer-focused values, and a culture that reinforces those values through its selection, appraisal and reward systems, and the messages it gives its employees at every level.

1.1.2 Internal customer relations

The satisfaction of *external* customers is the result of a range of satisfying *internal* relationships and transactions between colleagues and departments. Encouraging staff to consider the needs of their internal customers ('the next person to handle your work') will help to foster quality and service at the interface with external customers. Key factors in managing the quality of internal service operations include:

- The recruitment of skilled customer-facing people
- The supply of appropriate (and generous) training
- The empowerment of staff to take decisions that will attract and keep customers
- The reward and recognition of staff who deliver outstanding service

1.1.3 External customer relations

The delivery of customer care depends on:

- Gathering, analysing, communicating and acting upon customer **feedback**. Feedback enables an organisation to remain customer focused and to use the customer's experiences to trigger and drive necessary changes and improvements.

- Establishing a **partnership** approach to relationships with customers (and suppliers) in order to identify and meet needs more effectively at all links in the value-delivery chain.
- Reinforcing customer loyalty with **incentives and rewards**, to show that the organisation values its 'valued customers'.
- Establishing efficient **customer-friendly systems**. It is no good expecting staff to give great service to customers if the systems, procedures, technology and information flows do not support their efforts.

WORK BASED PROJECT TIP

application

What practical ways can you think of to **empower** front-line staff in your organisation to maintain customer care and service?

1.1.4 Commercial success

It must always be remembered that the point of the exercise (at least for commercial organisations) is profitability, survival and (usually) growth. Good customer care is not an end in itself. As we will see in Section 3 below, it represents:

- A **differentiating** competitive advantage: part of the package of benefits that helps to attract customers
- A powerful mechanism for sustaining **customer loyalty** – because retaining customers is more profitable than winning new ones.

1.2 Customer care and relationship marketing

Successful relationship marketing requires the integration of **customer service**, **quality** and **marketing** (Christopher et al 1992) which is the concept of **customer care**.

We introduced **relationship marketing**in previous chapters as an approach to marketing that aims at keeping customers – rather than merely attracting them. Relationship marketing involves:

- **Customer/supplier partnership**: entering into dialogue with customers to create mutually beneficial (win-win) exchanges
- **Personalisation of contact**: making customers feel that their business is valued and that their individual needs are being recognised and catered for
- **Continual deepening and improving of the relationship**: making sure that every contact with the brand satisfies – or delights – the customer.

Kanter (1991) describes five challenges for companies that want to develop genuinely close links with their customers.

- Understanding who the customer is
- Making the customer a member of one's own organisation
- Making the customer visible to all employees
- Rewarding faithful customers
- Having the flexibility to handle critical incidents

1.3 Customer care and the organisation

From the organisation's point of view, customer care is:

- Part of the overall package of **purchase benefits** that its product/service offers, and therefore an important part of the marketing mix in attracting customers

- A source of **differentiation** from competing products (particularly where globalisation has diluted the significance of product features and functionality), which may also attract customers
- A mechanism of **customer retention**, by creating 'pull' factors and minimising 'push' factors to make it more likely that customers will stay with the brand than go elsewhere.
- A way of creating **customer loyalty**: engaging customers' emotional involvement with the brand, making them feel valued and making on-going contact from the organisation (as part of a relationship marketing strategy) more welcome.
- A way of maximising positive (and minimising negative) **'word of mouth' promotion** by customers on the basis of their experience.
- A source of vital **feedback information** on customers' expectations and experience, to support more effective and efficient marketing in future. (We discuss this further below.)
- A source of **employee satisfaction** that enhances performance and enables the organisation to retain valuable human resources.
- A source of positive **employer branding** that enhances the organisation's ability to attract high-quality, customer-focused staff.

A survey by the Chartered Institute of Management highlighted the following key benefits of improving customer care.

Benefit	% of managers citing benefit
Retention of existing customers	68
Enhanced reputation of the organisation	58
Competitive advantage in the marketplace	53
Attraction of new customers	43
Increased profitability	28
Improved staff morale and loyalty	25
Cost efficiency	11

1.3.1 Internal Customer Care

Note that customer care is a source of **internal customer** satisfaction, commitment and retention – as well as external.

(a) A focus on (valued) customers adds value, responsibility and significance to jobs throughout the organisation. Peters and Waterman (1982) found that quality and customer-focused values was a key source of employee morale and motivation. Involving employees in the development and implementation of customer care initiatives (for example, through suggestion schemes, or quality/customer care circles or task forces) enhances this effect.

(b) Training and empowerment add to employees' flexibility, competence and employability, enhancing the organisation's human resource.

(c) Supportive customer care initiatives (including managing customer expectations, improving systems and responding to customer feedback) enhances the ability of staff to service customer needs effectively. This minimises the frustration and stress that otherwise leads to high staff turnover in customer service departments.

1.3.2 Not just for consumers!

These customer care imperatives apply not just to consumer (B2C) markets (where the advantages of brand differentiation, competition and customer retention are most obvious), but also to the:

(a) **Business-to-business (B2B) sector**. Customer/supplier relationship and partnership is a feature of industrial buying, as we saw in Chapter 3. The inertia that characterises industrial markets may work in the supplier's favour, but in the face of increasing global competition there is no room for complacency: once lost, a customer will not easily be regained.

(b) **Not-for-profit sector**. Schools, universities, museums and charitable and volunteer organisations still have 'customers' (as we saw in Chapter 1), and operate under more or less competitive conditions. A charity, for example, may be competing for volunteer labour and funding not only with other charitable causes but with a host of other uses for people's time and money. Customer service is integral to the mission and objectives of non-profit organisations, and delivering effective customer care may be essential to building and maintaining their image, staffing, public funding and ability to attract and retain paying customers (where relevant).

(c) **Public sector**. Despite traditionally operating under monopolistic or near-monopolistic conditions, the public sector is also subject to pressures for better customer care. Some activities will have to compete with the private sector (for example, in the case of local authority leisure and sports centres). They are often subject to external regulation and benchmarking, which impose standards of effectiveness and efficiency. In the UK, the public sector is going through a period of rapid change – from the old-established 'public servant' role to a more dynamic 'competitive' style in line with government policy.

1.4 Aiming for quality

Customer care is linked to quality – not just of customer service, but of the total offering marketed to and experienced by the customer.

A customer care orientation is akin to the quality management orientation which has been called **'total quality management'** or TQM.

concept

Quality is 'the degree of excellence' of a thing: how well made or performed it is, how well it serves its purpose, how it measures against rivals or benchmarks and how valuable it is *perceived* to be (for any number of subjective reasons).

TQM is the process of applying quality values and aspirations to the management of all resources and relationships within the firm, as a means of developing and sustaining a culture of continuous improvement which focuses on meeting customers expectations.

1.4.1 Quality control systems

The management of quality is not a new idea. **Control systems** have long been aimed at:

- Establishing **standards** of quality for products/services
- Establishing **systems and procedures** to ensure that quality standards are met, within acceptable tolerance levels
- **Monitoring** output/service quality and **comparing** it against standards
- Taking **control action** to adjust systems and procedures if actual quality falls unacceptably short.

2 Customer service

Customer service is the point of contact between the customer and the organisation at each point of the transaction process.

Key customer service activities can be depicted in a continuous cycle, as follows

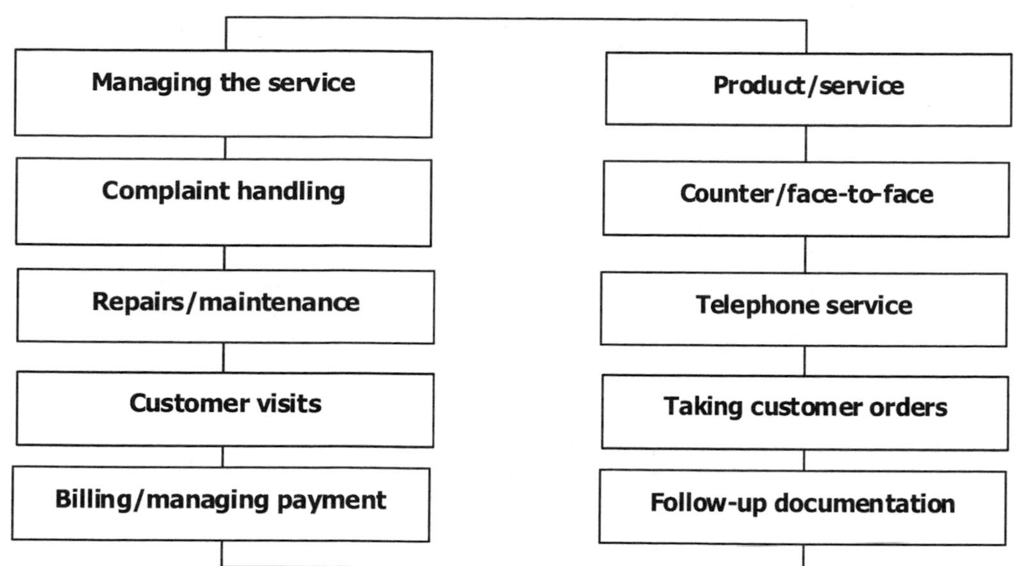

Key customer service activities

2.1 Key customer service values

Key customer service values include: reliability, responsiveness, competence, accessibility, courtesy, communication, credibility, security, understanding, tangibles, focus and TQM. Interpersonal skills, techniques and attitudes, as well as systems, are critical to effect customer service contacts, whether in person or by phone.

Customer service involves the following key values (Overton, 2002).

- **Reliability**: being dependable and consistent
- **Responsiveness**: being willing and ready
- **Competence**: skill and knowledge
- **Accessibility**: being easy to approach
- **Courtesy**: being polite, considerate, respectful and friendly
- **Communication**: being understandable, listening
- **Credibility**: being honest, believable, trustworthy
- **Security**: minimising danger, risk or doubt
- **Understanding**: appreciating customers' needs
- **Tangibles**: concrete evidence of the service
- **Focus**: an attitude that puts the customer first
- **TQM**: meeting quality requirements – or planning to meet them

2.2 Face-to-face customer service

Face-to-face encounters with customers can be easier and more effective than remote oral or written exchanges. As discussed in chapter 7, face-to-face communication allows for the use of non-verbal signals, more flexible feedback and interactivity in responding to customers. However, it is also more demanding.

- Staff have their appearance and non-verbal signals to think about as well as their verbal messages.

- Lacking the impersonality of the telephone, they may be more exposed to personal factors (for example, if the customer is upset or angry) and the stresses they cause.
- Their exchange with the customer may be audible to others, if not entirely public.

Staff will be able to respond effectively to customers if they follow some simple guidelines. (You might like to think of the mnemonic 'failure' to recall the following points.)

Element	Points to consider
First contact	• Immediate focus of attention (even if in the middle of something: an acknowledgement of the customer's presence and a promise to attend to him or her as soon as possible) • Greeting ('Good morning') • Engagement in the conversation ('Can I help you?')
Attention	• Concentration (single focus) • Eye contact (in cultures where this is a sign of attention and not, as in China – for example – an intrusion)
Information	• Not leaving the customer mid-contact for any reason, without informing him or her of what you need to do and how long it will take • Giving the customer the information (s)he requires, *or* making arrangements to do so, *or* offering other options
Language	• Avoiding technical jargon • Listening for what the problem/request/query really is
Understanding	• Show willing • Offer options, solutions, win-win approaches • Look for feedback that suggests satisfaction has not yet been achieved
Responsiveness	• Treat each customer as a special case: every contact matters • Respond to the customer – not the pressure of work problems or distraction (s)he represents • Dialogue – not monologue
Ending	• Confirm, sum-up, repeat back conclusions • Close with positive relationship-building ('Thank you')

WORK BASED PROJECT TIP

application

Draft a similar noticeboard (or staff web page) notice, with simple guidelines for staff in your organisation for **dealing with awkward customers**.

Use your own experience and common sense to suggest the content of your guidelines – or check the customer service manual (or similar) of your organisation.

2.3 Telephone customer service contact

Be aware, of the following points when considering the telephone as a means of customer communication.

(a) The telephone may be a customer's first or main point of contact with the organisation. The efficiency of the call answering and routing system, and the words and tone of voice of each person who responds, take on a front-line **ambassadorial role.**

(b) The telephone lacks the visual cues and feedback provided by face-to-face contact. Customer service staff will have to be alert to the implications of **oral cues** such as tones of voice, and confirm understanding by seeking and giving **feedback**.

(c) The telephone is not a 'neutral' piece of equipment. Customers may have strong **attitudes** towards being kept on hold, receiving unsolicited calls at home, hearing obviously scripted responses, calling a care line and finding an answer machine – and so on.

(d) The telephone costs money: calls should be handled as **efficiently** as possible.

Using the telephone effectively for customer care involves:

- **Interpersonal skills** in oral communication, and
- **Systems development** in order to take advantage of available technologies.

A **care line** is a phone number dedicated to customer care, usually printed on product packaging. Customers are encouraged to call if they have problems, or for further advice or information. Calls may be free or charged at local call rates. Care lines are intended to make customers *feel* looked after – even if they never use them! The purpose of this is theoretically to enhance customer loyalty, but research suggests that care lines actually have comparatively little impact on the purchase decision in the UK. (They are much more popular in the USA.)

WORK BASED PROJECT TIP

application

Think about the use of the telephone in your organisation, what are common practices? What improvements would you recommend?

3 Seeking customer feedback

3.1 The role of feedback in customer care

Organisations must gather systematic, specific and meaningful feedback in order to learn and grow.

Feedback, in this context, is part of a control system which reports back the results of a process or action, in order to compare them against the planned or intended outcome.

The gathering of feedback by customer-facing staff is important primarily so that:

- The organisation will have **customer-generated data** about customer needs and wants, in order to fine-tune the marketing mix, marketing communications (promotion) and customer care.
- Customers will **feel that they have been listened to** – and heard; that their satisfaction or dissatisfaction, and the reasons for it, are taken seriously by the organisation.
- Staff called upon to deal with customers have the ability to **influence organisational policy** (and even strategy) in areas that affect their work.
- **Information** keeps flowing into the organisation and through the organisation (particularly in an upward direction), creating opportunities for learning, innovation and adaptation.

Organisations which do not gather and utilise feedback become rigid and unable to adapt their behaviour to changing environments and customer demands. Crozier (1967) suggests that in large, hierarchical, bureaucratic organisations, the control mechanism – whereby feedback on errors is used to initiate corrective action – is hampered: bureaucracies cannot learn from their mistakes!

Complacent organisations may measure customer service performance in a vague or misguided fashion. The following are classic examples.

(a) The use of vague, generalised statements like 'quite good', 'getting better', 'world class'

(b) The counting of customer complaints in the belief that the incidence of complaints is a direct measure of customer satisfaction (without realising that, in most cases, only between 10 and 20 per cent of customers actually complain: the rest simply take their business elsewhere)

(c) Reliance on infrequent survey data about customer perceptions – and the selective application of the data thus acquired

(d) So-called 'improvements' that only address front-line 'customer care' features like answering the telephone within three rings – when what really matters is how customers are handled once the telephone has been picked up.

Organisations must gather systematic, specific and meaningful feedback in order to adapt, learn and grow.

- **Positive feedback** – satisfied responses – is useful to confirm organisational plans and strategies. It is also helpful in encouraging staff and reinforcing positive customer service behaviours through customer recognition and appreciation.
- **Negative feedback** – dissatisfied responses – is, however, even more useful in defining what it is that the organisation needs to do in order to gain and retain customers.

3.2 Encouraging customer complaints!

Customer service staff are gatherers of **customer feedback**, both formally and informally. They can be supported by training; feedback reporting systems; and culture and resources for encouraging feedback (and implementing solutions).

In other words, **customers should be encouraged to complain!** The following guidelines are given by *Johns* (1994).

- Make it easy for people to complain: eg by establishing free-call or local-call rate telephone numbers or complaint/feedback/review forms.
- Ask for feedback by selecting and approaching customers at random.
- Use random customer visits to sample the service first hand.
- Train staff to listen to complaints positively, as a learning opportunity, without becoming defensive.
- Act quickly and with goodwill to solve any problem identified, so complaints will be perceived to be worthwhile and positive. (This may mean replacing products or repeating services.)
- Communicate the intention to prevent recurrence of the problem.
- Reward customer feedback with appropriate incentives: discount vouchers, entry into Prize Draws and so on. Where feedback leads to change, customers should be thanked for their important contribution.

In addition, customer-facing staff have extensive opportunities to gather **informal direct and indirect feedback** by observing and talking to customers. They need to listen intentionally for explicit or implied complaints or suggestions for improvement. Returned products, for example, should be interpreted as non-verbal forms of complaint, as should returned mailings – or indeed, customer failure to recall company advertisements when asked.

3.2.1 Other possible sources of information

Feedback is not always negative, some customers actively seek ways to praise organisations that excel in customer service. The following table summarises the ways that information can be gathered to assess the level of customer service.

Formal feedback collection	Informal feedback methods
• Surveys, telephone, web based, questionnaire	• Front line staff-customer discussions
• Online forums (on organisations website)	• Online forums / review sites set up by third parties
• Suggestion boxes	• Press monitoring
• Analysis of formal complaints data	
• Review customer retention figures	
• Sales figure analysis	

3.3 Encouraging constructive use of feedback

There should be clear reporting lines for staff to convey customer feedback to appropriate decision-makers as swiftly (if necessary to resolve a current complaint) and as regularly as possible. Customer-facing staff are **gatekeepers** of information: they direct in-coming feedback to decision-makers – or do not. They need to know how to pass on feedback and to whom.

The concept of feedback as a **positive learning tool** should be marketed internally throughout the organisation.

- Staff should be trained and resourced to gather feedback (with appropriate forms, questionnaires and interpersonal skills).
- Staff should be recognised and rewarded for gathering feedback, especially if it is translated into constructive improvement suggestions.
- Suggestions for improvement should be rewarded, whether or not they result in action.
- The word 'failure' should be replaced by 'learning opportunity' in the corporate culture. If 'mistakes' are treated harshly, people will avoid gathering or sharing feedback.
- Senior management should model positive, feedback-seeking behaviour by welcoming upward feedback from staff.

It should be emphasised that encouraging feedback:

- Establishes dialogue and relationship with the customer
- Encourages customers to think about quality and service issues – attracting them to an organisation that demonstrably does the same.

Positive feedback – 'good news' and 'good reviews' – should be generously shared and celebrated.

WORK BASED PROJECT TIP

application

Begin to gather a portfolio of communications from organisations of which you are a customer that ask you to provide feedback on their product/services. (You might start with the Review Form at the back of this Study Workbook.) Include communications (such as announcements of product/service changes) that state or imply that customers' feedback has been taken into account by the organisation.

You may like to give your feedback, where requested, and see whether you feel that you have had a genuine 'say' or influence...

4 Setting up a customer care programme

Customer care is an organisation-wide orientation, which requires vision, leadership and cultural reinforcement – not just 'rules for customer service'. Nevertheless, a Customer Care Programme may provide a framework for planning, monitoring and evaluating customer service quality.

4.1 A systematic approach

Setting up a **customer care programme** involves standard-setting, systems development, training and control.

The following is a simple, systematic approach to setting up a customer care programme.

Step 1 **Identify key dimensions of service quality**, both inside and outside the organisation. This process may involve market research to identify existing levels of satisfaction of both customers and service personnel. The research could also be used to identify expectations of service quality and identify gaps between expectation and experience.

Step 2 **Establish a mission statement**. We have already discussed in chapter 7 the point that mission statements provide a means of focussing and uniting internal stakeholders towards working towards a shared goal. This is essential for a good customer care programme.

Step 3 **Set standards for service delivery**. These should be specific, measurable and realistic. Common standards specify, for example, a maximum queuing time (or length of queue) or a maximum time before a telephone is answered.

Step 4 **Establish a management process**. This will involve three key elements:

- **A systems for service delivery**. It is pointless setting targets if there is no operating system in place which will support and enable staff in meeting those targets. Attention should be given to organisation structures, information flows, use of technology and so on.
- **Analyse employee training needs**. Training should be relevant to the needs of staff: the gap between current performance and service standards should be analysed and tested if required.
- **Develop training programmes** to include (as required):

  Business and product knowledge

  Customer awareness

  Interpersonal skills

Step 5 **Establish a feedback and complaints system**. This will help **to measure and monitor success** in terms of achievement of the set targets. Again, systematic research and (internal and external) customer feedback may be required to examine post-implementation (and on-going) levels of:

- Employee performance (and satisfaction with the programme)
- Customer expectations and perceptions of actual current service quality

Some organisations also include a further step to help overcome any barriers to customer service.

Step 6 **Set up performance-related pay and recognition systems** for employees. Organisational commitment to service quality should be reinforced via key culture-change mechanisms such as motivation and reward. (Other such mechanisms include making customer care skills the criteria for employee selection, performance appraisal, career development and so on.)

5 Databases to assist customer service

5.1 Gathering customer information

Internet and database technologies offer some key advantages for gathering customer data. The key to their value is keeping the data up to date and relevant.

(a) Market research into customers' 'stated intentions' and perceptions can be replaced or augmented by actual **customer behaviour** and **demonstrated preferences**: Websites allow the tracking and storage of customer browsing (identifying areas of interest) and transaction/purchase history.

(b) **Market research** and **customer feedback gathering** can be carried out via such methods as:

- Online or e-mail-distributed questionnaires and feedback forms
- 'Message boards' on the website, allowing visitors to communicate with the company (and each other)
- Site monitoring to record hits, browsing and purchase patterns of users
- Inviting e-mailed comments and suggestions

Such methods are more convenient for the customer than face-to-face interviews and writing/mailing: they require less effort and allow 24-7 flexibility. From the company's point of view, they also facilitate the immediate analysis and integration of results, automatic 'thank you' messages and so on.

(c) Companies can also access **external online databases** compiled and managed by specialist data providers: market research publishers (for example, Mintel and Keynote), producers of statistical data (for example, the UK Central Statistical Office and Eurostat) and others.

5.2 Database marketing

Database marketing techniques can be used to personalise marketing media and channels, and to keep records of all customer contacts, in order to support further marketing planning and relationship marketing.

KEY CONCEPT

application

Database marketing has been defined as an interactive approach to marketing which uses individually addressable marketing media and channels to extend help to a company's target audience, stimulate their demand and stay close to them by recording and keeping an electronic database memory of customer, prospect and all communication and commercial contacts, to help them improve all future contacts and ensure more realistic planning of all marketing.

Customer data held in computerised databases can be interrogated and manipulated in various ways through the process of **data mining**.

Allen*et al* (2001) suggest the following projects which can be conducted using database marketing techniques.

(a) **Identify the best customers** (recency of the latest purchase, frequency of purchases and monetary value of all purchases) to determine which customers are most profitable to market to.

(b) **Develop new customers**. Collect lists of potential customers to incorporate in the database.

(c) **Tailor messages based on customer usage**. Target mail and e-mail based on the types and frequency of purchases indicated by the customer's purchase profile.

(d) **Recognise customers after purchase**. Reinforce the purchase decision by appropriate follow-up.

(e) **Cross-sell related and complementary products**. Use the customer purchase database to identify opportunities to suggest additional products during the buying session.

(f) **Personalise customer service**. Online purchase data can prompt customer service representatives to show that the customer is recognised, his needs known, and his time (eg in giving details) valued.

(g) **Eliminate conflicting or confusing communications**. Present a coherent image over time to individual customers – however different the message to different customer groups. (For example, don't keep sending 'dear first-time customer' messages to long-standing customers!)

5.3 Adding value

Database marketing supports customer service by targeting and personalising communications.

The two key points of this for adding value to customer service may be described as follows.

Targeting communications (mailing list management): greater relevance to the customer	• Targeting customers in particular geographic areas with information (suppliers, services, events) relevant to their local area • Targeting customers with relevant offerings, message content, and style, according to lifestyle, age group and other demographic/personal factors • Targeting customers with their preferred communication purposes (new product information, newsletters, special offers) and media (e-mail, phone, mail)
Personalising communications: greater relevance and sense of recognition for the customer	• Personally addressed mailed/e-mailed communications • Individual customer information made available in real time to call centre staff to personalise telephone contacts and streamline transactions (no need for the customer to supply details each time) • Contacts and product recommendations based on preferences and contact/transaction history: ('Since you enquired about...', 'As a regular purchaser of...', 'Since we haven't heard from you for some time...') • Relational use of personal information (for example, birthday cards)

Postma (1999) suggests that such techniques:

(a) **Build relationships**. 'Reacting to the personal behaviour of customers or prospects by responding to their obvious interests with an electronic message, a letter, a brochure or an offer actually fosters clients' feeling that you are becoming acquainted with their tastes and preferences and are taking them into consideration.'

(b) **Reinforce loyalty**. 'Loyal customers will value being recognised as such and receiving direct communications.'

(c) **Out-perform human beings**! 'An assistant in a fashion store may very well recognise a client's face after half a year, but will not instantly remember the client's measurements and tastes. A database, on the other hand, has no problem whatsoever retaining these facts or other information about the customer's average expenditure, quality standards or preferred brand. We won't even mention the fact that the employee who served the customer last time has moved on to a different job and been replaced.'

WORK BASED PROJECT TIP application

Suggest how a database could be used within your organisation to improve decision-making.

5.4 Data security and controls

Legislation and regulations exist in many countries to protect consumers from the misuse of personal details held on computer, unsolicited mail and invasion of privacy.

In the UK, controls on data usage include the following.

- **The Data Protection Act 1998** (and related Codes of Practice) provide that data controllers (organisations or individuals who control the contents of files of personal data and the use of personal data) must register with the Data Protection Registrar. They must limit their use of personal data (defined as any information about an identifiable living individual) to the uses registered, and not disclose data to third parties (including e-mail addresses sent in a 'cc' reference) without permission.
- **The Criminal Justice and Public Order Act 1994** makes it illegal to procure the disclosure of computer-held information, and to sell or offer to sell computer-held information.
- **The Mailing Preference Service** allows customers to state whether they would (and more often would not) be willing to receive direct mail on a range of specific areas. [This is the way to get taken off (or, if you are a Marketing Student, put on) mailing databases.]
- **The UK Privacy and Electronic Communications Regulations 2003**, requires proactive agreement (eg ticking an 'opt-in' box) to receive electronic communications such as e-mail marketing.
- Various countries have 'Do Not Call' registers enabling people to opt out of telemarketing call lists. (Australia for example implemented such a register in May 2007.)

Learning objective review

Learning objectives	Covered
1 Describe the concept of customer care and customer service in terms of how this helps to build relationships	☑ Customer care aims to close gaps between customer expectations and experience ☑ Relationship marketing- brings together customer service, quality and marketing
2 Describe how to set up a customer care programme	☑ Identify needs ☑ Establish a mission statement ☑ Set service levels ☑ Establish a management process ☑ Establish a complaints system ☑ Develop a control system
3 Explain the importance of collecting information and the measure used to monitor customer service	☑ Formal and informal customer feedback ☑ Helps to deal with complaint handling
4 Explain how IT and databases are essential to customer care and customer service	☑ Database is a collection of structured data ☑ Legislation exists to protect consumers from data misuse

References

Blythe, J. (2006) Principles and Practice of Marketing, Thompson, London.

Christopher, M., Payne, A. & Ballantyne, D. (1992) Relationship Marketing, Butterworth-Heinneman, Oxford.

Clutterbuck, D. (2001) communication competence and business success, International Association of Business Communicators.

Crozier, M. (1967) The Bureaucratic Phenomenon, University of Chicago Press, Chicago.

Jobber, D. (2007) Principles and Practice of Marketing 5th edition, McGraw Hill, London.

Johns, E. (1994) The Essential Marketing Sourcebook, 2nd edition, FT/Fitman, London.

Kotler, . 91999) Marketing Management, Prentice Hall, London.

Overton, R. (2002) Customer service, Business Basics, Sydney.

Peters, TJ. and Waterman R. (1982) In Search of Excellence, Harper 7 Row, New York.

Postma, P. (1999) The New Marketing Era, Mcgraw Hill, New York.

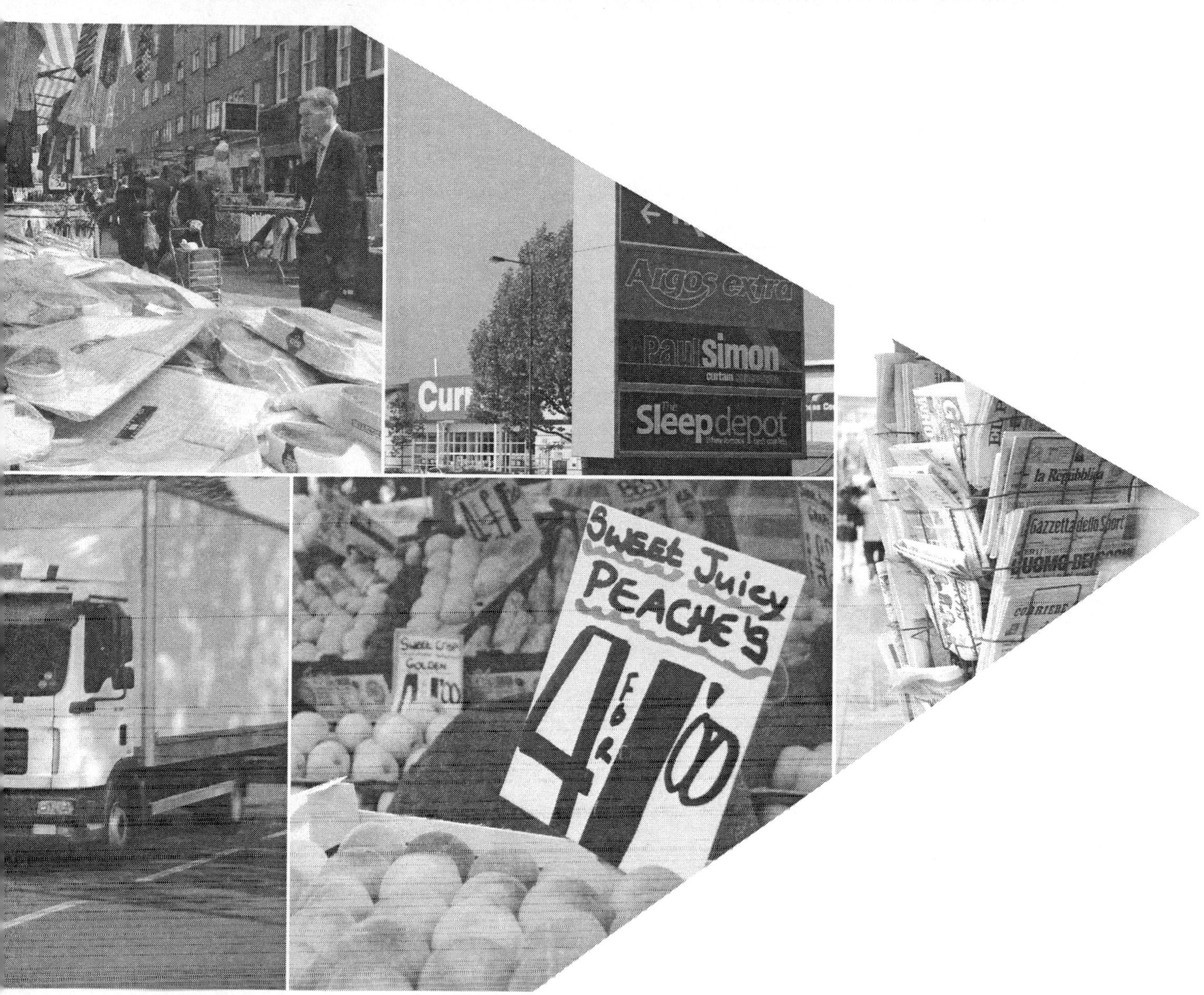

Chapter 9

Preparing for the examination

Topic list

1 The nature of the online exam
2 Revision tips
3 Online examination tips
4 Try an online mock exam

Introduction

Within this very brief chapter we look at the online exam and give you some useful tips to help you prepare and revise for this aspect of the assessment. We also give you the opportunity to try a free mock online test.

Syllabus linked learning objectives

By the end of the chapter you will be able to:

Learning objectives	Syllabus link
1 Prepare for the online examination	The entire unit 1 syllabus

1 The nature of the online exam

The online exam is designed to test your breadth of knowledge. In practice this means that you can expect to be tested on *any* and possibly even *all* areas of the unit 1 syllabus. You are expected to have a clear working knowledge of basic marketing concepts at this level of qualification and therefore marketing terminology and jargon will feature heavily in the exam.

1.1 Practical aspects

The exam is likely to take place at either your study centre or at a location organised by the CIM where you will have access to an internet linked computer.

As with any exam, there will be a specified time for the exam to take place. An invigilator will be present the whole time and expect you to adhere to exam conditions eg silence (except for keyboard tapping of course!). If you have any specific needs, you must ensure that you notify your study centre of these prior to the exam so that provision can be made with the CIM. You will be expected to take along your CIM membership card which will contain your student number, there may be other documentation that you will also need and this will have been outlined to you by your study centre and the CIM.

Your study centre will have organised for the online exam to be available between a pre-agreed set.

1.2 The exam format

You will have **one hour** to complete **50 multiple choice questions**.

Your time starts once you have accessed the online exam. **All questions are compulsory**.

The questions will give you three optional answers to select from. For example:

Question One
Marketing is defined as the identification, anticipation and satisfaction of customer:

1 service
2 needs
3 demand

(In this case the answer is 2- needs)

2 Revision tips

When it comes to actually revising, there are some essential strategies to address. Firstly, revision should not be left to the last minute and really starts the moment that you study a topic and complete your reading. Once you have completed the required topics, you should make sure that you fully understand the implications to a range of different contexts. Now is the time to start collecting examples of marketing practice by making notes of observations you have made through your own

work and on relevant articles you have read within the business and marketing press. This will be an invaluable exercise when you get to your final stage of revision.

Practice, practice, practice is key to passing CIM exams and throughout your course you should have been completing practice exam questions. Make sure that you complete the quick quizzes in chapters 1-4 and make use of our online mock exam.

2.1 Key steps in revision

This is a very important time as you approach the exam. You must remember three main things, which we will then break down into more detailed advice.

Point 1 Use your time sensibly

1 Be honest with yourself about h**ow much study time you have**? Remember that you must EAT, SLEEP, and of course, RELAX.

2 **How will you split that available time between each subject**? What are your weaker subjects? They will need more time.

3 **What is your learning style**? AM/PM? Little and often/long sessions? Evenings/ weekends?

4 Are you taking regular breaks? Most people absorb more if they do not attempt to study for long uninterrupted periods of time. Taking a five minute break every hour to make coffee or watch the news headlines can make all the difference.

Do you have quality study time? Unplug the phone. Let everybody know that you're studying and shouldn't be disturbed.

Point 2 Set yourself realistic goals

1 Have you set a clearly defined objective for each study period?

2 Is the objective achievable?

3 Will you stick to your plan? Will you make up for any lost time?

4 Are you rewarding yourself for your hard work?

5 Are you leading a healthy lifestyle?

Point 3 Believe in yourself

Are you cultivating the right attitude of mind? There is absolutely no reason why you should not pass this exam if you adopt the correct approach.

- **Be confident** – you've passed exams before, you can pass them again
- **Be calm** – plenty of adrenaline but no panicking
- **Be focused** – commit yourself to passing the exam

2.2 Scrapbook technique

When it comes to starting final revision, one of the most useful exercises you could do before the exam is to carry out what we like to call the scrapbooking activity. This will help you to remember the key theories but also to prepare bank of good marketing examples that may be easier to remember once you get into the exam room. To complete the activity you will need:

- A large piece of paper or a flipchart
- Some coloured pens
- Newspapers, marketing magazines, blog examples etc

Step 1 – Outline theories (list, mind maps, diagrams)

Aim to create one sheet per topic for the module you are revising. For example, if you are revising for Marketing Planning, you may have a sheet for pricing strategies. This is where you will need to think about how you like to remember information, so, for example, do you remember visually or do you list items in your mind, do you like diagrams, or pictures to words. If you are not sure, then think about how you might direct somebody to your house, would you be more likely to write a list of directions, draw a detailed map or a more basic diagram. The important point is that there are many books which tell you how to create mind maps or similar memory aides but at this stage you will not have time to master this and you need to be spending your time actually revising. Therefore, go with whatever works best for you, and get everything that you can think of about individual topics down on that piece of paper. Be creative with your colours if you wish, for instance, you may find it easier to colour code different subtopics.

Step 2 – Review your outline and add more detail

At this stage, you should go back to your notes and texts and add in more detail especially in terms of adding little bits of information about the good and bad points, advantages and disadvantages and contexts in which activities may be more or less appropriate. Now, complete this process for all the topics on the modules syllabus.

Step 3 – Adding examples

Move onto the example creation stage. Pull together as many copies of news reports, marketing press and business journals that you can from the last year. You will need scissors and some glue. You have probably guessed by now what you will be doing, well, yes, go through and stick as many examples as you can find about each of the topics onto your relevant sheets.

The result

By the time you have finished, you should have a huge bank, not only of the key theories and topics, but some good examples to add a depth to your understanding. Being in this position will help you interpret the online questions faster and more successfully.

Once you reach the final stages of your revision, you will need to reach the point where you are checking that you remember enough for your time in the online exam. It is here that you will want to be completing whole mock exams to check that you can answer quickly enough. You should also be testing yourself to check that you remember key theories and can commit them to memory. You would find BPP Learning Media's Passcards useful in this respect. Here, the sort of information you have included in your own flipchart scrapbook will have been reduced down to hand sized cards which you could use for a last minute memory jog. You may find it useful to write key words to trigger your scrapbooked marketing examples at the bottom of the relevant passcard page.

3 Online examination tips

When you sit online exams for the first time, they can be daunting for two reasons;

1 It is an exam!

2 It is computerised and you may not be familiar with online tests.

To overcome any fears you may have, it is therefore essential that you feel well prepared. Revision and practicing questions are essential for exam success. Here are a few additional tips for coping in the exam room.

3.1 The day of the exam

1 Set at least one alarm (or get an alarm call) for a morning exam.

2 Have something to eat but beware of eating too much; you may feel sleepy if your system is digesting a large meal.

3 Allow plenty of time to get to the exam hall; have your route worked out in advance and listen to news bulletins to check for potential travel problems.

4 Don't forget your student ID, CIM membership card or any other documentation you have been asked to take along.

5 Avoid discussion about the exam with other candidates outside the exam hall.

3.2 In the exam room

Try to remember the following when you are in the exam room.

1 **Let the invigilator know immediately if there are problems with your computer or the website used to access the exam.**

Don't become flustered if there are IT problems, the invigilator will take this into account and this will not 'cause' you to fail the exam

2 **Read the instructions (the 'rubric') about the test carefully**

Although it is difficult to misinterpret online multiple choice questions (compared to other exam formats) be aware of the information the CIM request at the beginning such as your membership number.

3 **Work through questions carefully**

Take each question in turn and try to answer it. If you are not sure about the answer you will have an option to 'flag' or 'mark the question. Once you have completed the paper you can return to the question later if you have time. Equally, it is very easy to make mistakes in multiple choice questions because often the available answers are similar and not necessarily straightforward.

4 **Check the time allocation for each question**

With 60 minutes available to answer 50 questions you have a maximum of 72 seconds per question. We suggest that you spend no longer than 60 seconds per question so that you leave ten minutes available to check through your answers at the end. With multiple choice questions, it is easy to rush through and accidentally answer incorrectly.

5 **Read the question carefully**

Read through the question again very carefully when you come to answer it. This advice is given based on points 3 and 4 above.

6 **Stay until the end of the exam**

Use any spare time checking and rechecking your answers.

7 **Don't worry if you feel you have performed badly in the exam**

It is more than likely that the other candidates will have found the exam difficult too. You will probably find out your score at the end of the exam. Please don't take this as confirmation of whether you have passed or failed, the CIM award passes- not computers!

4 Try an online mock exam

We have created an online examination for you to attempt as part of your revision. This exam has been made in-house at BPP Learning media and therefore will not look exactly the same as the CIM's version. The CIM have their own software for creating online exams.

Your study centre will be able to give you the details of the CIM's mock online exam. Your tutor may have planned this into teaching sessions or they may provide you with details of the website where you can access it. Either way, make sure that you do get used to the way the software works prior to the exam as well as using it an another opportunity to test your knowledge.

To access our online exam you should go to the following website:

www.bpp.com/lm/cim

You will be asked to register with us and there will be a few questions to verify that you have purchased this Study Workbook.

Once you have registered should go to the following sections:

Learning objective review

1. Select – Introductory Certificate in Marketing

2. Select – Mock online exam

If you have problems accessing the website for any reason then please email: cimrange@bpp.com

Learning objectives	Covered
1 Prepare for the online examination	☑ The nature of the exam ☑ Tips for planning your revision ☑ Tips for your time in the exam ☑ How to access the online mock exam

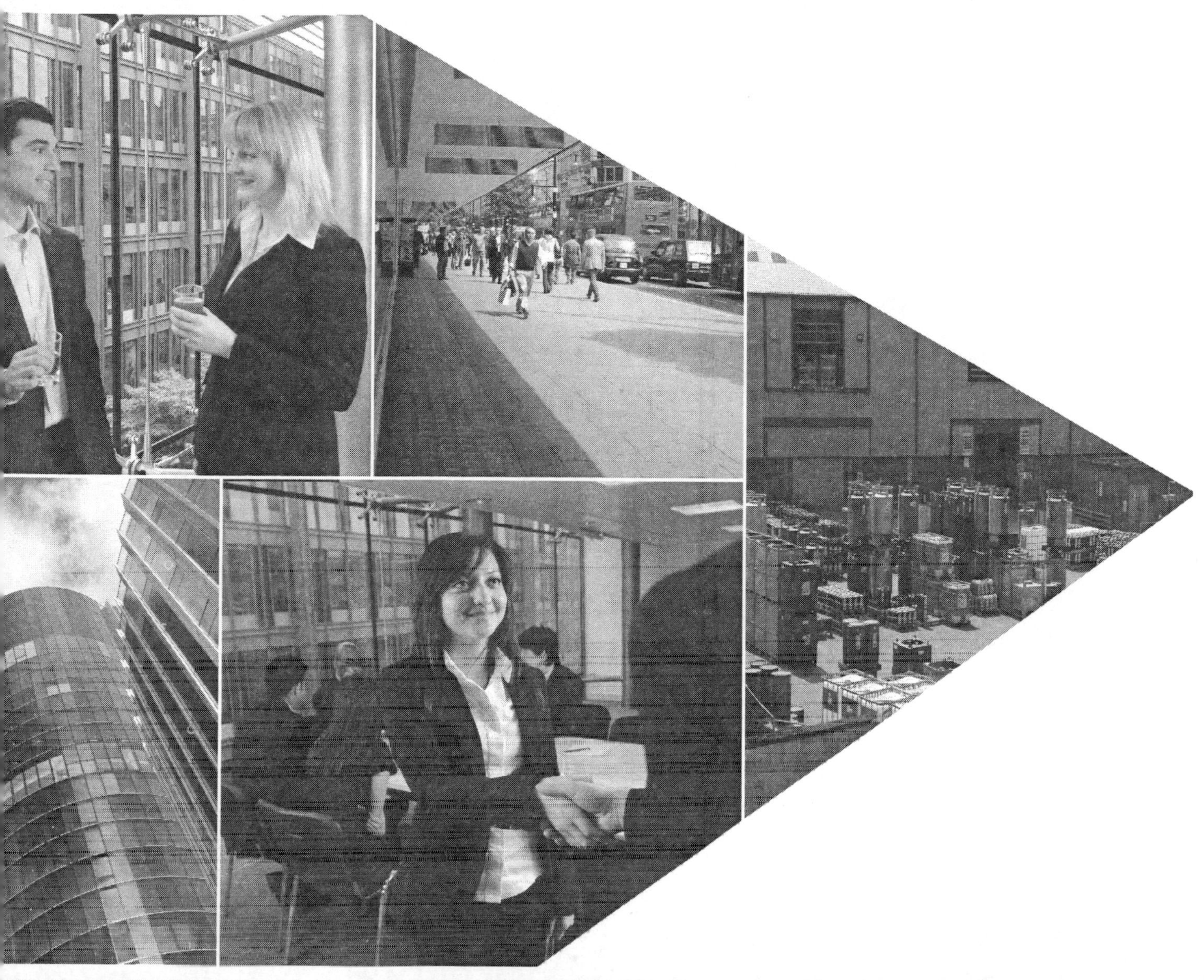

Chapter 10
Completing the work based project

Topic list

Introduction

For many students the work based project will be the most daunting and yet most useful aspect of their studies for this qualification. The CIM moved to project and assignment based assessment for all four levels of CIM qualification because they have been found to be highly useful in preparing aspiring marketers to function at an early stage within a marketing related role. Students often find projects and assignments useful because they enable you to consider more deeply the working practices of an organisation you are familiar with. They also provide the stating point for a portfolio of evidence of practical marketing to show potential employers.

Within this chapter we will explain what the CIM require you to demonstrate in the project, how to plan and research project, how to attempt the tasks in terms of preparing findings and finally how to present and submit your work. To do this, we use the specimen paper provided by the CIM to demonstrate how you might complete a similar project. Remember that for each assessment round the CIM prepare a new project. Once you are familiar however with the format and skills needed to complete this style of assessment, you should be in a position to attempt any of the projects prepared.

Syllabus linked learning objectives

By the end of the chapter you will be able to:

Learning objectives	Syllabus link
1 Explain the purpose of the work based project	Entire unit 2 syllabus
2 Approach the work based project and identify the key assessment criteria	Entire unit 2 syllabus, 4.10

1 The nature of work based projects

1.1 What is the CIM looking for students to demonstrate in work based projects?

There are a few key points to remember as you study and prepare for your CIM assessment with regard to the CIM's expectations of you. To put this into context try to remember the following:

(a) You are studying for a **professional** qualification. This means that you are required to use professional language and adopt a business approach in your work. Ten percent of the available marks are awarded for the 'format and presentation' of your work.

(b) You are expected to show that you have 'read widely'. Make sure that you read the quality press (and don't skip the business pages), read Marketing, The Marketer, Research and Marketing Week avidly. Adding real life examples into you work helps not only show that you have read widely but you are demonstrating that you understand how marketing works. One way to show you are well read is to make full use of the CIM's online Knowledge Hub. Your student membership entitles you to full access to this goldmine of both academic and non-academic press. The Knowledge Hub is an access point to lots of good sources you can use to demonstrate you have read widely in order to answer the specific assignment question posed. Also on the CIM's website, you will find a 'Shape the Agenda' section. This is another good source which enables you to show you are familiar with current CIM research programmes. Within the 'Shape the Agenda' pages you will find highly relevant and recent papers on current topics of importance to the CIM. New agenda papers are published every six months and in recent years topics have included: market segmentation; managing marketing; marketing metrics; relationship building communications and; social marketing.

(c) Become aware of the marketing initiatives you come across on a daily basis, for example, when you go shopping look around and think about why the store layout is as it is, consider the messages, channel choice and timings of ads

when you are watching TV. It is surprising how much you will learn just by taking an interest in the marketing world around you. This will help you build a portfolio of real like marketing examples to use in your assessment work.

(d) Get to know the way CIM write their exam papers and assignments. They use a specific approach which is referred to as The Magic Formula to ensure a consistent approach when designing assessment materials. Make sure you are fully aware of this as it will help you interpret what the examiner is looking for (we have referred to the Magic Formula throughout this workbook).

(e) Learn how to use Harvard referencing. This is explained in later in this chapter and is important to master because it is a key requirement of the CIM that you use it (in assignments). Harvard referencing refers to a system that helps you to organise and cite your source materials. Paraphrasing somebody else's ideas or directly quoting from a textbook or research paper, news report or article should all be clearly cited. The CIM requires you to use Harvard referencing for a number of reasons. Firstly, they need to ensure that your assignment is your own and an original piece of work. Plagiarising from someone else's work is a serious offence and if you were found to be copying from someone else or another source such as a textbook then you would fail. It is for this reason that the CIM requires assignments to be presented as both paper and electronic versions so that they can run your work through anti-plagiarism software.

The second reason for insisting on Harvard referencing is to demonstrate that you have read widely around the syllabus. It is important that you use a variety of sources in your assignments to justify and back up your ideas. In exams, although you are not expected to include references, if you can at least remember and add the names of key authors and sources then it adds more depth to your answers.

(f) Ensure that you read very carefully all assessment details sent to you from the CIM. They are very strict with regard to deadlines, completing the correct paperwork to accompany any assignment or project and making sure you have your CIM membership card with you at the exam. Failing to meet any assessment entry deadlines or completing written work on time will mean that you will have to wait for the next round of assessment dates and will need to pay the relevant assessment fees again.

1.2 The meaning of a 'work' based project

For your project you are encouraged in the tasks to use your own organisation to base your answers on. Of course if you are not currently working then you can:

(a) Find a host company who would be willing to let you use them (often charities and small local organisations are interested in any offer of free 'consultancy' work carried out as part of student projects).

(b) Consider whether a previous company you have worked with would be suitable.

(c) Discuss with your tutor the use of a case study company.

EXAM TIP

concept

Remember you are being assessed on your ability to relate to marketing and not whether you are working for a suitable type of organisation. Often the most interesting research proposals are written for the most unusual organisations so don't feel that because you may not work for a 'cutting edge' marketing orientated company you are disadvantaged in any way.

2 The format of the project

2.1 Format of the assignment

You assignment will have four compulsory tasks which together account for the 100% of the available marks.

2.2 The project/assignment brief

The project/ assignment brief is the document that sets out everything you need to know to complete your work-based project assignment:

- A rubric or set of instructions in regard to the marks available, the maximum word count for the project, and the documentation which should accompany the assignment
- Guidance Notes on teaching, project preparation and assessment
- Four tasks (each set out separately), setting out:
  - Brief background context to the topic
  - The scenario or role in which you are required to present a report, presentation or other project format
  - A list of tasks and their percentage contribution to the overall project
  - Maximum word and page counts for each task
  - A list of Syllabus References: that is, the learning objectives covered by the assignment
  - A list of the Assessment Criteria used to mark the assignment
- A Mark Scheme, with a breakdown of the marks available for each of the Assessment Criteria – cross-referenced to the CIM Magic Formula.
- Guidance on tackling the assignment, specifically related to the tasks and topics of the given Project Brief.

At this level within the CIM qualifications framework you will also be given a selection of appendix resources that you are expected to refer to.

2.3 The specimen assignment

The CIM uses a different assignment brief for each academic session. Ensure that you have the correct brief otherwise your work will not be accepted by the CIM. Within this workbook we will use the CIM's specimen assignment brief to illustrate the points that we make. Please be aware that no two assignment briefs will be identical however, the general advice that we give will enable you to tackle any assignment for this level. Your study centre will be able to access the specimen project brief from the tutor pages within the CIM website. Although we are not able to reproduce all the appendices mentioned, you should have access to these via the CIM Knowledge Hub and tracking them down will be a worthwhile activity to learn how to find your way around this vast bank of information.

The overall structure of the assignment is shown in the following table.

Task	Weighting	Word limit	You are to prepare...
1	25%	750 words	Prepare ten **presentation slides** and supporting notes about meeting different customer needs
2	25%	750 words	Construct an **internal email** discussing customer facing roles and the importance of interpersonal skills and communication
3	35%	1000 words	Prepare an informal **report** discussing how understanding customer needs benefits organisations
4	15%	500 words	Write **discussion document** to be used at your appraisal outlining your skills, objectives and measurement criteria

The assignment begins with a statement outlining your role.

Role

Your Manager is interested in developing a better understanding of the organisation's internal and external customers and wishes to know how this can assist in designing appropriate marketing activities that will engage and support customers, and in this way achieve long-term customer loyalty.

During a meeting with the Marketing team, it was felt that it would be useful to review different approaches that a range of other organisations use to develop their internal and external customer relationships.

In your role as a Marketing Assistant, you have been asked to review the case studies provided in the appendix, which profile different organisations and their individual approaches to managing customer relationships. Using the case studies as supporting material, address the following tasks:

Task One The customer facing role (25% weighting)

Using the resources provided on British Airways in the appendix of this document, produce a presentation consisting of **TEN** slides with supporting notes, suitable for presentation to the Marketing team.

The presentation should:

- briefly describe the specific initiatives adopted by British Airways to more closely meet customer needs
- compare these initiatives with those adopted by **ONE** of British Airways' competitors
- identify the strengths and weaknesses of **TWO** of these initiatives
- explain what other organisations can learn from these approaches.

Word count 750 words, excluding relevant appendices.

(Syllabus References 1.1, 1.4, 2.1, 2.3, 3.10)

EXAM TIP

format

We have shown the Assessment and Marking criteria within one table so that you can see how the two are similar. In the assignment you will be given these separately so look to see where marks are awarded for each assessment criteria.

Assessment / Marking Criteria	Marking Scheme- % Mark available
Brief description of specific initiatives adopted by British Airways to more closely meet customer needs	25 15=C 10=A
Comparison of initiatives with those adopted by **ONE** of British Airways' competitors	20 10=C 10=A
Identification of the strengths and weaknesses of **TWO** of these initiatives	25 15=C 5=A
Explanation of what other organisations can learn from these approaches	20 15=E 5+A
Layout, content and structure of slides produced	F=10

Task Two- The customer facing role (25% weighting)

With reference to the B&Q case study, your Manager has asked you to produce an email for circulation internally to all customer facing personnel that:

- identifies the qualities and interpersonal skills needed by customer facing staff as representatives of an organisation
- explains the importance of good verbal and non-verbal communication when dealing with customers, using llustrative examples.

Word count 750 words, excluding relevant appendices.

(Syllabus References 2.5, 3.3, 3.4,3.7)

Assessment / Marking Criteria	Marking Scheme- % Mark available
Identification of the qualities and interpersonal skills needed by customer facing staff as representatives of an organisation	30 30=C
Explanation of the importance of good verbal and non-verbal communication when dealing with customers, using illustrative examples	15, 15, 20 30=C 20=A
Format/layout/tone of email suitable for internal communication	20 20=F

Task Three Information for marketing decisions (35% weighting)

You are required by your Manager to produce an informal report for circulation to relevant departments to demonstrate how better understanding of customer needs can benefit organisations.

For your organisation, or one of your choice, prepare a report that covers the following tasks, using examples to illustrate your points:

- provide a background to your chosen organisation, its customer base and product/service range (two sides of A4 maximum)
- identify the needs of **TWO** different customer groups
- describe how internal and external information sources can help the organisation
- to understand the buying behaviour of these **TWO** customer groups
- outline the different methods that are used by the organisation to obtain feedback from these **TWO** customer groups
- recommend **TWO** promotional tools that could be used to develop and maintain relationships with these groups, giving reasons for your choice
- identify the internal departments to which your report should be circulated, giving reasons for your choice.

Appendix

- Brief background to the chosen organisation, its customer base and product/service range (maximum two A4 pages, no marks allocated)

WORK BASED PROJECT TIP

format

How to compile the company background requested here is covered later in the chapter.

Word count 1000 words, excluding relevant appendices.

(Syllabus References 1.1,1.4,2.6,3.3,3.5,3.10,4.4,4.5)

Assessment / Marking Criteria	Marking Scheme- % Mark available
Identification of the needs of **TWO** different customer groups	20 10=C 10=A
Description of how internal and external information sources can help the organisation to understand the buying behaviour of these **TWO** customer groups	20 20=C
Outline of the different methods used by the organisation to obtain feedback from these **TWO** customer groups	15 10=C 5=A
Recommendation of **TWO** promotional tools that could be used to develop and maintain relationships with these groups, giving reasons for choice	20 5=C 15=A
Identification of internal departments to which the report should be circulated, giving reasons for choice	15 15=E
Presentation, structure and flow of report	10 10=F

Task Four- Planning and measuring personal performance (15% weighting)

Having completed the previous tasks given and, in preparation for your appraisal with your Manager, you have been asked to obtain feedback about your skills, attributes and performance from a range of people that you know well. These may include fellow students, tutors, friends, family, colleagues and/or supervisors. You should interview a maximum of **FOUR** people.

Produce a discussion document for use at your appraisal that:

- summarises the feedback received on your skills, attributes and performance
- briefly analyses the feedback received, identifying your strengths and areas for development
- identifies a set of personal objectives for the next **12** months that addresses your areas for development
- outlines how your performance against these objectives would be measured

Word count 500 words, excluding relevant appendices.

(Syllabus References 4.4, 4.7)

Assessment / Marking Criteria	Marking Scheme- % Mark available
Summary of feedback received on skills, attributes and performance	**20** 20=C
Brief analysis of feedback received, identifying strengths and areas for development	20 10=C 10=A
Identification of a set of personal objectives for the next **12** months that addresses areas for development	25 25=A
Outline of how performance against these objectives would be measured	25 25=E
Presentation, structure and flow of discussion document	10 10=F

3 Tackling the project

3.1 Before you receive your assignment

There are a number of preparatory tasks that you can complete before you are given your assignment.

(a) Read the study text and complete the activities. It is particularly important that you complete the worksheet activities in chapters 5-8 because these have been written to help you gather evidence about your own organisation so that you can use it later whilst working on your project.

(b) Compile a company background. A formal company background features as a requirement within assessments. It is worthwhile constructing one at an early stage because it will help you to focus and explain your organisation better to your tutor. How to compile a company background is covered later in this section.

(c) Familiarise yourself with the CIM guidelines for the unit.

3.2 The CIM Guidance

The following notes pick out the key points that you **MUST** adhere to from the CIM's instruction for candidates. It also gives you tips about how to succeed by using these notes to your advantage.

3.2.1 Context

- The assignment should be **based on your own organisation** or an organisation you are familiar with. You should discuss the organisation you plan to use with your tutor.
- Do not include **sensitive data** from the chosen organisation or create an anonymous name for the organisation so that it cannot be identified from your work.
- Each assignment must be completed **individually**, not as part of a group.

3.2.2 Working with your tutor

- You are entitled to a minimum of **15 minutes individual tutorial** time for this unit.
- You are able to discuss with your tutor your **choice of organisation and any questions** about the assignment.
- You are allowed to gain **feedback on one written assignment draft**. Do not ask your tutor to look at your improved draft because they are not permitted by the CIM to coach you or provide any more feedback.
- Your tutor will **not** be able to tell you the grade a piece of work is likely to achieve.

3.2.3 Word count

Word counts always cause students concern. At the beginning it seems like a daunting task to be able to actually write the required number of words. Amazingly, by the time you have completed your first draft the problem is very likely to have transformed into a major word reduction exercise. Writing succinctly and clearly is far more difficult to achieve than endless pages of 'waffle'.

- You must remain within **+10%** of the specified word count. This means that if you have a word count of 1000 words you must not write more than 1100 words. In this unit you may be given a **page limit**, in which case you should stick to the number of pages requested.
- You must **state** the number of words on the **front page** of your assignment.
- Headings, index, references, bibliographies, appendices and tables **do not count towards** your word limit.
- **Diagrams and tables** are encouraged however if **all or most** of your work is presented in this format then they **will be counted** towards your word limit.

3.2.4 Plagiarism

Copying someone else's work or quoting from another source without referencing the source will be regarded as plagiarism. To avoid being suspected of plagiarism, ensure that you Harvard reference all sources as described in section 1 of this workbook.

Candidates found guilty of plagiarism may be:

- Disqualified from CIM membership
- Refused award of the unit or qualification
- Refused the right to retake the unit.

Remember to submit electronic copies of your work in the procedure specified by your tutor so that it may be passed through anti-plagiarism software by the CIM.

3.2.5 Assessment criteria, Mark schemes and Grade Descriptors

- **Assessment criteria and marking scheme**

  The assessment criteria is useful because it outlines what the examiner is looking for when assessing you. It is linked to the marking scheme which you will also be privy to. You should pay careful attention to these because they will give you a good indication of the level of content that is required in each section of your work.

format

It is highly advisable to use the assessment criteria as a basis for the structure of any reports that you are asked to complete as tasks. For example with the task 3 outlined in the specimen paper, you could use the following headings within your report to ensure that the examiner can easily find where to award you marks for each part of the marking scheme.

1 Background to the organisation
2 Customer groups
3 Information used to understand buyer behaviour
4 Recommendation for the use of promotional tools to develop relationships

5 Internal circulation
6 Summary

The headings follow conventional report style but are also linked to the specific points requested in the assignment brief. You will not leave the examiner searching for your points when they sit with the marking scheme and need to consider where to award your marks.

- **Grade descriptors**

  Grade descriptors are also available on the CIM website. You should look through these because they outline what candidates need to demonstrate in order to achieve the various grades.

3.3 Writing a company background

One item required within the appendix to accompany your assignment is a background to your organisation. In the sample assessment materials produced by the CIM, they stipulate in task three that you should include a

"*brief background to the organisation, it's customer base and product/service (2 sides A4 maximum, no marks allocated)*".

CIM examiners have said on many occasions that candidates frequently struggle to write clear and concise company backgrounds.

It is useful to first think about why you are being asked to provide this background. Imagine for a moment that you are an examiner faced with a few hundred scripts. Each candidate is likely to refer to a different company or division, the large majority of which will be unknown to the examiner. Unless the examiner is directly familiar with the company you are referring to, it is quite possible that they may take your responses out of context or misinterpret your meaning because they do not know the specifics or nature of your organisation. Think about when you first move to a new job, to begin it is difficult to see how the bigger organisational picture fits together because you may not know much about the industry, the culture of the organisation and key factors of influence. The same situation is true for the examiner and so your company background serves the purpose of your company background is to provide a brief induction document into these issues that will help put your answer into context.

Two points need to be remembered;

(1) The examiner may use your company background to put the rest of your answer into context.

(2) Your background should be clear, concise (no longer than two pages of A4) and well structured.

3.4 What should be included in the company background?

The following can be used as a checklist to ensure that you have included sufficient detail without rambling.

The organisation

- Organisations name including a parent company or more recognised brand.
- Type in terms of size, sector and ownership and legal structure.
- When established and major historical events.
- Growth and broad strategic aims.
- Mission statement
- Broadly outline any other details specific to the organisation which are important to the assignment tasks eg. culture, staff, structure, supply chain partners of importance etc

The market

- Market overview and the organisations position within the market eg market leader
- Approximate size of the market
- Key competitors
- Customer groups and their characteristics
- Broad key trends eg rapidly growing market...etc

Product/service range

- Description of the product/service range
- Key feature, associated benefits and unique selling proposition
- Historical developments of the product/service range
- Details of complementary products
- Details of substitutes

You are likely to find that not all of these points are relevant to your organisation but it will be useful to at least run through it in order to think about the key implications that will help put your company into an appropriate context for the examiner. Frequently when we work within organisations much of the knowledge we possess is unconscious. You may find it helps to show your final company background to someone who is not familiar with yours. Ask them to read your background and then in their own words to describe your organisation back to you- you will find this helps you to see whether you have produced a realistic impression.

3.5 An example organisational background

The following overview, for the purposes of demonstration the case study organisation and its situation are essentially fictional.

The Student House Company (SHC)

The Student House Company (SCH) is a UK based partnership specialising in premium property for students at leading universities.

Origins

The company began informally in 1981 when twin brothers Steve and Paul Newby purchased a house to share (and rent out spare rooms) whilst at university. The house was purchased using inheritance. Following their graduation, the brothers rented the house initially friends and then later to a series of unknown student tenants. Over the next five years, ten additional houses were purchased in the surrounding area as long term investments.

In 2001 the brothers decided to change careers and enter into the property business in a more formal capacity and established a formal partnership in the name of The Student House Company. (The original houses purchase in Manchester were not integrated into SHC but continue to be owned by the brothers and managed by a renting agency on their behalf.) A report by The Joseph Rowntree Foundation (2000) identified that the expansion in the UK HE sector had not been matched by increases in university provided accommodation leading to a 60% increase in the need for private housing in the sector. In order to differentiate their offering from existing private landlord, SHC identified a need for premium housing. A former 30 bedroom hotel in Bloomsbury, Central London was purchased and converted it into luxury student accommodation.

Corporate aim and customer proposition

The company aim from 2000 remains as:

"To provide luxurious accommodation for the discerning student who is willing to pay a premium to maintain a comfortable lifestyle whilst at university"

The product proposition for SHC is:

- High quality standard of rooms all with en suite and internet facilities
- Modern communal lounges and quiet study areas
- Fully serviced daily cleaning service and live in property manager

Rent paid by students at SHC is typically 50% higher than the average rent for student properties within the area.

Property portfolio

By 2005 SCH had rapidly expanded with a portfolio including similar properties in other major university towns. Locations were selected according to the following criteria:

- Size of student population with high socio-economic demographics
- Number of colleges/universities in close proximity to the property

The current portfolio of properties is shown in the following table:

Location	Properties
London	Property 1 – 30 rooms Property 2 – 40 rooms Property 3 – 45 rooms
Bath	Property 1 – 20 rooms Property 2 – 35 rooms
Manchester	Property 1 – 30 rooms Property 2 – 20 rooms
Cambridge	Property 1 – 20 rooms Property 2 – 30 rooms

Target market

Target consumers are students from affluent backgrounds with the desire for and propensity to live in premium accommodation. Parents are an important stakeholder group because they are central to the decision making process when students select their accommodation. In many instances parents pay rent directly on behalf of SHC's resident students.

Over 80% of tenants come from a privately educated background (60% of those boarded at boarding school). There is also a high proportion of overseas student tenants especially within the London, Oxford and Cambridge properties where on average 70% of students are foreign to the UK. Students from the US and China are key overseas markets for SHC.

The competitive market

The market has become increasingly competitive with large property developers entering the student accommodation market. Although individual private landlords (40%) and university halls of residents (25%) still possess the largest market shares, larger commercially branded properties account for 15% of student housing with the remainder living at home with parents or owning their own properties.

Key competitors are large property developers who have built large (average 100 rooms) halls of residence style accommodation. These properties have rooms which are functional in nature and are considered to be 'mid range' appealing to the mainstream student market.

- **Student Home** owns eight large properties in university towns including all SHC locations. The rent charged by Student Home is typically 40% less than SHC but this reflects the functional style of accommodation provided and shared bathrooms. It is 10% more expensive than the average rent.
- **Study House** own similar properties in five university towns (again all in SHC locations). Rent charged is 20% less than SHC because of their provision of en suite bathrooms within individual rooms.

The market is becoming increasingly competitive with new market entrants anticipated in the next two years.

3.6 Getting started once you receive your brief

When you receive the brief you will want to spend time familiarising yourself with what you need to do. It is important to consider the tasks in the context of the appendices that you given and so it is useful to look through these and use these as a basis for your initial research and gathering of further information.

Everybody has a personal style, flair and tone when it comes to writing. However, no matter what your approach, you must ensure your assignment meets the **requirements of the brief** and so is comprehensible, coherent and cohesive in approach.

Think of preparing an assignment as preparing for an examination. Ultimately, the work you are undertaking results in an examination grade. Successful achievement of all four modules in a level results in a qualification.

There are a number of positive steps that you can undertake in order to ensure that you make the best of your assignment in order to maximise the marks available.

Step 1 Work to the brief

Ensure that you identify exactly what the assignment asks you to do.

- If it asks you to be a marketing assistant, then immediately assume that role.
- If it asks you to prepare a report, then present a report, not an essay or a letter.
- Furthermore, if it asks for 500 words, then do not present 1,000 or 4,000.

Identify whether the report should be **formal or informal**; who it should be **addressed to**; its **overall purpose** and its **potential use** and outcome. Understanding this will ensure that your assignment meets fully the requirements of the brief and addresses the key issues included within it.

It would be a good idea at this point to check your understanding of the assignment with your tutor. Studying with a CIM centre means that you should expect a minimum **fifteen minutes** of tuition time specifically with the Unit 2 assignment in mind.

Step 2 Address the tasks and pay attention to the Assessment Criteria

It is of pivotal importance that you address **each** of the tasks within the assignment. **Many students fail to do this** and often overlook one of the tasks or indeed part of the tasks.

The Assessment Criteria that the CIM will use to assign marks is clearly shown on the assignment briefs. Make sure that you look at the criteria and think about whether you have fully addressed them. Likewise, make it easier for your examiner to identify where you are attempting to meet the criteria by wherever possible using similar terms for individual sections of you assignment.

Step 3 Information Search

Many students fail to realise the importance of collecting information to **support** and **underpin** their assignment work. However, it is vital that you demonstrate to the CIM your ability to **establish information needs**, obtain **relevant information** and **utilise it sensibly** in order to arrive at appropriate decisions.

You should establish the nature of the information required, follow up possible sources, time involved in obtaining the information, gaps in information and the need for information.

CIM are very keen that students are **seen** to collect information, **expand** their mind and consider the **breadth** and **depth** of the situation. We will cover more about this stage of your assignment when later in the chapter.

Step 4 Develop an Assignment Plan

Your **assignment** needs to be structured and coherent, addressing the brief and presenting the facts as required by the tasks. The only way you can successfully achieve this is by **planning the structure** of your Assignment in advance.

Step 5 Prepare Draft Assignment

It is good practice to always produce a **first draft** of an assignment. You should use it to ensure that you have met the aims and objectives, assignment brief and tasks related to the actual assignment. A draft document provides you with scope for improvements, and enables you to check for accuracy, spelling, punctuation and use of English.

Use the **'week in a drawer'** trick which involves completing your first draft and then not looking at it for at least a week. When you return to the draft areas where you are not entirely clear will be very apparent to you now. Your study centre tutor is only allowed by the CIM to give feedback on your written work once. It would therefore be advisable to make the most of this opportunity once you have reflected on areas of improvement after this week.

Your tutor will confirm whether they will review drafts of the complete assignment portfolio or on a task by task basis. Generally, if you plan your time carefully you should be able to have a draft of one task 'in the draw' whilst you are working on another task.

Step 6 **Prepare Final Document**

There are a number of components that should always be in place at the beginning of the assignment documentation, including **labelling** of the assignment, **word counts**, **appendices** numbering and presentation method. Ensure that you **adhere to the guidelines presented**, or alternatively those suggested by your Study Centre.

3.6.1 Time management for assignments

One of the biggest challenges we all seem to face day-to-day is that of managing time. When studying, that challenge seems to grow increasingly difficult, requiring a balance between work, home, family, social life and study life. It is therefore of pivotal importance to your own success for you to plan wisely the limited amount of time you have available.

Step 1 **Find out how much time you have**

Ensure that you are fully aware of how long your module lasts, and the final deadline. If you are studying a module from September to December, it is likely that you will have only 10-12 weeks in which to complete your assignments. This means that you will be preparing assignment work continuously throughout the course.

Step 2 **Plan your time**

Essentially you need to **work backwards** from the final deadline, submission date, and schedule your work around the possible time lines. Clearly if you have only 10-12 weeks available to complete three assignments, you will need to allocate a block of hours in the final stages of the module to ensure that all of your assignments are in on time. This will be critical as all assignments will be sent to CIM by a set day. Late submissions will not be accepted and no extensions will be awarded. Students who do not submit will be treated as a 'no show' and will have to resubmit for the next period and undertake an alternative assignment.

Step 3 **Set priorities**

You should set priorities on a daily and weekly basis (not just for study, but for your life). There is no doubt that this mode of study needs commitment (and some sacrifices in the short term). When your achievements are recognised by colleagues, peers, friends and family, it will all feel worthwhile.

Step 4 **Analyse activities and allocate time to them**

Consider the **range** of activities that you will need to undertake in order to complete the assignment and the **time** each might take. Remember, too, there will be a delay in asking for information and receiving it.

Always build in time to spare, to deal with the unexpected. This may reduce the pressure that you are faced with in meeting significant deadlines.

You may find it helps to plan your workload and individual tasks using the following table:

Time Plan

Task	Assessment brief released	Research and information gathering	Draft one complete by	Final draft complete by	Final submission date
Task 1					
Task 2					
Task 3					
Task 4					

Warning!

The same principles apply to a student with 30 weeks to do the work. However, a word of warning is needed. Do not fall into the trap of leaving all of your work to the last minute. If you miss out important information or fail to reflect upon your work adequately or successfully you will be penalised for both. Therefore, time management is important whatever the duration of the course.

3.7 Research and prep work on your assignment

You can simplify your early work by following a structured route to tacking the assignment.

Stage 1 – The initial read through

When you read through your assignment brief it is likely that a number of questions will spring to mind. We recommend that you read through once quickly to 'scan' the document and compile as table as we did in section 2 of this chapter when looking at the format of the assignment. A blank copy of this table is available within our online resources for you to download.

Stage 2 – The active read through cycles

Next, you will need to go through again but this time armed with a highlighter pen. If necessary photocopy the assessment or download an extra copy and make preliminary notes around the edges. Your aim is to go through and pick out the key information and first impressions. It is likely that you will have picked up cues within the assignment and particularly within the appendices that you missed on first reading. Think about the appendices you have been given and consider where they are relevant to the tasks you have been given.

Begin to group these ideas into key themes, using diagrams, mind maps, tables or lists. Generally it does not matter which format you use at this stage so long as it makes sense to you. It may take you a few readings before you have refined your notes and thoughts at this stage.

Stage 3 – Information gathering

By this point you should know what is required of you within your assignment and will have a list of topics and questions to address. Think about the likely sources. You should consider, the chapters you have read in this workbook eg task one of the specimen assignment considers the theory of the marketing concept so clearly much of the content in unit 1 will also be relevant. If we use task two as an example, you are asked to provide illustrative examples of the use of non-verbal communication. To research this you may wish to:

- Think about how you use non-verbal communications, how you react as a customer, think of good and bad instances
- Use the workbook (and especially your completed activities) and text books to research non-verbal communications theory
- Search for journal and press articles discussing non-verbal communications
- Conduct web based research initially using a search engine.
- Discuss with work colleagues, fellow students and other contacts their perceptions of non-verbal communication

Information requirements

Add topics and potential sources of information to the relevant spaces in a table similar to this. (This table is also available online as a resource for you to download.)

Task	Topics covered	Where is this covered in the study text	Other text chapters to refer to	Other sources of information	Internal organisational information
Task 1					
Task 2					
Task 3					
Task 4					

Stage 4 – Considering your findings and writing up

Your starting point for the write up will be to structure how you will present your work according to the format that has been requested. In the specimen example you therefore will be working within the confines of a presentation, an email, a report and a discussion paper.

As we have previously mentioned, use the assessment criteria as guidance for your structure.

Getting started is often the hardest part of writing. To fast track this often gruelling process there are a number of 'tricks' you can play, for example writing DRAFT at the top of your page can take the pressure off the feeling of a completely blank screen. Once you have something on the page, you have overcome the initial barrier to starting your write up.

4 Presenting and submitting your work

4.1 CIM requirements for submitting the assignment

You should always ensure that you prepare **two** copies of your assignment, keeping a soft copy on disc. On occasions assignments go missing, or second copies are required by CIM. The CIM also requires you to submit an **electronic copy** which may be scanned through anti-plagiarism software. You should save your assignment using the following convention for the title:

Centre name_ Unit title (abbreviated eg MIR/SM)_ CIM student registration number

You should also ensure that:

- Each assignment should be clearly marked up with your study centre, your CIM Student registration number and ultimately at the end of the assignment a word count. Do not under any circumstances put your name on the assignment because the CIM may not accept it. You cannot use fancy folders to present your work and should simply use a treasury tag in the top left hand corner. You will need to complete and attach a copy of the CIM's 'Assignment Front Sheet and Declaration Form' otherwise your work will not be accepted.
- The assignment presentation format should directly meet the requirements of the assignment brief, (ie reports and presentations are the most called for communication formats). You **must** ensure that you assignment does not appear to be an extended essay. If it does, you will lose marks.
- A word or page limit will be included in the assignment brief. These are specified by CIM and must be adhered to. Students who are +/- 10% risk their work failing. The word count does not include headings, references, bibliography, appendices or tables. Tables will however be counted if they are thought to constitute most or all of your assignment. When slides are presented, any word count will apply to the accompanying notes and not the slides. The word count is required at the end of your document.
- Appendices should clearly link to the assignment and can be attached as supporting documentation at the end of the report. However failure to reference them by number (eg Appendix 1) within the report is the key problem with many appendices. Only use an Appendix if it is essential and clearly adds value to the overall assignment and remember

that you cannot gain marks directly for items in the appendix. The Appendix should never act as a waste bin for all the materials you have come across in your research, or a way of making your assignment seem somewhat heavier and more impressive than it is.

4.2 Harvard referencing

Harvard referencing is the preferred method of the CIM for you to clearly state the materials you use to complete your written assessments. Referencing serves two purposes, firstly, it enables readers of your work to find the source documents for themselves to read further into the topic and secondly, it avoids the problems of plagiarism (it is more difficult for you to be accused of copying another's work and passing it off as your own if you have outwardly acknowledged their contribution).

Sometimes Harvard referencing is referred to as 'The Author, Date Method' and although it is the most commonly used and highly structured method, you will find that there are slight variations amongst guides about the exact way to state references. For example, some suggest book titles should be written in italics whilst others state that they should be underlined. Whichever convention you choose is fine so long as you stick to the same throughout.

4.2.1 When and how do you reference within your paragraph?

Any time that you refer to the writing of another, their thoughts, theories, drawings or sayings, you should clearly cite their work. In practice this means that there are two instances when you should state your reference. The first is within the paragraph where you are referring to their work and the second is at the end of your document where you should provide a list of references.

To demonstrate how you cite a source within the paragraph you can consider the following example. It is likely that at some point in your CIM studies that you will want to refer to the work of marketing guru Philip Kotler. You may find yourself writing something similar to:

Kotler (1994) outlined that the process of marketing involves stages of analysis, planning, implementation and control

There are a few things to note from this:

(1) The author Philip Kotler's name is used as part of the sentence. This means that their surname (Kotler) is used and is then followed by the year of publication (1994) which is shown in brackets

(2) If there were two authors then you would write Kotler and (year).

(3) If there were more than two authors then you would only use the surname of the first and refer to all others as et al. For example in this case if Kotler had co-authors then you would write Kotler et al. (1994).

If it did not seem appropriate to use the author's name within the sentence, you should still refer to them at the end of the sentence, for example you might have written:

The marketing process involves four essential stages; analysis, planning, implementation and control (Kotler, 1994). Should it be ; and then , - is this direct from Kotler – would have thought should be commas throughout?

Here you will see that before the final sentence full stop, you should have included in brackets the author's surname followed by a comma and then the year. There may be occasions that you find the same point is raised within more than one source. For example, you will be hard pressed to find a marketing text book which doesn't identify one of the key roles of marketing as identifying and meeting customer needs. Rather than trying to identify which is the most appropriate to use you should use as many as is necessary. For example, you may write:

Marketing should encompass the notion that there is a need to identify and satisfy customer needs (Blythe, 2007; Hill and O'Sullivan, 2004; Kotler, 1994).

You should notice that the order of the sources is alphabetical according to author surname and that they are separated by a semi colon.

If you take a direct quote from the author, it should be referenced as shown in the example below: ***"Marketing means working with markets to actualize potential exchanges for the purpose of satisfying human needs and wants"*** **(Kotler, 1994 p.12)**

Again, you should use the author's surname and date within brackets following the italicised quote, but as it is a direct quote then you should provide more information to enable to reader to find it, for example by including a page reference.

Now that you have cited the source at the point that you refer to it, you should remember to add the entry to your reference list placed at the end of your document.

4.2.2 How do you cite different types of material within a reference list?

At the point within the sentence/ paragraph where you cite your source, you will always use the author's surname and date regardless of whether the source was a book, newspaper or website. When you come to compile your reference list however, the nature of the material will determine how you structure your reference.

Examples of a number of types of materials are shown below along with examples of the convention being put into practice. As the convention is summarised, make sure that you pay attention to the use of underlining, italics, bold and grammatical marks.

A Book

Author surname, Initial. (Year) Book title, Edition if more than one, Publisher, City.

Kotler, P. (1994) Marketing Management: Analysis, Planning, Implementation and Control, Eighth Edition, New Jersey, Prentice Hall.

Blythe, J. (2006) Principles and Practice of Marketing, Thompson, London.

Hill, L. and O'Sullivan, T. (2004) Foundation Marketing 3rd Edition, Prentice Hall, Oxford.

An edited book

Editor surname, Initials (ed) (Year) Book title, Edition if more than one, Publisher, City.

Bateson, J.E.G. (ed) (1991)Managing Services Marketing: Text and Readings, Second Edition, The Dryden Press, Orlando.

A Chapter or readings in a book

Author surname, Initials (Year) '*Chapter, reading, article title*' In Editor surname, initial (ed) Book title, Edition if more than one, Publisher, City, pages.

Chase, R.B (1991) '*Where does the customer fit in a service operation?* In Bateson, J.E.G. (ed) Managing Services Marketing: Text and Readings, Second Edition, The Dryden Press, Orlando, pp171-177.

A newspaper or magazine

Author surname, Initials or Anon (Year) '*Article title*' Journal or Newspaper, Date

Cowlett, M. (2007) ' *PR Leagues*' Marketing, 23rd May

An academic journal

Author surname, Initials (Year) '*Article title*' Journal, Volume, (Issue or Special Edition), pages.

A website

Author, initials (Year) '*Title*' [Online] Company/ website owner details, Available at: web address [accessed date].

Boots Group Plc., (2003). '*Corporate social responsibility*'. [Online]. Boots Group Plc.
Available at: http://www.Boots-Plc.Com/Information/Info.Asp?Level1id=447&Level 2id=0 [accessed 23 July 2005].

A blog etc.

Author, Initials., (Year). *Title of document or page.* [type of medium]. Website Address Locating details(eg. Breadcrumb) [Accessed date]

Jay, S. (2008) '*Good affiliates are just ahead of the curve*' [Online blog], available at: http://www.thedigitalmarketingblog.co.uk/2008/02/index.html [accessed 12.3.08].

A recorded broadcast

Author, Initials, (Year). *Title of document or page.* [type of medium]. Locating details [Accessed date]

Anon (2007) 'The Edwardian Larder' [Television programme] BBC 4, [First Aired Monday 11 June 2007 10.50pm-11.50pm]

An annual report

Corporate author, (Year). *Full title of annual report,* Place of Publication: Publisher

Advertising Standards Authority (2006) ASA Annual Report, London: Advertising Standards Authority.

All references should be placed in alphabetical order. If you are referring to more than one source written by the same author, references should be listed in chronological order (earliest first).

4.2.3 How to work practically with Harvard Referencing

There are software packages available such as Endnote which can be used to file, sort, organise, insert within your text and automate your final reference list. Microsoft Word 2007 also now has referencing functionality which will do the same. Although these packages will make referencing appear easier, for the size of documents you will be working probably wouldn't warrant the investment. With this said, you will need to become highly organised as you read and start to make citations.

A few tips worth trying :

(1) Create a separate master document in which you complete the full reference list style citation in table format as shown below as you refer to the source;

Author/Year	Reference
Kotler (1994)	Marketing Management: Analysis, Planning, Implementation and Control, Eighth Edition, Prentice Hall, New Jersey,
Hill, L. and O'Sullivan, T. (2004)	Foundation Marketing 3rd Edition, Prentice Hall, Oxford.
Anon (2007)	The Edwardian Larder' [Television programme] BBC 4, [First Aired Monday 11 June 10.50pm-11.50pm]
Jay, S.(2008)	'*Good affiliates are just ahead of the curve'* [Online blog], available at: http://www.thedigitalmarketingblog.co.uk/2008/02/index.html [accessed 12.3.08].

Open a blank table in a separate document which you call References for task x (the specific task you are working on), As you insert a citation into your work, copy and paste the reference from your master document.

When you have finished your answer, sort the table alphabetically, merge the cells, tweak any line breaks etc and make sure that you clear the border lines from around and within the table. The reference list below was formatted this way.

References

Anon (2007) The Edwardian Larder' [Television programme] BBC 4, [First Aired Monday 11 June 10.50pm-11.50pm]

Hill, L. and O'Sullivan, T. (2004) Foundation Marketing 3rd Edition, Prentice Hall, Oxford.

Jay, S.(2008) '*Good affiliates are just ahead of the curve'* [Online blog], available at: http://www.thedigitalmarketingblog.co.uk/2008/02/index.html [accessed 12.3.08].

Kotler (1994) Marketing Management: Analysis, Planning, Implementation and Control, Eighth Edition, Prentice Hall, New Jersey.

4.2.4 So what is the difference between a list of references and a bibliography?

A bibliography will include all items that you have read throughout your studies which have helped to shape your thinking to be able to answer a particular question. A reference list will include only those sources which you directly cite.

A bibliography should be placed directly after a reference list. This is not as relevant to your work and so you may wish to only use a list of references.

4.2.5 Useful online guides to referencing

Anglian Ruskin University (2008) '*Harvard System of Referencing Guide*' [Online] available at: http://libweb.anglia.ac.uk/referencing/harvard.htm?harvard_id=40#40 [accessed 20.3.08].

Sheffield University (2008) '*Harvard Referencing Guide*' [Online] available at: http://www.shef.ac.uk/library/libdocs/hsl-dvc1.pdf [accessed on 20.3.08].

Learning objective review

Learning objectives	Covered
1 Explain the purpose of the work based project	☑ CIM requirements ☑ Expectations of a student ☑ What 'work' based means
2 Approach the work based project and identify the key assessment criteria	☑ Preparing before you receive the assignment ☑ The format of the assignment ☑ Tackling the assignment ☑ Presenting the assignment

Key concepts and Index

Key concepts

Index

Review form & Free prize draw

All original review forms from the entire BPP range, completed with genuine comments, will be entered into one of four draws on 31 July 2009/2010 and 31 January 2010/2011. The names on the first four forms picked out on each occasion will be sent a cheque for £50.

Name: ______________________ **Address:** ______________________

____

____

1.How have you used this Text?
(Tick one box only)

☐ Self study (book only)

☐ On a course: college______________

☐ Other ______________

2. During the past six months do you recall seeing/receiving any of the following?
(Tick as many boxes as are relevant)

☐ Our advertisement in *The Marketer*

☐ Our brochure with a letter through the post

☐ Saw website

3. Why did you decide to purchase this Text?
(Tick one box only)

☐ Have used companion Passcards

☐ Have used BPP Texts in the past

☐ Recommendation by friend/colleague

☐ Recommendation by a lecturer at college

☐ Saw advertising in journals

☐ Saw website

☐ Other ______________

4. Which (if any) aspects of our advertising do you find useful?
(Tick as many boxes as are relevant)

☐ Prices and publication dates of new editions

☐ Information on product content

☐ Facility to order books off-the-page

☐ None of the above

5. Have you used the companion Passcards? Yes ☐ No ☐

6. Your ratings, comments and suggestions would be appreciated on the following areas.

	Very useful	*Useful*	*Not useful*
Introductory section (How to use this text, study checklist, etc)	☐	☐	☐
Introduction	☐	☐	☐
Syllabus linked learning outcomes	☐	☐	☐
Activities and Marketing at Work examples	☐	☐	☐
Learning objective reviews	☐	☐	☐
Magic Formula references	☐	☐	☐
Content of assessment material	☐	☐	☐
Index	☐	☐	☐
Structure and presentation	☐	☐	☐

	Excellent	*Good*	*Adequate*	*Poor*
Overall opinion of this Text	☐	☐	☐	☐

7. Do you intend to continue using BPP CIM Range Products? ☐ Yes ☐ No

8. Have you visited bpp.com/lm/cim? ☐ Yes ☐ No

9.If you have visited bpp.com/lm/cim, please give a score out of 10 for it's overall usefulness **/10**

Please note any further comments and suggestions/errors on the reverse of this page.

Please return to: Dr Kellie Vincent, BPP Learning Media, FREEPOST, London, W12 8BR.

If you have any additional questions, feel free to email cimrange@bpp.com

Review form & Free prize draw (continued)

Please note any further comments and suggestions/errors below.

Free prize draw rules

1. Closing date for 31 January 2010/11 draws are 31 December 2009/10. Closing date for 31 July 2009/10 draws are 30 June 2009/10.
2. Restricted to entries with UK and Eire addresses only. BPP employees, their families and business associates are excluded.
3. No purchase necessary. Entry forms are available upon request from BPP Learning Media. No more than one entry per title, per person. Draw restricted to persons aged 16 and over.
4. Winners will be notified by post and receive their cheques not later than 6 weeks after the relevant draw date. List of winners will be supplied on request.
5. The decision of the promoter in all matters is final and binding. No correspondence will be entered into.